X
XI
XII
XIII
4
6
8
21
26

FEASTING UPON THE WORD

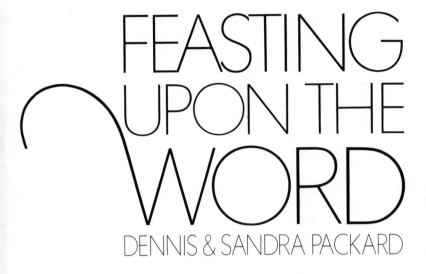

FEASTING UPON THE WORD

DENNIS & SANDRA PACKARD

Foreword and afterword by
Arthur Henry King

Deseret Book Company
Salt Lake City, Utah
1981

Library of Congress Cataloging in Publication Data

Packard, Dennis J.
  Feasting upon the word.

  Includes index.
    1. Bible—Study. 2. Mormon Church—Sacred books—
Study and teaching. I. Packard, Sandra, 1950-.
II. Title.
BS600.2.P28   220'.07   81-12446
ISBN 0-87747-879-1   AACR2

To our children: Jay, Hannah, Alisia, and Nathan.
May they teach us from the scriptures.

Contents

Foreword

Arthur Henry King

I used to listen to my father read the scriptures to us every day before breakfast. I can still hear him reading to me the parable of the prodigal son. My father was accidently killed when I was nine years old, but I had heard him read the scriptures for three or four years and those passages are still in my mind. That was the most important part of my education.

There is no substitute for the scriptures—and by "scriptures" I mean, of course, canonized scriptures, ancient and modern, as well as writings of the prophets of the Church, which, as we know, are also scripture. Reading about the scriptures, instead of reading from them, will not do; reading "simpler" versions will not provide scriptural milk, but merely someone else's milk and water.

Nor will it do to make the center of our reading any other version of the scriptures than that which the Church recommends. The Authorized Version of the Bible (the King James Version) is the one that English speakers should primarily use (though by all means use others cautiously as aids). Joseph Smith told us that the best version he knew was the one by Luther, which is available to German speakers. The Book of Mormon is translated into a style similar to that of the Authorized Version. The Doctrine and Covenants is written in several different styles; Joseph Smith's account of his own life is in still another style; but they are all consistent with the King James tradition.

So, there is no alternative to reading the scriptures themselves, which are written in a language that becomes more and more foreign to us, not simply generation by generation, but year by year. Still, we can comfort ourselves with the thought that we as children learned language mainly by hearing it constantly about us in contexts that enabled us to understand it. Our children, hearing the scriptures day by day and absorbing them from the very beginning of their lives, will be at home with the language of the scriptures. No other way of learning to read the scriptures is as good.

So, it is our duty to read the scriptures aloud daily with our children, no matter what age they may be. If we do not, they will never learn to read the scriptures half so well by themselves. The public schools will not teach them — they cannot teach them to read even contemporary language, let alone the language of the early seventeenth century. Besides, by an American manifestation very different from that of Providence, the public schools do not teach the scriptures. When I was brought up, my father's reading the scriptures aloud at home was supplemented later by scripture lessons at school; and, as I grew into my teens, by lessons about historical background, archaeology, and so on.

All this the Church has to do for itself, and of course it does it better than the public schools could, as it is no use teaching these things without faith. And, increasingly, the leaders of the Church are telling us that this instruction must be given in the family rather than at Church meetings, although it may be supplemented by instruction at such meetings. But if this instruction outside the family were not based upon instruction inside the family, our children would not grow to love and understand the scriptures as part of their deeper life, for the profound things grow in us from the family. We impede our children in their way to eternal life if we neglect this.

But this means that we must be prepared to answer

our children's questions, and that may well be the greatest
incentive we shall ever have to learn to read the scriptures
properly ourselves. The scriptures are so important that
they must be the center of all our education. From where
else, except inspiration and the patient teaching of the
Lord himself, did Joseph Smith derive his first-class
education? The same absorption in the scriptures enabled
John Bunyan to write his *Pilgrim's Progress,* and John
Woolman to set down his *Journal.* Many of us today may
think ourselves educated, but unless we are versed in the
scriptures, we may be certain that those of our ancestors
who *were* versed in the scriptures were better educated
than we are.

Furthermore, the scriptures are a guide by which we
may judge the value of all other literature. When we have
learned to read the scriptures, we have learned to read
from the right point of view anything and everything else,
from Shakespeare to the newspaper. "In the beginning
was the Word," and the Word is from *Alpha* to *Omega.* All
good words lead toward the Word of words. Bad words,
bad language of all kinds, lead us away.

The ultimate choices of our lives are always between
good and evil. Only in the scriptures are those choices
always shown as being that way. From the scriptures we
can therefore learn to judge how far other literature ac-
cords with this ultimate choice between good and evil. We
shall be able to see that the greatest writers are what they
are because they came nearest to the values of the scriptures. We have a way of judging good from bad in
literature. The rest of the world is losing or has lost it.
Our way is thus of inestimable advantage to us. But, of
course, it is only of that advantage if we learn to read the
scriptures themselves and apply their standards to other
good literature — and to the bad literature people so often
use to entertain themselves. The scriptures enable us by
contrast to recognize trash. My grandmother was quite
an "uneducated" woman, but she was well versed in the
scriptures and knew for herself what was trash: she had no
interest in sentimental or violent literature and was
always telling us children not to read it.

Nor does the influence of the scriptures end there.
The greatest music and the greatest art in the past have

sprung from and been devoted to the values of the gospel.
The standards of the scriptures that we apply to other
literature, we can also apply to the other arts. We can
distinguish good from bad in art, in music, and in dance
(including athletics and games). To live our lives with the
scriptures means to lead better lives, whether it be by the
objects we put in our homes or the things we listen to, the
pictures we look at or the shows we go to.

Nor does it end even there. The judgments we base
on the scriptures may be carried over into the assessment
of specialist writing, whether on natural science, the life
sciences, medicine, the social sciences, or law. Behind all
these lie certain preconceptions, which a wise scientist or
scholar may use as scaffolding, always knowing that these
conceptions will change. A great scientist knows that the
values of natural science have changed from epoch to
epoch, and now change from generation to generation,
just as he knows that he works with changing observations
of facts, not with facts themselves. But the moral values of
the gospel endure forever.

It is in the light of all this that I ask you to look at this
book. It may open up ways of thinking and feeling for you
that will, if they have not already been developed, set up
within yourself, within your family, and among you and
your friends and brethren and sisters, a dialogue that will
never end—the profound dialogue of eternal progression.

Of course, this book is not the first, nor is it the final
word. There will be other books from the same authors,
and, we hope, many books from other writers that will
help us all, with the aid of the Holy Ghost, to have a
deeper, more total feeling for scripture as we read it from
Moses or hear it from the lips of our living prophet.

This book should prove most useful for parents to
share with their teenagers. Chapter 12, however, is
specifically for parents who want to read the scriptures to
their young children. In general, by reading and
understanding this book, parents will find themselves able
to make the scriptures more open and available to all their
children.

Our surrounding culture tempts us away to pleasures
that prove boring and demand to be succeeded by ever
more violent pleasures, which, in their turn, also prove

boring. Our principal enemy is the idea that the scriptures are boring. The main reason our children may think
so is not because the scriptures are boring, but because
the false values of our surrounding culture tempt us to enjoy the fleeting, the frivolous, the easy, and the vain.
Rightly interpreted, the scriptures are the most interesting of all writings, because they deal with life as it
really is.

Application and patience are needed to acquire
everything worthwhile. A boy will spend hours getting the
ball into the net, a girl in practicing her dance steps. Such
application and patience are fundamental to education.
Let us try to give our children (and ourselves) what so-
called education may have failed to give them (or us): the
power to concentrate on a good thing—in this case
reading the scriptures, our guide to eternal life.

Acknowledgments

We are grateful to Arthur Henry King. We wanted to know more of what he knew about reading the scriptures, and so offered to help him do a book. He counter-offered: he would help us do a book. He has met with us often, sharing his insights, reading one draft after another, coaching us along like an experienced riverboat pilot who knows the sights you don't want to miss and the shoals you don't want to crash into.

Many others have read drafts of the book and given us helpful comments and suggestions. Thanks to all our friendly critics: Jay Packard, Virginia Bradford, Lon and Debra Packard, Von and Ann Packard, Terry Warner, Neal A. Maxwell, David Yarn, Frank Flake, Camille Williams, Jim and Jan Faulconer, Paul and Beth Hedengren, Monte Shelley, James Moss, John Welch, and Leonard Wald.

Thanks also to Jeffrey R. Holland for permission to use his article "Daddy, Donna and Nephi" in Chapter 2.

Wherefore, if ye shall press forward, feasting upon the word of Christ, and endure to the end, behold, thus saith the Father: Ye shall have eternal life.

2 Nephi 31:20

Learning to Feast

The scriptures are intended for us to feast upon. (2 Nephi 32:3.) When we approach the scriptures properly, we feast and are filled. But in our age, we approach the table laden with foods and delights only to discover that we have no utensils. Quite simply, we are unaccustomed to the careful reading the scriptures require, that the daily newspapers do not require. The careful reader ponders as he reads, finding in the scriptures "wisdom and great treasures of knowledge, even hidden treasures." (D&C 89:19.)

1

Pondering the Scriptures

Some people love the scriptures. Anciently, Nephi declared, "My soul delighteth in the scriptures." (2 Nephi 4:15.) Today, Howard W. Hunter of the Council of the Twelve tells us that studying the scriptures "is the most profitable of all study in which we could engage." (*Ensign,* Nov. 1979, p. 64.) Jeffrey R. Holland, President of Brigham Young University, writes, "Surely the best of the 'best books' are the scriptures." (*Ensign,* Sept. 1976, p. 7.)

On the other hand, a dedicated Sunday School inservice teacher with a master's degree asks in a candid moment, "Why aren't the scriptures better written? They are so hard to understand." A stake leader warns her teachers, "You will have to use the scriptures for some of the lessons in the manual. There is no other way." A devoted father wonders, "Why should I read the scriptures if I live and teach the gospel principles?" Many good Latter-day Saints are comfortable in that same opinion. They prefer a one-sentence message on forgiveness to reading the parable of the prodigal son.

A sacrament meeting speaker, apparently concerned with putting people to sleep, apologizes for reading a verse of scripture. A yawn contagiously spreads throughout the tabernacle as a speaker in general priesthood meeting begins to read a passage from the Book of Mormon. A bishop in desperation urges his members at least to hold the scriptures once a day and see if perhaps the book will open and they will find themselves reading.

Obviously, active and faithful members of the Church do not always love the scriptures. We've asked ourselves why.

The Savior, after a lengthy discourse, told the Nephites they needed time to ponder and pray about his word: "I perceive that ye are weak, that ye cannot understand all my words which I am commanded of the Father to speak unto you at this time. Therefore, go ye unto your homes, and ponder upon the things which I have said, and ask of the Father, in my name, that ye may understand." (3 Nephi 17:2-3.) He has repeated this counsel in our day: "My friends, I leave these sayings with you to ponder in your hearts, with this commandment which I give unto you, that ye shall call upon me while I am near—Draw near unto me and I will draw near unto you; seek me diligently and ye shall find me; ask, and ye shall receive; knock, and it shall be opened unto you." (D&C 88:62-63.) So, when we don't enjoy the scriptures, when we don't understand and appreciate them, the Lord's counsel is to ponder and pray about them. What does it mean to ponder? It means "to weigh in the mind; to view with deliberation; to examine carefully; to consider attentively."

The Lord's advice is good, but perhaps we worry what will become of us if we take it seriously. For one thing, most of us are unaccustomed to pondering: "I hardly ever have to read anything with that much attention. It sounds like a lot of hard work." Perhaps we are also preoccupied with the cares and ways of the world: "I read the scriptures, but I can't really think about them—too many problems I've had to worry about. Besides, if I really start trying to understand the scriptures, I might start thinking I need to make changes in my life, and I am doing the best I can for now." Or maybe we don't trust ourselves to probe very deeply: "I'll start asking silly questions and feel stupid—I might even start asking weird questions that will just get me confused and make me think the scriptures can't hold up, and then I might become a heretic and lose my testimony." Or perhaps we haven't yet realized that *we* can discover something new in the scriptures: "I really don't know how the Lord let it happen, but the scriptures are usually boring—the same old thing over and over again—or else obscure. Maybe the Lord intended the boring parts for those who have to be told over and over, and the perplexing parts for the scriptorians, who like that sort of thing." But whatever the cause, the result of not thoughtfully, prayerfully considering the scriptures as we read them is the same: we endure them when we could delight in them.

But why, we might ask, do the scriptures have to be pondered to be appreciated? After all, we don't need to ponder the newspaper. We understand it at first reading. What makes the scriptures different?

Perhaps an analogy will help. The scriptures seem to us like a symphony. The problem with a symphony, if it can be called a problem, is that there is so much going on at the same time that an inexperienced listener feels bewildered, not knowing what to listen for nor how to connect all the parts. But the music lover knows what to listen for. He will pick out a theme carried by the string section, compare it to a variation of that theme by the oboes, and hear the composer being playful or reflective or joyful. In short, the experienced listener, unlike the novice, hears and feels the effects of the details that give the symphony its power and impact.

The ability to notice and interpret details often distinguishes an expert from a layman. When an architect looks at a cathedral, a bridge, or a house, he sees more than most of us do, and not because he has better eyesight. What he sees is there for all to see. Rather, he knows what things to look for and he takes time to look for them. Likewise, a person who appreciates a painting looks at it differently than one who doesn't. His eyes move differently, stopping at different places, connecting new points, tracing previously unnoticed patterns. When most of us listen to someone speaking, we listen for the gist of his message. But when a man of discernment listens to someone, he notices the tone of voice, the expression on the face, and the choice of words, and he sees the man's

soul. Brigham Young was such a man. Hugh Nibley
writes: "A big black leather chair stood in Brigham
Young's office by the Lion House; it faced the window on
the opposite wall and the President's desk in the middle of
the room. First-time visitors to the office were invited to
sit on that chair, facing the strong light of day and the
calm blue eyes of Brother Brigham, who sat there at his
desk, his back to the window, quietly waiting for his guest
to say something. After all, the man had come to see him,
and it was only right to let him state his business: President Young, according to Grandfather [Charles W.
Nibley], would never say a word for the first three
minutes. And at the end of those first three minutes he
always knew exactly the sort of man he was dealing with,
and the nature — greedy, benign, or sinister — of his
business. "And he *never* (here Grandpa smote the arm of
his chair) had to change his mind!" — his psychoanalytical
techniques, black leather couch and all, were deadly ac-
curate . . . Brigham Young used to say that no man, if
allowed to speak, could possibly avoid revealing his true
character." (BYU Studies, Autumn, 1970, p. 61.)

Like symphonic music, cathedrals, paintings, and our
own speech, the scriptures are rich with details that
pondering helps us discover and appreciate. And it is
precisely the richness of the scriptures, the intricately
woven truths they contain, that makes them enduring,
that makes us want to go back to them again and again.
They aren't like most popular books or songs whose total
content is exhausted in one quick reading or hearing.
The scriptures are to feast upon, whenever we return to
them, time after time.

What does one do, then, who wants to love the scriptures more? He ponders the scriptures, asking questions
that help him see and understand the details of what he is
reading. He is full of questions, good, sincere questions
he asks himself, questions he asks others, questions he
takes to the Lord in prayer. If he reads a verse that leaves
him perplexed or bored, he doesn't put it aside or force
himself to read on. He stops and ponders. If he isn't learning anything, he wonders what he has missed. If there is
repetition, he looks for the reasons for the repetition. If
there seems to be no connection between two verses, he

tries to discover how the verses relate to each other. And if he is teaching a class and gets no response to a scripture, he doesn't proceed to new material. He discusses with the class the details of the passage.

In the remainder of this chapter, we ponder some passages of scripture, exploring details. First, we consider *setting*. We look at two passages and pose questions about their setting or context. Then we go on to other important and perhaps less familiar details in the scriptures, posing more questions in other areas besides setting.

We suggest you try to answer the questions before reading our answers. That way, instead of merely learning more of what *we* think, you'll learn more of what *you* think—more about pondering. Remember, the comments we make are simply *our* response to the scriptures, given our understanding, experience, and study. They aren't definitive in any way, doctrinally or otherwise. Your response is what's important for you, and your insights may change and grow each time you reread a passage of scripture.

The best questions to ask may vary from one verse of scripture to another. So, we end this chapter with a list of the study questions in various areas we've found most useful. (Note: We have added italics to many of the quotations in this book for emphasis. *"Teachings"* refers to *Teachings of the Prophet Joseph Smith,* selected by Joseph Fielding Smith [Salt Lake City: Deseret Book Company, 1938].)

Setting

The setting of a passage of scripture helps us better understand the passage. It might include the geography of the area, the customs of the people, or the past behavior of the individuals involved. Frequently, key aspects of the setting are found in the scriptures themselves. And it is often helpful to look further in history or reference books. Of course, to know what circumstances are relevant, we need to know something of the passage itself. The two work together: the more we understand the passage, the more we know what in the setting is relevant; and the more we know the relevant setting, the more we understand the passage. Following are some examples of trying to understand the setting of scriptural passages:

Nephi wrote a passage of scripture similar to the psalms of David; it is often called the Psalm of Nephi. (2 Nephi 4:17–35.) Nephi begins the psalm, "O wretched man that I am! Yea, my heart sorroweth because of my flesh; my soul grieveth because of mine iniquities." Question: Why is Nephi so disturbed?

Here is what we've found. Just before the psalm, Lehi dies and the older brothers become angry with Nephi. Just after the psalm, the family separates. Nephi must have wanted to keep the family together, for he had seen in vision what separation would mean—wars and contentions and ultimately the annihilation of his people. (1 Nephi 12:1–3, 19.) But without Lehi, trying to keep the family united must have been so frustrating that Nephi calls himself "wretched." Before the psalm ends, however, Nephi has turned to the Lord and found peace, setting the example for us: we too can find peace in the Lord.

The story of David and Bathsheba marks a terrible transition in the life of David. (2 Samuel 11–12.) What led to David's fall? (Hint: See verse 1 of chapter 11.)

Verse 1 says, "And it came to pass, after the year was expired, at the time when kings go forth to battle, that David sent Joab, and his servants with him, and all Israel; and they destroyed the children of Ammon, and besieged Rabbah. But David tarried still at Jerusalem." So, instead of leading his armies in battle, as other kings would have, David tarries at Jerusalem. The writer seems to be tactfully saying that King David's irresponsibility as commander of his armies led, in part, to his immoral behavior. We might have missed this connection between irresponsibility and immorality if we hadn't asked about the setting.

Meaning of Words and Phrases

Understanding the plain sense of a passage of scripture is obviously important. Dictionaries, concordances, and other translations of the Bible can help us understand the meanings of unfamiliar words and phrases in the scriptures. Here are some examples:

good example

What is the meaning of the word "betimes" in the scripture that begins, "Reproving betimes with sharpness, when moved upon by the Holy Ghost . . ."? (D&C 121:43.)

For this question, a dictionary is the most helpful reference book. According to the dictionary, "betimes" doesn't mean "at times," as is commonly supposed; it means "early, speedily, in due time, before it is too late." So, if we let our children's misbehavior pile up without saying anything and then end up exploding, we've done wrong; we've waited too long. Solomon wrote, "He that loveth [his son] chasteneth him betimes." (Proverbs 13:24.)

When Jesus asked John the Baptist to baptize him, he justified his request by explaining, ". . . for thus it becometh us to fulfil all righteousness." (Matthew 3:15.) Wasn't Christ already righteous?

A dictionary will not help us with this question. A concordance, however, tells us that the phrase, "to fulfil all righteousness," occurs also in 2 Nephi 31:5-7. In this passage, Nephi asks and answers our very question. Baptism is an outward witness of our willingness to be obedient in keeping the commandments. Christ, who was already righteous, still needed to give witness of his willingness to be obedient, thus showing that we, who are not so righteous, must do likewise. This is just one example of other scripture clarifying the meaning of a phrase from a biblical passage.

Matthew, describing John's baptism of Jesus, writes, "And Jesus, when he was baptized, went up straightway out of the water: and, lo, the heavens were opened unto him, and he saw the Spirit of God descending like a dove, and lighting upon him." (Matthew 3:16.) Do the pronouns he, him, he, him, refer to John or to Jesus? (Hint: See John 1:32-34.)

John's account illuminates Matthew's. It seems that the first and last of these pronouns refer to Jesus, who was baptized and on whom the Spirit descended, while the middle two refer to John, who witnessed the heavens opening and the Spirit descending on Christ. Pronouns are used frequently in the scriptures and can be confusing if we don't determine to whom or what they refer.

In the Word of Wisdom, the Lord says, "All grain is good for the food of man; as also the fruit of the vine; that which yieldeth fruit, whether in the ground or above the ground." (D&C 89:16.) What does "fruit" mean in this passage, since fruit doesn't grow under the ground?

In the usual sense of the word *fruit,* there are no fruits under the ground. Hence, the Lord must be using *fruit* in the broader sense of *produce,* which includes vegetables. In the same way, when Christ says, "Ye shall know them *by their fruits*" (Matthew 7:16), he means "by what they produce."

What did Jesus mean when he told the woman of Samaria, "Whosoever drinketh of this water shall thirst again: But whosoever drinketh of the water that I shall give him shall never thirst; but the water that I shall give him shall be in him a well of water springing up into everlasting life"? (John 4:13–14.)

Jesus was speaking of spiritual things in terms his listener would understand: as water is to the thirsty, so Christ is to man a source of life; but unlike the life that water gives, the life that Christ gives is enduring.

The scriptures are rich with figurative language that helps us understand the things of the Spirit through familiar things like rocks, bread, water, birth, death, and marriage. And as we come to comprehend spiritual things through familiar ones, we sense much of the beauty and power of the scriptures.

Speaker's Attitude

When someone speaks or writes for any length of time, he reveals his attitude toward his subject, his listeners, and himself. This is particularly true of speakers and writers in the scriptures, where the attitude or spirit conveyed is especially important.

What was Pilate's attitude towards Christ and the truth when he said to Jesus, "What is truth?" (John 18:38.)

We don't believe Pilate was sincerely asking about the truth. He seems cynical about anyone, including Christ, ever coming to know what truth is. Try asking Pilate's question cynically.

*What was the attitude of the Lord when he said of the Saints'
enemies, "Let them bring forth their strong reasons against the
Lord"? (D&C 71:8.) Did he really think they had strong reasons
against him?*

The Lord, it seems, was being ironic. By appearing to
agree that they had "strong reasons," he was in effect saying how foolish it is to argue with him. Try saying this
line ironically.

*Isaiah speaks of Lucifer's fall from heaven, saying that Lucifer
thought in his heart, "I will ascend into heaven, I will exalt my
throne above the stars of God: I will sit also upon the mount of the
congregation, in the sides of the north: I will ascend above the
heights of the clouds; I will be like the most High." (Isaiah
14:13–14.) What is Lucifer's attitude here?*

These words clearly show Lucifer's extreme pride.
Five times he says, "I will," and ends up insisting he will
be like God. Try saying Lucifer's words boastfully, as he
might have.

When we study the attitudes of the speakers in the
scriptures, we learn what they feel and how their
language shows their feelings. As a result, we also learn to
listen to each other more closely, to discern and evaluate
more accurately the attitudes we all reveal, every day, in
the way we use language.

Scriptural Comparisons

Many things in the scriptures can be compared — individuals, attitudes, events, reactions. When we make
comparisons, we look for similarities and differences. In
fact, we look for the similarities in light of the differences,
and the differences in light of the similarities — both are
instructive. Frequently in the scriptures, two comparable
items — two things similar in important ways and different
in other important ways — are placed side by side so we
can better understand both of them. Often it also helps
our understanding to compare events or individuals in the
scriptures to those we are familiar with outside the scriptures.

*In recounting the events preceding the First Vision, Joseph
Smith describes both his reaction to the clergy (Joseph*

Smith — History 1:8–9) and his reaction to the passage in James that begins, "If any of you lack wisdom . . ." (Joseph Smith — History 1:12). How do these two experiences compare?

Joseph's experience with the clergy left him feeling confused and disturbed (verses 8 and 9); on the other hand, the passage in James came with great power and force into every feeling of his heart (verse 12). The difference between these two experiences must have deeply affected Joseph. Having tasted the bitter, he could recognize and prize the sweet when he received it. This is how we all learn — by seeing and feeling contrasts.

When Adam and Eve are asked by the Lord if they've partaken of the forbidden fruit, they don't say simply, "We did." Instead, Adam says, "The woman thou gavest me, and commandest that she should remain with me, she gave me of the fruit of the tree and I did eat." Eve says, "The serpent beguiled me, and I did eat." (Moses 4:18–19.) How are their answers similar?

Though Adam and Eve both admit they've eaten the forbidden fruit, they both want to place responsibility elsewhere, Adam on Eve, and Eve on the serpent. Today, we still look for "extenuating circumstances" when we feel guilty. When the scriptures describe two people in the same situation or the same person in two similar situations, comparing their behavior is often enlightening.

When Joseph Smith recalls his decision to ask God which of all the churches was right, he uses the words "venture" and "attempt." (Joseph Smith — History 1:13–14.) Do these words remind you of any passage of scripture with similar words?

The words "venture" and "attempt" remind us of the word "experiment," which occurs in Alma's sermon on faith: "Awake and arouse your faculties, even to an experiment upon my words." (Alma 32:27.) The Joseph Smith story is an example of faith exercised the way Alma said it should be. Joseph, having felt the words of James begin to enlarge his soul and enlighten his understanding, experimented upon the words by doing as James directed: asking God.

Implied Messages

The scriptures imply much more than they actually state. Hence, the more we learn to read between the lines, the more we'll learn from them.

In Doctrine and Covenants 20:5–6, the Lord says of Joseph Smith, "After it was truly manifested unto this first elder that he had received a remission of his sins, he was entangled again in the vanities of the world; But after repenting, and humbling himself sincerely, through faith, God ministered unto him by an holy angel, whose countenance was as lightning, and whose garments were pure and white above all other whiteness." What do these verses imply about the First Vision?

The angel with white garments must have been Moroni. (Compare Joseph's description of Moroni in Joseph Smith—History 1:32.) So, before Moroni's visit, presumably at the First Vision, Joseph was told that his sins were forgiven him. (Compare D&C 29:3.) This fact isn't recorded in the Pearl of Great Price account of the First Vision, though it is in other accounts. (See Milton V. Backman, Jr., *Joseph Smith's First Vision* [Salt Lake City: Bookcraft, 1971].)

After the Lord sends down fire to consume Elijah's offering on Mount Carmel, and then wind and a great rain to end the drought that Elijah had earlier decreed on Israel, Elijah meets the Lord on Mount Horeb: "And, behold, the Lord passed by, and a great and strong wind rent the mountains, and brake in pieces the rocks before the Lord; but the Lord was not in the wind: and after the wind an earthquake; but the Lord was not in the earthquake: And after the earthquake a fire; but the Lord was not in the fire: and after the fire a still small voice. And it was so, when Elijah heard it, that he wrapped his face in his mantle." (1 Kings 19:11–13.) What do you think all this implies about how the Lord deals with his children?

Those who are hardhearted, like the Israelites during Elijah's ministry, seem only to know the Lord when he speaks with the voice of wind and earthquake and fire. But to the righteous, like Elijah, the Lord speaks in a still small voice, apparently the way he prefers to speak.

What Is or Is Not Included

Frequently we expect to find something in a passage
of scripture that isn't there. Or, we are surprised to find
something there we hadn't expected. Whenever this happens, we should ask why that particular part was or wasn't
included in the scriptures.

*While journeying in the wilderness, Lehi dreams about a dark
and dreary wilderness and a tree of life. Nephi records this dream
and Lehi's ensuing concern for his children in 1 Nephi 8, beginning
with verse 2. But in verse 1 of the same chapter he records, "And it
came to pass that we had gathered together all manner of seeds of
every kind, both of grain of every kind, and also of the seeds of fruit
of every kind." Why is the fact of the seed-gathering recorded here?
It doesn't seem to have anything to do with Lehi's dream, or does it?*

The gathering "of seeds of fruit of every kind" prepares
our minds for the central symbol of Lehi's dream: the fruit
of the tree of life, a fruit "desirable above all other fruit"
(verse 12); the "seeds" anticipate Lehi's concern for his
own "seed" (verse 3); and the repetition of "every kind"
foreshadows the many kinds of people and paths in the
dream. The gathering of the seeds also suggests that they
were ready for a long journey that would take years, and
that this was therefore the right time for Lehi to receive
his historic vision.

*According to Matthew, Christ said to his disciples,
"Whosoever is angry with his brother without a cause shall be in
danger of the judgment." (Matthew 5:22.) But in the Book of
Mormon, Christ tells the Nephites, "Whosoever is angry with his
brother shall be in danger of his judgment." (3 Nephi 12:22.) Why
isn't the phrase "without a cause" in the Book of Mormon account?*

First, we might ask ourselves what it means to be "in
danger of the judgment." Other translations of this phrase
are: "brought to judgment" *(New English Bible)* and "will
answer for it before the court" *(Jerusalem Bible).* So it appears that an angry person isn't necessarily a sinful
one—only that he had better be able to justify his anger.
Christ seems to be saying, "If you are angry, watch out!"
We know that the Lord himself becomes angry on occasion, but godly anger, like godly sorrow, must be quite

different from worldly anger, which, like worldly sorrow, works death, not repentance. (See 2 Corinthians 7:10.) And most human anger seems to us worldly, not godly. The phrase "without a cause" thus seems unnecessary. If you do have a just cause, and your answer "holds up in court," you won't be condemned. But if you don't, then you will be condemned. Too, it seems that the phrase "without a cause" would too easily allow anyone to excuse his anger: after all, who is ever angry without some kind of cause? The *Jerusalem Bible* translates the verse: "Anyone who is angry with his brother will answer for it before the court." This translation corroborates the Book of Mormon verse.

Organization

The scriptures aren't organized like a treatise, but this doesn't mean they aren't organized. Their organization is subtler and far richer than that of most things we are accustomed to reading. We need to look closely within and between verses at how things are ordered and how they relate to each other. Then the scriptures will have a more unified, powerful effect upon us.

The second chapter of 1 Nephi begins, "For behold, it came to pass that the Lord spake unto my father, yea, even in a dream . . ." In that dream, Lehi was warned to flee from Jerusalem and the Jews who sought his life. Why does Nephi begin the verse with "For behold"? What relationship is he implying between the material that goes before it and the material that comes after it?

At the end of the first chapter, we read, "I, Nephi, will show unto you that the tender mercies of the Lord are over all those whom he hath chosen, because of their faith, to make them mighty even unto the power of deliverance." Nephi then proceeds in the second chapter to do just that, showing how the Lord's mercy in warning Lehi made Lehi "mighty even unto the power of deliverance." So, Nephi wasn't using the words "For behold" out of mere custom or habit, but as a signal to the reader that he was about to explain how he knew the Lord supports those who place their trust in him. Connecting words like "for," "but," and "thus" imply relationships of explanation or contrast between passages. It's easy to miss these relationships, if we don't, as a matter of habit, ask ourselves why those particular connecting words are used.

What is the effect of having to wait until the very end of the following verse to find out what is going to happen? "And thus commandeth the Father that I should say unto you: At that day when the Gentiles shall sin against my gospel, and shall be lifted up in the pride of their hearts above all nations, and above all the people of the whole earth, and shall be filled with all manner of lyings, and of deceits, and of mischiefs, and all manner of hypocrisy, and murders, and priestcrafts, and whoredoms, and of secret abominations; and if they shall do all those things, and shall reject the fulness of my gospel, behold, saith the Father, I will bring the fulness of my gospel from among them." (3 Nephi 16:10.)

Putting so much material at the beginning suspends the final clause, making us wait for it, thus emphasizing it by delaying it.

Repetition of Ideas, Words, and Sounds

A word, an idea, or a sound makes a more lasting impression when repeated. Little children delight in the repetition they hear in their favorite stories, for example, Little Red Riding Hood saying, "Oh, grandmother, what big eyes (ears, teeth) you have!" In the scriptures, repetition is an art. And when we become sensitive to it, we, like our children, will delight in it.

What phrases repeat the same ideas in the following instructions from the Lord to Martin Harris? "Therefore I command you to repent — repent, lest I smite you by the rod of my mouth, and by my wrath, and by my anger, and your sufferings be sore — how sore you know not, how exquisite you know not, yea, how hard to bear you know not." (D&C 19:15.)

The phrases "by my wrath" and "by my anger," and "by the rod of my mouth" repeat the same idea, as do the three phrases "how sore you know not," "how exquisite you know not," and "how hard to bear you know not." This warning, after we hear it, is not easily forgotten; the drumming continues in our ears. Paul wrote that scripture is "profitable for doctrine, for reproof, for correction, for instruction in righteousness." (2 Timothy 3:16.)

Repetition helps to powerfully convey that doctrine, reproof, and instruction.

What words are repeated in James 1:6, which reads, "But let him ask in faith, nothing wavering. For he that wavereth is like a wave of the sea driven with the wind and tossed"?

"Wavering," "wavereth," and "wave" are all variations of the same root word.

How does this repetition make you feel?

These variations of the word "wave" create a feeling of instability and lack of direction — the wavering we avoid if we "ask in faith."

Quickly read the first twenty-two verses of Doctrine and Covenants 19, a section addressed to Martin Harris, and identify the words most frequently repeated.

The words *repent, suffer,* and *punishment* are repeated over twenty times. Try finding them.

What is the effect of this repetition?

It is sobering, to say the least. After hearing these words repeated again and again, Martin was probably more willing to listen to the Lord. Does the repetition have the same effect on you?

After warning Martin Harris in the first half of Doctrine and Covenants 19, the Lord entreats him in verse 23, "Learn of me, and listen to my words; walk in the meekness of my Spirit, and you shall have peace in me." What repeated sounds do you notice in this verse, and what is their effect?

We notice these sounds: *l* (*l*earn, *l*earn), *m* (*m*e, *m*y, *m*eekness, *m*y, *m*e) and *s* (*l*i*s*ten, meekne*ss*, *S*pirit, pea*c*e). These sounds bind the verse together and help convey the peaceful compassion of the Lord as he beckons to Martin and to us. Even young children who don't yet read can hear sounds like these and tell how the passage makes them feel. Now, with an awareness of the sounds, try re-reading this verse aloud: "*L*earn of *m*e, and *l*isten to *m*y words; walk in the *m*eekne*ss* of *m*y *S*pirit, and you shall have pea*c*e in *m*e."

What sounds stand out in the following passage from Nephi's vision of the last days, and what is the effect? "And I also saw gold, and silver, and silks, and scarlets, and fine-twined linen, and all manner of precious clothing; and I saw many harlots." (1 Nephi 13:7.)

We hear the *l* and *s* sounds. Can you pick them out? Notice how these sounds create in this verse a different effect than in the previous verse. Sounds support messages, and here the message is different. The repeated sounds in this verse build up to the last word, "harlots," emphasizing the wealth and depravity of the great and abominable church. Note how the rhyming word "scarlets" also reinforces "harlots."

What sounds are repeated in Isaiah 13:8, which reads, "And they shall be afraid: pangs and sorrows shall take hold of them; they shall be in pain as a woman that travaileth: they shall be amazed one at another; their faces shall be as flames"?

The long *a* sound is repeated in th*ey*, afr*ai*d, t*a*ke, th*ey*, p*ai*n, trav*ai*leth, th*ey*, am*a*zed, f*a*ces, and fl*a*mes. The result: an ailing, moaning sound conveying the despair of those described by Isaiah. Throughout Isaiah, sounds help communicate the message. But, you might point out, we are reading a translation, and the sounds in the original were probably different. True, but depending on the quality of the translation, the overall message and effect should be similar. Try rereading this verse, with an awareness of the repeated sound.

Emphasis

Because the spoken word is richer than the written word, we better understand and appreciate the scriptures when we read them aloud, even in individual study. A major advantage of the spoken word is emphasis. That is, when we emphasize certain words as we read aloud, we better express the meaning and power of the scriptures.

Young Joseph Smith was deeply affected when he read the scripture from James which begins, "If any of you lack wisdom, let him ask of God . . ." (James 1:5.) Read aloud Joseph Smith—History 1:12, empahsizing those words you think Joseph would emphasize if he were telling you the story.

We read the verse emphasizing the words we've italicized: "Never did *any* passage of scripture come with *more* power to the heart of man than *this* did at *this* time to mine. It seemed to enter with *great* force into *every* feeling of my heart. I reflected on it *again* and *again,* knowing that if *any* person needed wisdom from God, *I* did; for *how* to act I did *not* know, and unless I could get *more* wisdom than I *then* had, I would *never* know; for the teachers of religion of the different sects understood the *same* passages of scripture *so* differently as to destroy *all* confidence in settling the question by an appeal to the Bible."

When this verse is read with understanding, with key words emphasized, the powerful effect that James 1:5 had on Joseph is easy to see.But when the verse is read flatly, without emphasis or understanding, we adjust our position on the chair, look at the clock, and proceed to another verse. When we read with understanding, without having to work at it or be dramatic, the emphasis comes out right. Proper emphasis is particularly important for children, who will understand or fail to understand a passage of scripture simply by how we read it.

Should the word "all" or the word "faith" be emphasized in the following verse from the Doctrine and Covenants? "And as all have not faith, seek ye diligently and teach one another words of wisdom." (D&C 88:118.)

If the word "faith" is emphasized, the verse says that diligently seeking and teaching one another words of wisdom is the next best thing to having faith. But if "all" is emphasized, it says that diligently seeking and teaching one another words of wisdom is a way to help everyone gain faith. Changing the emphasis changes the meaning. Perhaps only one of these meanings is intended, perhaps both are.

After her husband's death, Ruth was encouraged by Naomi, her mother-in-law, to return home to her own people. Read aloud Ruth's beautiful response (Ruth 1:16–17), emphasizing the words you think should be emphasized.

The passage could be read with emphasis as follows: "And Ruth said, *Intreat* me not to *leave* thee, or to return from following *after* thee: for whither *thou* goest, *I* will go;

and where thou *lodgest, I* will lodge: *thy* people shall be *my* people, and thy *God my* God: Where thou *diest,* will *I* die, and *there* will I be buried: the Lord *do* so to me, and *more* also, if *ought* but death part thee and me." Emphasis in this passage carries the message, helping us feel the tremendous love and faith of this convert and ancestress of Christ.

Phrasing

Pausing in the right places as we read aloud is one of the best and simplest ways of making the scriptures more understandable and interesting. Most important is where to take a full pause and catch a breath. As a general rule, take breaths at all punctuation marks except commas — at all periods, dashes, colons, semi-colons, exclamation marks, and question marks.

Read aloud the following passage and notice what is conveyed by taking breaths where marked: "Therefore, get ye straightway unto my land; (breath) *break down the walls of mine enemies;* (breath) *throw down their tower, and scatter their watchmen.* (breath) *And inasmuch as they gather together against you, avenge me of mine enemies, that by and by I may come with the residue of mine house and possess the land.* (breath) *And the servant said unto his lord:* (breath) *When shall these things be?* (breath) *And he said unto his servant:* (breath) *When I will;* (breath) *Go ye straightway, and do all things whatsoever I have commanded you* (breath)." (D&C 101:57-60.)

Read this way, the Lord's instructions in the first sentence are emphatic. And when the Lord says "When I will," we hear him pointedly telling his servant to leave the Lord's coming up to the Lord and to do as commanded until then.

What is conveyed in the following passage by taking breaths according to the punctuation? "For unto us a child is born, unto us a son is given: (breath) *and the government shall be upon his shoulder:* (breath) *and his name shall be called Wonderful, Counseller, The mighty God, The everlasting Father, The Prince of Peace* (breath)." *(Isaiah 9:6.)*

The last phrase conveys a fulness, an abundance, a sense of majesty.

Conclusion

President Kimball writes, "I am convinced that each of us, at some time in our lives, must discover the scriptures for ourselves." (*Ensign*, Sept. 1976, p. 4.) For us, the discovery of the scriptures has come through learning to ponder. We've found that when we ponder more, we learn more. We've made it a practice when teaching a family home evening lesson, an MIA class, or a priesthood or Sunday School class, to select a passage of scripture, prepare some questions like those in this chapter, and then with our family or class read the passage aloud, a portion at a time, and ponder what we read. It's simple. And the result is a closing prayer in which it is said, "We thank thee for the scriptures thou hast given us."

Study Questions for the Scriptures

Setting

1. Are any of the following important in understanding the passage: the political situation, the laws and traditions of the time, the geography of the area? (Consult a Bible encyclopedia or Church history book for answers.) What about previous instructions or prophecies from the Lord?

2. What were the characters doing before and after the events described in the passage? Is the behavior of the characters consistent with their previous and subsequent behavior?

3. Has the Lord said anything about the persons described in the passage? What do others say about them? What do they say about themselves?

4. What prompted the speaker in the passage to say what he said? Joseph Smith wrote, "I have a key by which I understand the scriptures. I enquire, what was the question which drew out the answer, or caused Jesus to utter the parable?" (*Teachings,* pp. 276–77.)

5. What led to the prophet's receiving the revelation? Was he grappling with a question or trying to solve a problem?

Meaning of Words and Phrases

1. What does a word or phrase mean? What did it

mean at the time it was uttered? Does or did it have several meanings? How is it used elsewhere in the scriptures? (Consult a dictionary, a concordance, or another translation.) To what or whom do the pronouns refer?

2. Is the language figurative? If so, what is the literal meaning of the passage? Why is the message put figuratively? What are the important symbols in the passage, for example, in Lehi's dream? What are they meant to symbolize? Why are the symbols good ones? That is, what attributes are shared by the symbols and what they represent? For example, how is the fruit of a tree like the love of God? How far should the comparison between the symbol and what it represents be carried? For example, should we make anything of the fact that an iron rod could rust? Obviously not.

3. Does the passage make sense? Could the words and phrases be understood in such a way that the passage would make more sense? Could there be translation problems? What do other translations say, including the Joseph Smith Translation of the Bible? If someone other than the Lord or his prophet is speaking, could he be mistaken or even lying?

Speaker's Attitude

1. What is the attitude of the writer or the speaker? Is it matter-of-fact, remorseful, joyful, ironic, cynical? Do particular words or actions reveal the attitude? What is the effect of the speaker's attitude on his listeners? What is its effect on you? Is the attitude and its effect good or bad, desirable or undesirable?

Scriptural Comparisons

1. How does a person in the passage compare to someone else in the scriptures, in history, or today? How does he compare to you? How are their actions, speech, or attitude alike or different?

2. How has a person in the passage changed? How does his present behavior compare to what it was or will be? Has he matured, repented, sinned, learned a lesson, or stayed about the same? Does his behavior in different situations show that he has changed or remained the same?

3. What are the similarities and differences between events recorded in scriptural passages? To which situa-

tions does the Lord react similarly? To which differently? For example, when does the Lord send missionaries to a wicked people, and when does he destroy a wicked people? How do different individuals react in similar situations? How does the same individual react in comparable situations? For example, how does Christ's reaction to Pilate compare to his reaction to Herod, and what do you learn about Pilate and Herod from the differences? What situations in your own life are spiritually or morally similar to those described in the passage? What are the similarities and differences between various accounts of the same event or various descriptions of the same person? For example, how do the accounts of Christ's life in the four gospels compare?

4. Could the scriptural passage, its words or phrases, have reasonably been written differently? If so, why was it written as it was? For example, why does the Lord say the church shall be "terrible as an army with banners" (D&C 5:14), rather than "powerful as an army with banners"?

5. How might a person in the passage have acted differently? How should he have acted? How would most individuals have acted? How would the Lord have acted in that situation?

6. Does the passage remind you of another passage of scripture? Does it seem consistent with other scriptures and doctrine? If not, what have you misunderstood?

Implied Messages

1. Does the passage imply something it doesn't directly say? Was the speaker or writer aware of the implication? If so, why did he say it indirectly?

2. What do the words of the writer or speaker imply about his intentions, feelings, or knowledge? For example, when Sherem the anti-Christ says that no man can tell of things to come (Jacob 7:7) and then that he knows there will never be a Christ (verse 9), what do we learn about his state of mind?

3. Does the passage imply something about the way people or affairs actually are? What does it imply about the way they should be?

What Is or Is Not Included

1. Why does a passage or story from the scriptures include a particular part or incident?

2. Why are other facts or incidents omitted when it would seem natural to include them?

3. What does the inclusion or exclusion of particular material tell us about the author's purpose?

Organization

1. Why are the chapter and verse divisions the way they are? Are they appropriate?

2. What are the major divisions within a chapter, series of chapters, or section? Why does a particular passage occur next to another within a chapter or section? What is the relationship between them?

3. Is there a particular order in which things are presented? Is it chronological, negative to positive (such as the Word of Wisdom, where what we shouldn't eat is mentioned before what we should eat), abstract to concrete (such as D&C 93, in which relevant doctrine is presented before specific instructions), or question to answer (such as D&C 121, where Joseph's petition to the Lord is recorded before the Lord's answer)?

4. If an event is told out of a particular order, such as out of chronological order, why is it told that way?

5. What do transitional words like "for," "but," and "thus" imply about the organization of the passage? What phrases or verses do these transitional words connect? Why are they appropriate to the passage? Do they indicate an explanation, a causal relationship, a contrast?

6. Is the word order in a verse unusual? If so, what is the effect? Are particular words emphasized because the order is unusual?

7. Does the organization create suspense by leading you to expect something and then delaying it?

Repetition of Ideas, Words, and Sounds

1. What ideas are repeated in the passage? In what order are they repeated? That is, are they repeated in the same order, in reverse order, or in some other order? What is the effect of the repetition? Does it make the idea seem more important to you? Does it help you remember the idea? Does it have an emotional effect on you?

2. What words are repeated in the passage? In what order are they repeated? What is the effect of the repetition, emotionally and intellectually?

3. When the passage is read aloud, what sounds stand out? How do the sounds feel — harsh, gentle, lyrical, stern? Do the sounds reinforce the message or thought? Is a change in thought accompanied by a change in sound? Do the repeated sounds bind phrases or verses together? Do they emphasize a word? Do they make a phrase harder to articulate, hence emphasizing it by slowing it down?

Emphasis

1. What words or syllables should be emphasized when the passage is read aloud? Are there several alternative ways of correctly placing emphasis?

2. Does a change in emphasis result in a change in meaning?

3. Which patterns of emphasis best carry the passage along rhythmically? Which patterns best highlight the points the writer is making?

Phrasing

1. Where should you pause when reading the passage aloud? Where should you make a full pause and take a breath? Does the punctuation correctly indicate where you should pause?

2. Do the pauses help emphasize what is important in the passage?

3. Do the distances between successive breaths differ? What is the effect of the similarity or variation in distance between breaths?

2

Discussing the Scriptures

"The greatest temporal and spiritual blessings which always come from faithfulness and concerted effort, never attended individual exertion or enterprise." That is what the prophet Joseph Smith said. (*Teachings,* p. 183.) We believe it is true of scripture study. Put simplistically, two heads are better than one.

One way to learn how to ponder the scriptures, one of the best ways and in the end perhaps the only way, is by simply reading and discussing the scriptures together as a group or a family. In a family, the little children will learn from the older ones and from their parents. The older children and the parents will learn from each other and, if they are ready for it, from the little children. We think of a discussion brought on by a little girl. She was told how Heavenly Father saved baby Jesus from Herod's swords by warning his parents to flee. Her question, asked in all innocence, was, "Didn't Heavenly Father love the other babies, too?" It may take an adult to answer that question or even to attempt an answer, but it takes the simplicity of a child to ask it.

Thanks to a delightful piece written by Jeffrey R. Holland, president of Brigham Young University, we can look in on a father and his daughter discussing the Book of Mormon together. As you might expect from the last chapter, questions guide the discussion. While you read "Daddy, Donna and Nephi," list those questions. Most often they are followed by question marks. But sometimes they aren't, as when Daddy says, "And maybe there's another reason for having the Book of Mormon begin like this." The question he is asking is, of course, "Why does the Book of Mormon begin the way it does?" You might want to make two lists, one for the questions Daddy asks and one for those Donna asks, ignoring the questions listed in the right-hand margin — our list of all the questions — until you've finished.

An Excerpt from "Daddy, Donna and Nephi" by Jeffrey R. Holland (Ensign, Sept. 1976, pp. 8-10)

Let's take the first chapter of the first book of Nephi. This is probably the most familiar material in the book to most of us; and yet if we are not alert, we will miss much of its meaning, for it was very carefully written and must be read that way.

Let's assume that a father is helping his twelve-year-old daughter get started in this first chapter. She is a delightful, fun-loving girl who has tried reading the Book of Mormon a few times but hasn't been able to get too interested. We might overhear a conversation something like this:

Dad: O.K., sweetheart, let's read the first chapter of the first book of Nephi. It's only twenty verses long, less than two pages of print. Think about it as you read. Ask yourself questions.

Donna: What kind of questions?

Dad: Oh, questions like "Why should this be the first chapter of the book?" or "What does this verse have to do with that one?"

Donna: Well, I don't know anything about those things but I do want to know why we don't start off reading about those Jaredites. They were here first.

Dad: That's *exactly* the kind of question to ask — and here you've waited at least a minute and a half to ask it. Now — when you begin to find the answer to questions like that —

Donna: Daddy! Surely you're going to tell me the answers if I can finally think up the questions!

Dad: Tut, tut, Impatience. When you begin to find the answers to questions like that, the whole Book of Mormon will open up to you. You'll find out why the Book of Ether should come exactly where it does when you read it *very* carefully. We'll talk about that when we get to it, which is nearly the very end of the book. Now, let's start reading.

Donna: Whatever you say, Dad. *(Donna begins reading, silently. With a furrowed brow or two she makes it to the end of the first chapter.)* O.K., I've read it.

Why should this be the first chapter of the book?

What does this verse have to do with that one?

Why doesn't the Book of Mormon begin with the Jaredites, who were here first?

Dad: Good. What do you think it says?

What does the first chapter say?

Donna: Daddy, I said I *read* it. I didn't say I knew what it meant.

Dad: Well, then we have to read it again, only a little slower this time. And out loud. We'll talk as we go.

Donna: Whatever you say, Dad. *(Reading aloud)* "I, Nephi, having been born of goodly parents . . ."

Dad: Now why do you think Nephi starts his book like that?

Why does Nephi start as he does?

Donna: Maybe he's a nice man.

Dad: Maybe. What else?

Donna: Maybe it's going to be about his family.

Dad: Maybe. What else?

Donna: Maybe he wants us to know who is telling the story.

Dad: Maybe. What else?

Donna: Daddy! This could go on all night and I have school tomorrow. If I read this slowly in class my teacher would bean me. Now let me read it clear through and don't stop me unless I ask you something. O.K.?

Dad: O.K. *(Donna reads the chapter aloud. Slowly. With one eye on her father.)*

Dad: Good. *Now.* What does that chapter say?

What does the chapter say?

Donna: *(With a wry smile because she had known he was going to ask her that question)* It's about a man named Lehi who has a vision and warns his people about their destruction. But they don't like him.

Dad: *(With a wry smile because he had known she was going to read more thoughtfully)* Terrific! What do we call a man like Lehi?

What do we call a man like Lehi?

Donna: A prophet.

Dad: What did he do that brought the vision?

What did Lehi do that brought his vision?

Donna: I don't know. It doesn't say.

Dad: Yes it does. Look. In verse 5.

Donna: *(Reading)* Oh. He prayed. I didn't notice that. I guess I turned the page too fast. It's kind of hidden there near the bottom, you know.

Dad: That's O.K., honey. You're not the only one moving too fast to remember to get the prayer worked in.

Donna: What?

Dad: Nothing. Now exactly what did Lehi see in his vision?

What did Lehi see in his vision?

Donna: He saw that Jerusalem was going to be destroyed.

Dad: Hold on! You're going too fast. *How* did he see that Jerusalem was going to be destroyed?

How did Lehi see that Jerusalem was going to be destroyed?

Donna: *(Rereading)* Well, some heavenly messengers brought him a book and he read it.

Dad: Can you tell who the heavenly messengers are?

Who were the heavenly messengers?

Donna: I think one of them sounds like Jesus.

Dad: I think he does, too. Now you said that when Lehi tries to tell the people about Jerusalem being destroyed, they don't like it. What do they do?

What did the people do after Lehi warned them?

Donna: *(Rereading)* They get mad and make fun of him.

Dad: How mad do they get?

How mad did they get?

Donna: Well, finally they try to kill him.

Dad: Let's just put down on paper a little outline of this chapter. I think it would look something like this:

a prophet prays
has a vision
sees heavenly messengers
    (apparently including
    Jesus)
receives a book
is rejected by most of the
    people

Now that's a rough outline of the story you described in chapter 1. Does it look at all familiar to you?

What is the story of Lehi similar to?

Donna: I don't believe so.

Dad: Think about it.

Donna: Well, it does

sort of sound like Joseph
Smith's experience. Hey! It
sounds a *lot* like Joseph
Smith's experience. That's
neat. Why is that Daddy?

*Why are Joseph's and Lehi's
experiences so similar?*

Dad: Terrific com-
ments! It seems to me one
possible answer to your
question is that all prophets
usually have some very
similar experiences. In any
case one thing we *know* they
have in common is receiving
revelation from the Lord.
Joseph Smith once said that
revelation is the rock on
which the Church of Jesus
Christ will always be built
and there would never be
any salvation without it. I
think we're going to find,
Donna, that this whole book
will be one long revelation
about revelation. And Jesus
is going to be at the center of
it all. These first 20 verses
tell an awfully lot about what
is to follow. You can't do
much better than that in an
opening chapter.

And maybe there's
another reason for having
the Book of Mormon begin
like this. Maybe it helps in
its own way to teach that if
we accept Lehi and the Book
of Mormon, we surely have
to accept Joseph Smith as a
prophet of God. On the
other hand, when we accept
Joseph Smith as a prophet,
we must accept and faithful-

*Why does the Book of Mor-
mon begin with the story of
Lehi?*

ly live by the teachings of this book which he helped bring forth.

In a way, Donna, this record is not only the testimony of Nephi and Alma and Mormon and Moroni, but it is also the testimony of Joseph Smith and Brigham Young and Harold B. Lee and Spencer W. Kimball. Maybe that's why the Church wasn't even organized until the Book of Mormon was completely translated and published. The Prophet Joseph Smith once called it "the keystone of our religion," and I think most of us do not yet understand how essential the Book of Mormon was to everything that would happen after Moroni handed those plates over to the seventeen-year-old Prophet. When I think of what the Church has become since Joseph's first vision and the delivery of this book I want to shout with Lehi in verse 14: "Great and marvelous are thy works, O Lord God Almighty!" Donna, I love this book with all my heart and I know it's the word of God.

Donna: Daddy, I've never heard you talk like this before.

Dad: Well, I've never had my twelve-year-old

daughter read the Book of
Mormon to me before.

Donna: Whillikers! It's
past 10:00! We've been talking more than forty-five
minutes on one little
chapter. I've got to get to
bed. You're going to bean
me.

Dad: I doubt it. But
then I might. Scurry, Abish.

Donna: Abish? Who's
Abish?

Who's Abish? (Answer: See Alma 19.)

Dad: Just someone I
read about once. Scoot!
Now! Pronto!

With a kiss and a hug for
her dad, Donna dashes off to
bed, more assuredly on her
way to a testimony of the
truthfulness of the Book of
Mormon and the reality of
the restoration than she
realizes.

Of course, what Donna's
father knows — and what she
is about to find out — is that
every chapter is charged
with meaning, often many
meanings, and always
meanings that illuminate
and inspire.

Conclusion

Donna, we found, asked three questions in this story:
1. Why doesn't the Book of Mormon begin with the Jaredites, who were here first?
2. Why are Joseph Smith's and Lehi's experiences so similar?
3. Who's Abish? Or, why are you calling me Abish?
Donna didn't ask as many questions as her father, but hers were just as significant. It is easy to imagine a sequel

to the story: The next night, Donna, still puzzled, asks her father again, "Who was Abish, anyway?" Her father gives her a hint: "Try looking in the Book of Mormon index." She does; they start reading Alma 19; and one question leads to another, and then to another. Before long, Donna is full of questions, asking them and attempting to answer them.

We, too, can come to the scriptures with searching and illuminating questions. When we do, we will gain much and give much, for no two of us will ask just the same questions, nor find exactly the same answers. We each bring to and take from the scriptures something personal, yet something that can enrich the lives of our families and our brothers and sisters in the gospel.

The farmer, for instance, knows what it is like when a hen gathers her chickens under her wings and will ask himself why Christ used that particular metaphor. Parents will ask themselves what Christ meant when he said that unless we become as little children, we cannot enter the kingdom of heaven. A convert, studying the Joseph Smith story, will notice how Joseph felt as he went from church to church searching for the right one, and will compare his own feelings to Joseph's.

In reading the scriptures, as with the rest of the gospel, "the body is not one member, but many." (1 Corinthians 12:14.) Ours is a lay ministry, and if we all are scripturally literate, then "all may be edified of all.' (D&C 88:122.)

Feasting upon the Word

Ours is a fast-paced age. We eat on the run, read on the run, even make friends and sometimes marriages on the run. There is so much to do, so much to buy, no time to waste. We are in a train rushing past houses and buildings, and the faster we go, the more everything begins to look alike. Nothing seems very good, nothing very bad, everything rather average.

And when we mistake the scriptures for a quick meal instead of a feast, we choke, trying to down something too rich too fast. The scriptures, like all "the things of God are of deep import; and time, and experience, and careful and ponderous and solemn thoughts can only find them out." (*Teachings,* p. 137.)

In this section, we slow down, take our time with the scriptures, and feast. We ponder by asking the types of questions we have been discussing. As in the previous section, try to find your own answers to the questions before reading our answers.

3

A Father and His Two Sons
— Luke 15:11–32

What is the setting of this parable? What prompted Jesus to give it? (Hint: See the first part of chapter 15.)

We like what Joseph Smith writes about the setting: "While Jesus was teaching the people, all the publicans and sinners drew near to hear Him; 'and the Pharisees and scribes murmured, saying: This man receiveth sinners, and eateth with them.' This is the keyword which unlocks the parable of the prodigal son. It was given to answer the murmurings and questions of the Sadducees and Pharisees, who were querying, finding fault, and saying, 'How is it that this man as great as He pretends to be, eats with publicans and sinners?'" (*Teachings,* p. 277.)

In fact, the Lord answers the murmurings of the scribes and Pharisees with three parables. The first is the parable of the lost sheep; the second, the parable of the lost piece of silver; and the third, the parable of the prodigal son. About these first two parables, Joseph Smith, continuing, writes: "The hundred sheep represent one hundred Sadducees and Pharisees, as though Jesus had said, 'If you Sadducees and Pharisees are in the sheepfold, I have no mission for you; I am sent to look up sheep that are lost.' . . . He also gave them the parable of the woman and her ten pieces of silver, and how she lost one, and searching diligently, found it again, which gave more joy among the friends and neighbors than the nine which were not lost; like I say unto you, there is joy in the presence of the angels of God over one sinner that repenteth, more than over ninety-and-nine just persons that are so righteous; they will be damned anyhow; you cannot save them." (*Teachings,* pp. 277–78.)

How are these three parables the same, and how is this last one different?

When the lost sheep and the lost piece of silver are found, there is rejoicing, just as there is in heaven over the repentant sinner. The third parable continues the theme, with a father rejoicing over the return of his repentant son. But this parable is clearly more complex: besides the joy of the father, we have the repentance of the son (the lost sheep and piece of silver can't repent), the envy of the elder brother at his father's rejoicing, and the father's response to the envious brother. So, we see the Lord waiting until the third parable to show the Pharisees and scribes what they were up to: criticizing him for eating with sinners is just like criticizing one's father for receiving home a repentant younger brother.

11   And he said, A certain man had two sons:

12   And the younger of them said to his father, Father, give me the portion of goods that falleth to me. And he divided unto them his living.

13   And not many days after the younger son gathered all together, and took his journey into a far country and there wasted his substance with riotous living.

14   And when he had spent all, there arose a mighty famine in that land; and he began to be in want.

15   And he went and joined himself to a citizen of that country; and he sent him into his fields to feed swine.

16   And he would fain have filled his belly with the husks that the swine did eat: and no man gave unto him.

What do you think "divided unto them his living" means? (Verse 12.)

The father divides up his property, deciding what each of his sons will inherit. The younger son here asks and is generously allowed to receive his inheritance *before* the father dies. So now, all the father's remaining wealth, including its subsequent increase, goes to the elder son. We aren't told whether the elder son, like the younger, received any of his inheritance early. But given that the father is in charge of things throughout the rest of the parable, he must have retained control over the bulk of the remaining property.

What does "gathered all together" mean? (Verse 13.)

The son sells the property he received, converting it into cash.

What sound stands out in the phrase "and there wasted his substance with riotous living?" (Verse 13.) What word does the repeated sound emphasize?

We hear the *s* sound building up to the word "riotous": "and there wa*s*ted his *s*ubstan*c*e with riotou*s* living." Assuming we have a good translation, Jesus would also have emphasized the son's riotous living, though not necessarily through the repetition of *s* sounds.

What is emphasized by repeating the word "living" at the end of verses 12 and 13?

To us, it emphasizes the sinfulness of the son as he spends his inheritance in riotous living, using his wealth in ways his father would highly disapprove of.

In verse 15, the son "joins" himself to a citizen of the country. The word join *suggests a rather indefinite arrangement, one that must have contrasted sharply with the family relationships the son had left. What do you think the "employer-employee" arrangements were between the citizen and the son?*

Apparently the son, being destitute in a famine, puts himself under the care of the citizen and agrees to carry out his biddings for whatever the citizen chooses to give him, which certainly isn't much, as he becomes hungry enough to eat the food given to the pigs. The pigs are cared for better than he is.

What does his having to feed swine tell us about the condition of the son?

Ask one who has slopped hogs, and he will tell you that it is a distasteful chore; it is difficult to feed them without getting the slop splashed on you by the eager, hungry pigs. More importantly, to the Jews swine were unclean and so not fit to eat. Some Jews, in fact, actually get sick to their stomachs at the thought of eating pork. The younger son's task must have been particularly disgusting for a Jew. He had hit rock bottom.

What does "fain" mean? (Verse 16.)

Webster tells us that it means "willingly." The son would willingly have eaten husks, which were carob pods. (See the footnote in the LDS edition of the Bible.) But no one responded to his need.

What sounds are prominent in verses 15 and 16, and what do they emphasize?

The *f*, *ee*, and *s* sounds bind together verses 15 and 16 and serve to intensify the distress of the prodigal son: "And h*e* went and joined him*s*elf to a *c*itizen of that countr*y*; and h*e* *s*ent him into his *f*ields to *f*eed *s*wine. And h*e* would *f*ain have *f*illed his bell*y* with the hu*sks* that the *s*wine did *ea*t: and no man gave unto him." Notice that it's a little difficult to say "fields to feed swine." You have to say the phrase slowly, which emphasizes the last word, swine.

17 And when he came to himself, he said, How many hired servants of my father's have bread enough and to spare, and I perish with hunger!

18 I will arise and go to my father, and will say unto him, Father, I have sinned against heaven, and before thee,

19 And am no more worthy to be called thy son: make me as one of thy hired servants.

20 And he arose, and came to his father. But when he was yet a great way off, his father saw him, and had compassion, and ran, and fell on his neck, and kissed him.

21 And the son said unto him, Father, I have sinned against heaven, and in thy sight, and am no more worthy to be called thy son.

22 But the father said to his servants, Bring forth the best robe, and put it on him; and put a ring on his hand, and shoes on his feet:

23 And bring hither the fatted calf, and kill it; and let us eat, and be merry:

24 For this my son was dead, and is alive again; he was lost, and is found. And they began to be merry.

What does "came to himself" mean? (Verse 17.)

These words, used to describe the son's repentance, suggest almost a return to consciousness—consciousness of his sinfulness and the dire circumstances it has put him in. The phrase reminds us of Jacob saying to his brethren, "shake yourselves that ye may awake from the slumber of death." (Jacob 3:11.)

What sounds are significant in verse 17?

The younger son, thoroughly humbled by his circumstances, begins to repent of having left his family. We see him exhausted, hungry, heavy-hearted—all these feelings suggested by the repeated *h* sound: "*H*ow many *h*ired servants of my father's *h*ave bread enough to spare, and I perish with *h*unger!" Try reading this softly, slowly, with weariness, slightly emphasizing the *h* sounds.

What words should be emphasized in verse 17?

Emphasizing the words "servants" and "perish" brings out the contrast between what the son now has and what even the servants of his father had.

Is the attitude expressed in verses 17 and 18 typical of repentance?

Elder Howard W. Hunter of the Council of the Twelve spoke about this parable, saying, "Repentance is but the homesickness of the soul." When we repent, we long for the "food"—the spirit of peace and love—experienced in our families, earthly or heavenly; and we resolve to arise and go back home.

There is an interesting paradox in the speech the son plans to give his father in verses 18 and 19. Can you pick it out?

He plans both to address his father as "father" and to say he isn't worthy to be the son of his father. He doesn't really feel like a servant toward his father.

In verse 21, the son starts into the speech he had planned even after his father's overwhelming expression of forgiveness in verse 20. What does this tell you about him?

It seems to us that he was remorseful, and also nervous.

The fact that the father sees the son when "he was yet a great way off" (verse 20) implies what?

That his son was on his mind, that he was watching for him. Many times before, he must have looked at approaching figures, hoping to see his son.

Verse 20, which describes the father's initial response to his son, is beautiful. In the second sentence of verse 20, part of the beauty comes from pairs and triples of words with repeated vowel sounds. For example, when yet; great way. Can you find others?

There are several others: off, saw; had compassion, ran; fell, neck; his, kissed him. These repeated sounds bind together the phrases in which they occur, creating a movement and beauty that conveys the father's intense joy at his son's return.

Now, with an awareness of these sounds, try reading the sentence aloud, allowing yourself to feel the father's joy.

"But when he was yet a great way off, his father saw him, and had compassion, and ran, and fell on his neck, and kissed him."

What is conveyed by the rapid succession of active verbs — saw, had compassion, ran, fell, kissed?

This communicates a joy that couldn't be contained, that had to be expressed in action.

The verb phrases continue in verses 22 and 23. Can you pick them out?

Bring, put, put, bring, kill, let.

The son tells his father, "I . . . am no more worthy to be called thy son." (Verse 21.) Does his father reply to this?

The father replies not in words, but in action. He cuts short his son's speech, and gives directions for a great feast to celebrate his son's return. By this action he reaffirms the father-son relationship and rejects any idea of a master-servant relationship. The details of the celebration are significant: *The Interpreter's Bible* says that the best robe was reserved for distinguished guests on special occasions, and the ring and shoes were both signs of sonship — only slaves went without shoes. Notice also how the father says, "this my son," which is more emphatic than just saying "my son."

What is conveyed by the dead-alive and lost-found metaphors? (Verse 24.)

There are few contrasts of greater magnitude than the one between life and death, or between losing and finding. These metaphors seem to highlight the difference between the son's past and his present, emphasizing the importance of the present.

What doesn't the father do that other fathers in similar circumstances might have done?

The father doesn't probe into the past, demanding, "Where have you been all this time?"; nor into what led the son to return, asking "Have you learned your lesson?" All that seems important is that he has returned. Like the sheep, he was dead and is alive; and like the piece of silver, was lost and is found. Just as it would have been absurd to question the sheep or silver, so a cross-examination of the son is inappropriate.

25 Now his elder son was in the field: and as he came and drew nigh to the house, he heard musick and dancing.
26 And he called one of the servants, and asked what these things meant.
27 And he said unto him, Thy brother is come; and thy father hath killed the fatted calf, because he hath received him safe and sound.
28 And he was angry, and would not go in: therefore came his father out, and intreated him.
29 And he answering said to his father, Lo, these many years do I serve thee, neither transgressed I at any time thy commandment: and yet thou never gavest me a kid, that I might make merry with my friends:
30 But as soon as this thy son was come, which hath devoured thy living with harlots, thou hast killed for him the fatted calf.

Now the parable focuses on the elder son's reaction. This son is initially out "in the field." (Verse 25.) What does this tell us about him?

He must have been a hard worker.

When he approaches the house and hears the "musick and danc-ing" he calls one of the servants for an explanation. (Verse 26.) Why does the elder son ask the servant what's happening instead of just going in himself to see?

He is perhaps already annoyed that a party is going on without his knowledge and wants to get all the facts to plan his response.

The elder son responds angrily to the servant's explanation. (Verse 28.) Do you think he would have been less angry had the servant said something like, "Thy brother is home! And he is safe and well! And thy father hath killed the fatted calf"? Would the ser-vant have then shown a different attitude?

Put that way, the servant would have seemed glad and excited that the son had returned. As it is, his speech sounds to us rather studied, not spontaneous. Like a detached observer, he says, "Thy brother is come," and then shows how excited the *father* is. His speech ends with hissing *s* sounds: "Because he hath received him *s*afe and *s*ound." The servant seems to be meddling, feeling the elder son out, wondering how he'll react, construing events in a way so the son will feel his position and in-heritance threatened. The elder son responds angrily, at least in part, because he seems to have lost face in front of the servant.

Try reading the servant's speech (verse 27) in a way that would make the elder son angry—as if the servant were saying, "Now what are you going to do?" Say the word "brother" with a teasing in-tonation.

What does the servant then do? (Verse 28.)

Apparently, the servant tries to encourage the elder son to go into the party, which would make the son lose face all the more; for the account says, "He . . . would not go in."

How does the father know the son is outside?

The servant must have gone in himself and reported the elder son's reaction to the father.

The father comes out to his elder son. (Verse 28.) What do you think most fathers in those days would have done?

We would expect the father, being the patriarch, to have summoned his son to him. It seems a great concession for him to go out to the elder son, even more of a concession than his going out to meet the younger one, which occurred under exceptional circumstances.

What does the father's coming out tell us about him?

We feel his love for his sons. In his concern for them, he disregards the deference due him. There is no holding back on the father's part, no waiting for his sons to make the first move. The younger son had to first "come to himself" before his father could go to him, but when he had repented, the father ran out to meet him. The father also goes out to meet his unrepentant elder son.

The elder son's speech seems to reveal his character; most obvious is his selfish disregard for his father and brother. What sounds are prominent in the speech in verse 29 and what do they convey?

The elder son's "my" attitude comes through with the repetition of *m* and *i* sounds in verse 29: "Lo, these *m*any years do *I* serve thee, neither transgressed *I* at any t*i*me th*y* co*mm*and*m*ent; and yet thou never gavest *m*e a kid, that *I* *mi*ght *m*ake *m*erry with *m*y friends."

The son begins his speech by saying "Lo." What does lo *mean?*

It is the equivalent of "see here"—a reproach to his father.

In verse 29, rather than saying "I served thee these many years; I neither transgressed thy commandment at any time," the elder son says, "these many years do I serve thee, neither transgressed I at any time thy commandment." The unusual word order emphasizes the phrases "these many years," "neither transgressed I," "at any time." Why does the son emphasize these phrases?

The elder son seems to be stressing his superiority to his younger brother.

What does the elder son's sureness that he had never transgressed his father's commandments tell us about him?

He must have interpreted his father's commands very mechanically or pharisaically, giving himself points for each act of obedience. Otherwise, it would be difficult for him to know that he hadn't transgressed.

Compare the elder son's speech in verses 29 and 30 with the younger son's speech in verse 21. How does each son feel toward his father?

Though the younger son doesn't feel worthy to be his father's son, he still comes to him and addresses him as "Father." The elder son, on the other hand, won't come to his father and doesn't address him at all. Further, he emphasizes his service to his father and his expectation of pay, concerns of a servant rather than a son. So he acts like a servant though he claims to be a son, whereas the younger son acts like a son though he is asking to be a servant. The younger son's actions clearly show respect; the elder son's do not.

How does the elder son refer to the younger son? (Verse 30.)

In verse 30 he says "thy son" instead of "my brother." This appears to be a rebuttal to the servant's "thy brother" in verse 27. Apparently, the elder son would like to disown his brother.

Even though it appears the family had no word about the younger brother while he was away, the elder son assumes the worst — "devoured thy living with harlots." (Verse 30.) What does this imply about the elder son?

Perhaps that is what he would have done. While the younger son — like one portion of humanity — indulged his unrighteous desires, the elder son — like the Pharisees — may have repressed his and felt superior for not giving in to those desires. If so, his outward behavior may have been "correct," but his heart wouldn't have been right.

Why does the elder son say that the father never gave him a kid (verse 29), rather than say that he never gave him a calf?

A kid is a young goat. The inference is, "You never gave me even a kid."

Do you think the elder son's accusation was true?

It was probably untrue or true in some way that wronged the father. Maybe the elder son didn't like parties, which is why the father never gave him one. It seems the kind of thing one says in anger. The parable shows the father to be a generous person.

31 And he said unto him, Son, thou art ever with me, and all that I have is thine.

32 It was meet that we should make merry, and be glad: for this thy brother was dead, and is alive again; and was lost, and is found.

The elder son has unjustly accused his father. But his father responds without recrimination. Why isn't he angry?

The father sees his son not as an enemy, but as a child who needs reassurance and a better understanding of his father's actions. Thus, he first reassures and then teaches.

How does the father reassure his son? (Verse 31.)

He addresses him as "Son" and tells him that all the remaining wealth is his inheritance — hence there is no need for him to feel threatened.

Does the phrase "all that I have is thine" remind you of anything else in the scriptures?

It reminds us of a part of the oath and covenant of the priesthood, in which the Lord says, "And he that receiveth my Father receiveth my Father's kingdom; therefore all that my Father hath shall be given unto him." (D&C 84:38.) Apparently, in the heavenly scheme, all can be given to each, without diminishing what each receives.

What is significant about the way the father refers to the younger son in verse 32?

The father says "thy brother," as opposed to the elder brother's "thy son" in verse 30, reminding the elder son that the younger son is still his brother.

What does the father teach his son in verse 32?

Without argument, the father simply affirms the appropriateness of the celebration, saying, "It was *meet* that we should make merry, and be glad." And though it will

use up part of the father's wealth—the elder son's inheritance—that is how their wealth should be used. It is a
time for rejoicing, because the son "was dead and is alive,
and was lost and is found." The repetition of this phrase
helps us see even more how much his son's return means
to the father. But the phrase also serves as a response to
the elder brother's "devoured thy living with harlots."
Again, what seems important is not the past sinful
behavior, but the return home.

*Here the parable ends. But we aren't told whether or not the
elder brother joins in the celebration and accepts his brother back as
a member of the family. Why not?*

The omission is deliberate. The parable has come
around at last to the accusation: "This man receiveth sinners, and eateth with them." The elder brother represents
the Pharisees and their spiritual kin, and the parable is an
appeal to them to receive the outcasts. Jesus was waiting
for their decision.

*Now, read the whole parable aloud, letting your increased
understanding come through in the way you read.*

4

Ask of God —
Joseph Smith — History 1:1-20

1 Owing to the many reports which have been put in circulation by evil-disposed and designing persons, in relation to the rise and progress of the Church of Jesus Christ of Latter-day Saints, all of which have been designed by the authors thereof to militate against its character as a Church and its progress in the world — I have been induced to write this history, to disabuse the public mind, and put all inquirers after truth in possession of the facts, as they have transpired, in relation both to myself and the Church, so far as I have such facts in my possession.

2 In this history I shall present the various events in relation to this Church, in truth and righteousness, as they have transpired, or as they at present exist, being now the eighth year since the organization of the said Church.

3 I was born in the year of our Lord one thousand eight hundred and five, on the twenty-third day of December, in the town of Sharon, Windsor county, State of Vermont. . . . My father, Joseph Smith, Sen., left the State of Vermont, and moved to Palmyra, Ontario (now Wayne) county, in the State of New York, when I was in my tenth year, or thereabouts. In about four years after my father's arrival in Palmyra, he moved with his family into Manchester in the same county of Ontario —

4 His family consisting of eleven souls, namely, my father, Joseph Smith; my mother, Lucy Smith (whose name, previous to her marriage, was Mack, daughter of Solomon Mack); my

brothers, Alvin (who died November 19th, 1824, in the 27th year
of his age), Hyrum, myself, Samuel Harrison, William, Don
Carlos; and my sisters, Sophronia, Catherine, and Lucy.

*Joseph begins his account with one long matter-of-fact
sentence. In that sentence, he tells us why he is writing the account.
What reasons does he give?*

Joseph wants to "disabuse the public mind" and "put
all inquirers after truth in possession of the facts." "Evil-
disposed and designing persons" have "abused" the public
mind, exciting it and filling it with falsehoods about the
Church. Joseph, we'll see later, refers to his own mind as
if it had been similarly abused while he searched for which
church to join. These designing persons have also made it
hard to find the truth, if one wanted to, among so many
false reports. So, Joseph is "induced" to give us this account, not because of a particular fondness for making
spiritual experiences public, but because the public mind
must be disabused and those who want the truth must be
given a chance to find it.

*If you were Joseph and wanted to "disabuse the public mind,
and put all inquirers after truth in possession of the facts," how
would you present your account? Would you try to persuade people
of what had happened to you, try to make them feel what you had
felt, tell them who you approved or disapproved of? What would or
wouldn't you do if you were Joseph?*

Because Joseph wants to calm the agitated public, he
gives what seems to us a cool, factual account. Rather
than try to persuade us, he simply presents the facts. He
doesn't try to make us feel what he felt, as it seems Oliver
Cowdery is trying to do in his rather overdone account of
the coming of John the Baptist at the end of the Pearl of
Great Price, but instead, he carefully describes what happened. Even when he expresses his disapproval, we'll see
that he does it indirectly and with a good deal of irony, so
as to approach his readers with firmness but without
anger, with courtesy but with clarity.

*What do you think Joseph's attitude is toward his readers when
he says at the end of verse 1, "so far as I have such facts in my
possession"?*

Joseph doesn't end the first verse saying heavy-handedly that he is going to give the reader the facts, but softens it by adding "so far as I have such facts." A writer's admission of his own limitations is a gesture of friendship.

In verse 2, Joseph tells us that he will present his account "in truth and righteousness"? Who is he contrasting himself with?

Joseph contrasts himself with those he mentioned in verse 1 who made reports on the Church from an evil disposition and an ulterior design. In verse 3 he plunges into the facts.

5 Some time in the second year after our removal to Manchester, there was in the place where we lived an unusual excitement on the subject of religion. It commenced with the Methodists, but soon became general among all the sects in that region of country. Indeed, the whole district of country seemed affected by it, and great multitudes united themselves to the different religious parties, which created no small stir and division amongst the people, some crying, "Lo, here!" and others, "Lo, there!" Some were contending for the Methodist faith, some for the Presbyterian, and some for the Baptist.

6 For, notwithstanding the great love which the converts to these different faiths expressed at the time of their conversion, and the great zeal manifested by the respective clergy, who were active in getting up and promoting this extraordinary scene of religious feeling, in order to have everybody converted, as they were pleased to call it, let them join what sect they pleased; yet when the converts began to file off, some to one party and some to another, it was seen that the seemingly good feelings of both the priests and the converts were more pretended than real; for a scene of great confusion and bad feeling ensued — priest contending against priest, and convert against convert; so that all their good feelings one for another, if they ever had any, were entirely lost in a strife of words and a contest about opinions.

The account in verses 1–4 is matter of fact, without much expression of approval or disapproval. But in verses 5–6, Joseph begins to express his disapproval, not directly, but by his choice of words. He tells us that an unusual religious excitement commenced, soon became general, and, indeed, seemed to affect the whole district. What image does this description bring to mind?

To us, it brings to mind the image of a contagious disease.

Verse 5 also seems to convey the feeling that something overdone and rather ridiculous was going on. Read the last part of verse 5, emphasizing the words that convey this feeling.

". . . *great* multitudes united themselves to the different religious parties, which created no small *stir* and *division* amongst the people, *some crying, "Lo, here!"* and others, *"Lo, there!" Some* were *contending* for the Methodist faith, *some* for the Presbyterian, and *some* for the Baptist."

In verse 6, the ironic disapproval increases in another long, powerful sentence. Several phrases in this verse are ironic. Can you pick them out as you read?

We have put single quotation marks around the phrases that seem ironic to us: "For notwithstanding the 'great love' which the 'converts' to these different faiths expressed at the time of their 'conversion,' and the 'great zeal' manifested by the respective clergy, who were active in 'getting up and promoting' this 'extraordinary scene of religious feeling,' in order to have everybody 'converted,' as they were 'pleased' to 'call' it, let them join what sect they 'pleased'; yet when the converts began to 'file off,' some to one party and some to another, it was seen that the seemingly 'good feelings' of both the priests and the converts were more pretended than real; for a scene of great confusion and bad feeling ensued — priest contending against priest, and convert against convert; so that all their 'good feelings' one for another, if they ever had any, were entirely lost in a strife of words and a contest about opinions."

Do the phrases "getting up and promoting" and "filing off" bring any particular images to your mind?

"Getting up and promoting" sounds to us like advertising for a circus. "Filing off" sounds like the military, or perhaps like dividing up for a game of some kind.

Rather than use irony, why doesn't Joseph just come out and say that ridiculous, corrupt ministers were manipulating the people?

Such a direct statement, even if true, would no doubt inflame rather than calm an agitated public mind. By using irony, Joseph is able both to calm and to inform.

Joseph concludes verse 6 by calling the affair "a strife of words and a contest of opinions." Later, he calls it a "war of words and tumult of opinions." (Verse 10.) From these phrases, what do you think Joseph found most objectionable in the religious discussions of the clergy?

The words "strife," "contest," "war," and "tumult" leave no doubt that Joseph was disturbed that the religious debate was so contentious. Surely alleged ministers of the Prince of Peace should engage in more peaceful discussion. Joseph also seems disturbed that the ministers had no power beyond mere "words" to resolve their differences of "opinion." He later speaks of "the powers of both reason and sophistry" used by the various denominations in trying to prove others in error. Where was the power of godliness—the power that would bring real understanding and certainty?

(If you'd like to read an interesting comparison to this portion of the Joseph Smith story, read aloud Nephi's description of the last days, particularly 2 Nephi 28:3-6. Try to catch the ministers' attitude as you read aloud verse 3.)

7 I was at this time in my fifteenth year. My father's family was proselyted to the Presbyterian faith, and four of them joined that church, namely, my mother, Lucy; my brothers Hyrum and Samuel Harrison; and my sister Sophronia.

8 During this time of great excitement my mind was called up to serious reflection and great uneasiness; but though my feelings were deep and often poignant, still I kept myself aloof from all these parties, though I attended their several meetings as often as occasion would permit. In process of time my mind became somewhat partial to the Methodist sect, and I felt some desire to be united with them; but so great were the confusion and strife among the different denominations, that it was impossible for a person young as I was, and so unacquainted with men and things, to come to any certain conclusion who was right and who was wrong.

9 My mind at times was greatly excited, the cry and tumult were so great and incessant. The Presbyterians were most decided against the Baptists and Methodists, and used all the powers of both reason and sophistry to prove their errors, or, at least, to make the people think they were in error. On the other hand, the Baptists and Methodists in their turn were equally zealous in endeavoring to establish their own tenets and disprove all others.

Joseph says in verse 7 that his family was "proselyted" to the Presbyterian faith. He doesn't say they joined the Presbyterian faith. What does the word "proselyted" imply about what took place?

Joseph seems to be emphasizing the pressure put on his family rather than their willingness to join.

The ministers probably tried to "proselyte" Joseph too, but unsuccessfully. What does this tell us about him?

It shows he was strong in resisting pressure to accept something he wasn't fully convinced of.

Joseph says nothing of his family "proselyting" him. What does this imply?

Joseph appears to have had complete religious freedom within his family.

Joseph uses the word great, *or variations of it, five times in verses 8 and 9. Three times he uses it to describe what was going on outside of him ("time of great excitement," "so great were the confusion and strife," "the cry and tumult were so great") and twice to describe what was going on inside of him ("great uneasiness," "my mind at times was greatly excited"). What does Joseph convey by using the same word to describe the confusion outside and inside himself?*

We feel the tumult of the times reverberating in Joseph's soul. Although cautious when it came to action, Joseph seems to have been sensitive mentally and emotionally. His mind was agitated and worked on by the clergy, and he appears at times to have been almost unnerved by the constant barrage of words. In verse 11, Joseph describes himself as "laboring under the extreme difficulties" caused by the clergy and in verse 13 as being in "darkness and confusion." In all this, Joseph shows how similar he was to many of his intended readers: he, like they, had been subjected to the propaganda of "evil-disposed and designing persons."

In verse 8, Joseph tells us that in time he became "somewhat partial" to and had "some desire to be united with" the Methodists. Why didn't he join the Methodists?

A weak inclination must not have been sufficient for Joseph. Apparently, he wanted certainty, which he couldn't seem to get, given the great confusion among the sects and his inability to understand what these men were up to.

In verse 9, Joseph describes his current understanding of what the clergy was then doing. He says the clergy used all the powers of both reason and sophistry to prove the errors of other sects, or at least to make people think they were in error. What is the difference between reason and sophistry?

Sophistry is corrupted reason; it is reasoning that has a false look of genuineness or truth.

Why do you think the ministers used sophistry in addition to reason?

Reason alone couldn't establish which church was right. It hasn't the power to. So, the clergy had to use sophistry to make it appear that they had established the rightness of their churches. With "powers" we are introduced to a theme — namely, what powers men accept and what they use them for. Here we have men using their power of reason foolishly. In the next several verses we see Joseph using his power of reasoning in a fruitful way.

10 In the midst of this war of words and tumult of opinions, I often said to myself: What is to be done? Who of all these parties are right; or are they all wrong together? If any one of them be right, which is it, and how shall I know it?

11 While I was laboring under the extreme difficulties caused by the contests of these parties of religionists, I was one day reading the Epistle of James, first chapter and fifth verse, which reads: *If any of you lack wisdom, let him ask of God, that giveth to all men liberally, and upbraideth not; and it shall be given him.*

12 Never did any passage of scripture come with more power to the heart of man than this did at this time to mine. It seemed to enter with great force into every feeling of my heart. I reflected on it again and again, knowing that if any person needed wisdom from God, I did; for how to act I did not know, and unless I could get more wisdom than I then had, I would never know; for the teachers of religion of the different sects understood the same pas-

sages of scripture so differently as to destroy all confidence in settling the question by an appeal to the Bible.

13 At length I came to the conclusion that I must either remain in darkness and confusion, or else I must do as James
directs, that is, ask of God. I at length came to the determination
to "ask of God," concluding that if he gave wisdom to them that
lacked wisdom, and would give liberally, and not upbraid, I
might venture.

*In verse 10, Joseph asks himself, "Who of all these parties are
right; or, are they all wrong together?" Why does he say, "all wrong
together" rather than just "all wrong"?*

"Together" implies a unity among the churches. Apparently, Joseph wonders if the churches, though violent-
ly at odds over particulars, are fundamentally more
similar than dissimilar. The Lord later tells Joseph that
they are: they each have a form of godliness, but they all
deny the power thereof.

*In verse 11, Joseph speaks of "the contests of these parties of
religionists." This phrase is big-sounding, but actually ironical.
Why?*

"Contesting" is out of character for the truly religious.
Also, the word "religionists' suggests a zealous, insincere
religion.

*While under the troublesome influence of these "religionists,"
Joseph finds in James an answer to his confusion. Verse 12, which
describes his reaction, is a beautiful verse, written in such a way
that one cannot miss the proper tone of voice or the proper emphasis.
Read verse 12 aloud, emphasizing the words you think should be
emphasized.*

Never did *any* passage of scripture come with *more*
power to the heart of man than *this* did at *this* time to
mine. It seemed to enter with *great* force into *every* feeling
of my heart. I reflected on it *again* and *again,* knowing that
if *any* person needed wisdom from God, *I* did; for *how* to
act I did *not* know, and unless I could get *more* wisdom
than I *then* had, I would *never* know; for the teachers of
religion of the different sects understood the *same* passages
of scripture *so* differently as to destroy *all* confidence in
settling the question by an appeal to the Bible."

How does Joseph's reaction to the passage in James compare to what he had been feeling? (Verses 6 and 8.)

Joseph says that the scripture in James came to him with power and with great force into every feeling of his heart. This feeling must have been very different from the "religious feelings" of the clergy and converts (verse 6), and the confused, anxious feelings he had labored under before (verse 8). It was substantial, something he could "reflect" on "again and again," until he reached the firm conclusion that if he didn't ask of God, he would have to remain in darkness, for without God, reason and scripture were insufficient, though they were important in leading him to seek God. "At length" (he must have reflected for some time), he decides to ask of God. If God will answer him without condemning him, he has nothing to lose and wisdom to gain. It all seems quite reasonable to him.

14 So, in accordance with this, my determination to ask of God, I retired to the woods to make the attempt. It was on the morning of a beautiful, clear day, early in the spring of eighteen hundred and twenty. It was the first time in my life that I had made such an attempt, for amidst all my anxieties I had never as yet made the attempt to pray vocally.

15 After I had retired to the place where I had previously designed to go, having looked around me, and finding myself alone, I kneeled down and began to offer up the desire of my heart to God. I had scarcely done so, when immediately I was seized upon by some power which entirely overcame me, and had such an astonishing influence over me as to bind my tongue so that I could not speak. Thick darkness gathered around me, and it seemed to me for a time as if I were doomed to sudden destruction.

16 But, exerting all my powers to call upon God to deliver me out of the power of this enemy which had seized upon me, and at the very moment when I was ready to sink into despair and abandon myself to destruction—not to an imaginary ruin, but to the power of some actual being from the unseen world, who had such marvelous power as I had never before felt in any being—just at this moment of great alarm, I saw a pillar of light exactly over my head, above the brightness of the sun, which descended gradually until it fell upon me.

17 It no sooner appeared than I found myself delivered from the enemy which held me bound. When the light rested upon me

I saw two Personages, whose brightness and glory defy all description, standing above me in the air. One of them spake unto me, calling me by name and said, pointing to the other — *This is My Beloved Son. Hear Him!*

18 My object in going to inquire of the Lord was to know which of all the sects was right, that I might know which to join. No sooner, therefore, did I get possession of myself, so as to be able to speak, than I asked the Personages who stood above me in the light, which of all the sects was right — and which I should join.

19 I was answered that I must join none of them, for they were all wrong; and the Personage who addressed me said that all their creeds were an abomination in his sight; that those professors were all corrupt; that: "they draw near to me with their lips, but their hearts are far from me, they teach for doctrines the commandments of men, having a form of godliness, but they deny the power thereof."

20 He again forbade me to join with any of them; and many others things did he say unto me, which I cannot write at this time. When I came to myself again, I found myself lying on my back, looking up into heaven. When the light had departed, I had no strength; but soon recovering in some degree, I went home. And as I leaned up to the fireplace, mother inquired what the matter was. I replied, "Never mind, all is well — I am well enough off." I then said to my mother, "I have learned for myself that Presbyterianism is not true."

In describing his decision to ask God, Joseph uses the words "venture" (verse 13) and "attempt" (verse 14). Do these words remind you of anything else in the scriptures?

They remind us of the frame of mind described by Alma in the Book of Mormon: ". . . if ye will awake and arouse your faculties, even to an experiment upon my words." (Alma 32:27.)

In verse 14, Joseph says, "It was the first time in my life that I had made such an attempt." He then gives the reason he hadn't made the attempt to pray vocally before. What is the reason?

It must have been that his anxieties had kept him from prayer. It is unlikely that the clergy would have told him to ask God, and whatever they did encourage him to do may well have kept him back from doing what he should have done and was now about to do.

Notice how carefully he relates the details in verse 15 — he went

to the place he had previously decided on, looked around, and find-
ing himself alone, knelt down to pray. Is it significant that Joseph
had previously decided on a place?

We think so. It tells us that Joseph had carefully
thought out what he would do beforehand. Joseph seems
serious in what he's doing.

Why did Joseph look around to see if he was alone?

Obviously, he didn't want an audience. This was a
private matter, not one done for show. Again, we sense
his inclination to keep spiritual experiences private: he's
not telling this story for publicity.

Why doesn't Joseph tell us who the evil "power" or "being"
was? (Verse 15.)

At the time, he probably didn't know who the evil
power was. Joseph is relating the facts as he experienced
them.

How does the evil power's influence over Joseph compare to the
religionist's influence over him?

Both put him in darkness and keep him from prayer.

Why at the end of verse 15 doesn't Joseph simply say "Thick
darkness gathered around me, and I felt doomed to sudden destruc-
tion"? After all, it would be more dramatic to leave out the phrase
"it seemed to me for a time as if."

Joseph, we see, isn't trying to be dramatic, and he
qualifies his sense of being doomed. The experience isn't
of overriding importance.

Verse 16 is another long sentence. Just after the emotional
climax of the sentence, "at the very moment when I was ready to
sink into despair and abandon myself to destruction," Joseph inserts
a parenthesized explanation, "not to an imaginary ruin, but to the
power of some actual being," and then resumes with a less emo-
tional phrase, "just at this moment of great alarm." What is the ef-
fect of this insertion?

It makes the account less dramatic; consequently, we
don't feel Joseph is trying to work on our emotions. He is
just carefully telling us what happened. And, of course,
this makes the story all the more believable. From the way
he writes, we sense this man is telling us the truth.

Does Joseph's experience with Satan remind you of anything else in the scriptures?

It reminds us of Moses' encounter with Satan. Moses, like Joseph, experienced the power of Satan, and after calling upon God for deliverance, was visited by the Lord. (Moses 1:12–42.)

In verse 16, Joseph carefully describes the movement of the pillar of light as he remembers it, using the phrases "just at this moment," "exactly," and "gradually." What does this description tell us about his state of mind at the beginning of the vision?

Joseph wasn't swept away into some mystical ecstasy. He retained his rationality and his capacity for careful observation.

Why does Joseph use the phrases "two Personages," "one of them," and "the other" to refer to the Father and the Son? (Verse 17.)

The phrase "two Personages" is matter-of-fact and yet seems respectful. Joseph doesn't say two "persons" or "men" or "beings" or "gods," but two "Personages." Given what he knew at the time, that was about all he could have called them. He refers to them individually as "One of them" and "the other." These are God the Father and the Son! But again, Joseph isn't trying to make us feel awe or reverence or fear. His object is just to explain what happened.

How does Joseph respond to the two Personages differently than another fourteen-year-old boy might have? (Verse 18.)

Joseph gets "possession of" himself in order to ask his question. He doesn't seem terror-struck. He was horrified with the power that seized him before, but he doesn't appear horrified now, though he still needs to get sufficiently in possession of himself to speak. And he does—a fourteen-year-old boy. You'd think he would be either so frightened that he couldn't say a word or so amazed that he would forget what he came to ask about. But no: Joseph calmly and rationally asks the question he came to ask.

In verse 19, the Lord tells Joseph to join none of the churches. He gives three reasons and then elaborates on them in reverse order. What are the reasons?

First, the churches were all wrong. Second, their creeds were an abomination. Third, their ministers were corrupt. In elaborating, the Lord says first that the ministers were corrupt as only their words drew near the Lord, not their hearts; second, their creeds were merely men's ideas taught as doctrine; and third, the churches were wrong in that they recognized only reason and scripture as sources of knowledge, denying the power of godliness, the power Joseph was experiencing.

In verse 20, Joseph describes finding himself lying on his back. There is nothing dignified about lying on ones' back, so why does Joseph mention such a detail?

Again, we see Joseph being matter-of-fact. He doesn't seem out to create a particular impression of himself, only to relate the facts.

After Joseph says he came to himself, he says, "When the light had departed, I had no strength." (Verse 20.) Does he mean the light departed after he came to himself and that he might have experienced part of the vision while he was unconscious?

We don't think so. Joseph is apparently telling us what happened earlier — when the light *had* departed. The sentence, "When the light had departed, I had no strength" explains why Joseph found himself lying on his back: after the light had departed, he had no strength and must have collapsed from exhaustion. Moses, too, was exhausted after *his* vision: "And the presence of God withdrew from Moses, that his glory was not upon Moses; and Moses was left unto himself. And as he was left unto himself, he fell unto the earth. And it came to pass that it was for the space of many hours before Moses did again receive his natural strength." (Moses 1:9–10.)

Joseph, coming to himself, "soon" recovers sufficiently to go home. (Verse 20.) Notice that he doesn't struggle to get up or anything dramatic like that. Tired, though, he leans up to the fireplace. We picture him, head on his hand, arm on the mantle, probably reflecting. His mother asks him what's the matter. What would you then expect a boy of fourteen to tell his mother after an experience like the one Joseph had just had?

You'd think he would say something like, "Guess what just happened to me." But he doesn't. He is much more serious than that. He quickly brushes off any need to be concerned about his health and comes right out and tells his mother something of interest to her. He had learned for himself, not from the clergy, that Presbyterianism, the faith his mother had adopted, was not true. His single-mindedness in light of all that has happened to him is sobering. Through it all, he never loses touch with his desire to find the true church.

5

A Wife for Isaac — Genesis 24

1 And Abraham was old, and well stricken in age: and the Lord had blessed Abraham in all things.

2 And Abraham said unto his eldest servant of his house, that ruled over all that he had, Put, I pray thee, thy hand under my thigh:

3 And I will make thee swear by the Lord, the God of heaven, and the God of the earth, that thou shalt not take a wife unto my son of the daughters of the Canaanites, among whom I dwell:

4 But thou shalt go unto my country, and to my kindred, and take a wife unto my son Isaac.

5 And the servant said unto him, Peradventure the woman will not be willing to follow me unto this land: must I needs bring thy son again unto the land from whence thou camest?

6 And Abraham said unto him, Beware thou that thou bring not my son thither again.

7 The Lord God of heaven, which took me from my father's house, and from the land of my kindred, and which spake unto me, and that sware unto me, saying, Unto thy seed will I give this land; he shall send his angel before thee, and thou shalt take a wife unto my son from thence.

8 And if the woman will not be willing to follow thee, then thou shalt be clear from this my oath: only bring not my son thither again.

9 And the servant put his hand under the thigh of Abraham his master, and sware to him concerning that matter.

The story of Isaac and Rebekah begins, "And Abraham was old and well-stricken in age." "Old" and "well-stricken in age" mean essentially the same. Why is Abraham's age emphasized?

For all Abraham knew, he would soon die. Sarah had recently died. Isaac needed a wife, and if Abraham was to have any say in the matter, it was time to act.

How old was Abraham at this time? (See Genesis 21:5 and 25:20.)

The scriptures say, "Abraham was an hundred years old, when his son Isaac was born unto him" (Genesis 21:5) and "Isaac was forty years old when he took Rebekah to wife" (Genesis 25:20). Thus, Abraham was 140 years old at this time. But he was far from being on his deathbed. He died when he was 175 (Genesis 25:7-8), and in the meantime had another wife and six children (Genesis 25:1-2).

Abraham says in Genesis 15:2 that the steward of his house is Eliezer of Damascus. Unless Eliezer died in the meantime, he is probably the servant spoken of in this chapter. But he is never referred to by name. Why?

Perhaps he is supposed to be remembered not as a particular individual, but as a steward, or even more, as a good example for all stewards. One of the things to look for in this chapter is how a good steward acts.

Why does Abraham tell Eliezer to put his hand under Abraham's thigh while taking the oath? (Verse 2.)

The *Interpreter's Dictionary of the Bible* says the purpose of this custom was to relate the oath-taker to the source of life in the other person. Given the nature of Eliezer's task, this must have been an appropriate way to swear the oath: Eliezer was to make a journey to see that Abraham would have descendants under the covenant.

The Joseph Smith Translation changes the line, "Put, I pray thee, thy hand under my thigh" to "Put forth I pray thee thy hand under my hand." However, this change is not made later in Genesis when Israel says to Joseph exactly what Abraham says to Eliezer, "Put, I pray thee, thy hand under my thigh." (Genesis 47:29.) Perhaps the idea was for Abraham to hold Eliezer's hand under his hand and against his thigh.

Why does Abraham select his steward for the important mission of finding Isaac a wife? Why didn't he go himself to arrange the marriage?

The five-hundred-mile trip from the Beersheba-Hebron area to Haran was likely an arduous one, especially difficult for someone of Abraham's age — perhaps another reason why his age is emphasized at the beginning of the chapter.

Why doesn't Abraham want Isaac to take a wife from among the Canaanites? (Verse 3.)

For one thing, the Canaanites probably didn't possess the right to the priesthood. From Abraham 1, we learn that the right to the priesthood was partly a matter of lineage. It appears that Canaan, one of the sons of Ham, was cursed pertaining to the priesthood, and it was this same Canaan who settled the land of Canaan. (Genesis 9:18-27; 10:6, 15-19; Abraham 1:21-22, 26-27.) One of Canaan's sons was Heth (Genesis 10:15), and when Esau later married two of the daughters of Heth, those marriages "were a grief of mind unto Isaac and to Rebekah." (Genesis 26:34-35.) Rebekah tells Isaac, "I am weary of my life because of the daughters of Heth: if Jacob take a wife of the daughters of Heth, such as these which are of the daughters of the land, what good shall my life do me?" (Genesis 27:46.) Abraham would have been particularly aware of priesthood rights; he says, "The records of the fathers, even the patriarchs, concerning the right of Priesthood, the Lord my God preserved in mine own hands." (Abraham 1:31.) At any rate, it is unlikely that a woman of Canaan, unless converted, would have raised Isaac's children to believe in Abraham's God. They might even have persuaded Isaac to believe in their gods. Abraham probably knew the fate of Lot and his children, some of whom had intermarried with the unbelieving inhabitants of Sodom and were consequently destroyed with them. (Genesis 19:14.) He may also have felt that a woman separated from her kindred and culture was more likely to come under his and Isaac's influence than one living among her relatives.

Why does Abraham want to take Isaac a wife from among his own kin? (Verse 4.)

Perhaps his kin were the best available people that Abraham knew. Even though it appears that they were idolatrous (Genesis 31:19), which was most likely the reason the Lord wanted Abraham to leave them in the first place, still it is likely that they had some understanding of the Lord and devotion to him. (See Genesis 24:31.) Marrying next-of-kin wasn't imperative, however. Joseph married "Asenath the daughter of Potipherah priest of On" (Genesis 46:20), and their son Ephraim received the birthright blessing. Another possibility is simply that the Lord told Abraham to take a wife for Isaac from among his own kin.

The servant responds to Abraham in verse 5. Immediately he anticipates a possible difficulty in fulfilling the oath he will make to Abraham, and further proposes a way to overcome the difficulty, namely, to bring Isaac along. What does this response tell us about him?

Eliezer's mind is quick and active in the exercise of his stewardship; in this, as in other incidents, he is the model of a good steward. He is also conscientious—he doesn't want to take an oath he might not be able to keep. And of course, he won't be able to keep it if the woman won't follow him. Abraham is sensitive to Eliezer's unspoken wish not to make an oath he can't keep, and in verse 8 states the conditions that will free Eliezer from the oath.

Abraham's answer to his servant in verses 6 to 8 forms a "chiasmus." The following abbreviation of the speech shows the form:
   a. Bring not my son
      b. Lord's oath
         c. Angel to go before
            d. take a wife from thence
         c. Woman to follow
      b. Abraham's oath
   a. Bring not my son

Notice the similar ideas in the a *lines and the contrasting ideas in the* b *lines and in the* c *lines. In a chiasmus, once the ideas are stated, they are repeated again in reverse order. The center of the chiasmus in verses 6 to 8 is: ". . . thou shalt take a wife unto my son from thence." This is the most important part, and so occurs in the middle. Why is Abraham's speech structurally formal? What does the formality emphasize?*

The formality reinforces the significance and seriousness of what is being said. God's promise to Abraham, "Unto thy seed will I give this land," is linked with Eliezer's promise to Abraham that he will take a wife from his kindred for Isaac. For God's promise to be fulfilled, Eliezer had to fulfill his. It was a solemn occasion. Eliezer must have left feeling no uncertainty about the importance of his task.

In verses 6 and 8, when Abraham says, "Bring not my son thither again," is he implying that Isaac has been in Haran before?

"Thither again" probably means "back to the place we (Abraham and Eliezer) came from" and does not imply that Isaac was ever in Haran.

Why doesn't Abraham want Isaac to go with Eliezer? (Verses 5-6, 8.)

The length of the trip and the possible dangers along the way may account for why Abraham didn't send Isaac along. Even though Isaac was forty years old, Abraham was probably still a protective father; Isaac was his only son by Sarah, one for whom he had waited numerous years, and then had nearly lost at Moriah. Abraham may have also been concerned about how long Isaac would be away. Now that Sarah was gone, he must have especially wanted Isaac near.

How does Abraham know the Lord will send his angel before Eliezer? (Verse 7.)

We are not told. It may have been that the Lord specifically told Abraham he would; more likely, Abraham has faith that the Lord will do so in order to fulfill his promise about Abraham's seed. Eliezer probably doesn't know how Abraham knew either but he nevertheless trusts Abraham.

Eliezer takes the oath in verse 9, though he probably doesn't know yet how he will fulfill it. Why is he willing?

Eliezer apparently believes, as Abraham states, that the Lord will help him, and he acts on that faith.

10 And the servant took ten camels of the camels of his master, and departed; for all the goods of his master were in his hand: and he arose, and went to Mesopotamia, unto the city of Nahor.

11 And he made his camels to kneel down without the city by a well of water at the time of the evening, even the time that women go out to draw water.

12 And he said, O Lord God of my master Abraham, I pray thee, send me good speed this day, and shew kindness unto my master Abraham.

13 Behold, I stand here by the well of water; and the daughters of the men of the city come out to draw water:

14 And let it come to pass, that the damsel to whom I shall say, Let down thy pitcher, I pray thee, that I may drink; and she shall say, Drink, and I will give thy camels drink also: let the same be she that thou hast appointed for thy servant Isaac; and thereby shall I know that thou hast shewed kindness unto my master.

Beginning in verse 10, Eliezer proceeds to do what's needed to find Isaac a wife, without further instructions. Abraham completely turns over this important task to Eliezer just as he had previously put all his goods "in his hand." What does this tell us about Abraham and Eliezer's past relationship?

Eliezer was obviously a trustworthy steward who, by his past initiative and good judgment in managing Abraham's affairs, had gained Abraham's confidence. Abraham trusts his faithful steward, feeling no compulsion to hover over him like a mother hen, afraid to relinquish control. This is how a good servant-master relationship should be, including ours with the Lord. Remember, "for he that is compelled in all things, the same is a slothful and not a wise servant." (D&C 58:26.) Notice how the words "servant" and "master" are repeated in verses 9 and 10, drawing our attention to the relationship as a good example.

Verse 10 says the servant went to "Mesopotamia, unto the city of Nahor." Genesis 25:20 calls Rebekah's father "Bethuel the

Syrian of Padanaram." And in Genesis 28:10 we read that Jacob went "toward Haran" to find Laban. Where exactly did Abraham's kindred live?

A good Bible dictionary is helpful in unraveling this. We find that Mesopotamia (which included the country between the Tigris and Euphrates rivers) was a part of Syria, and that Padanaram was another name for Mesopotamia. Haran, the city in Mesopotamia where Rebekah lived, was the name of Abraham's brother who died in Ur of the Chaldees. (Genesis 11:27–28.) Evidently the city of Haran was named for him. The probable reason it is also called the "city of Nahor" is that Nahor, Abraham's other brother and Rebekah's grandfather, settled there.

If we figure ten miles per day, the five-hundred-mile trip to Haran would have taken Eliezer about seven weeks — plenty of time to think. By the time he arrives in Haran, he has formulated a plan. He arrives in the evening when the women come out to draw water; then he proposes a plan to the Lord and asks for his help in making it successful. Eliezer tells the Lord, "This is what I propose to do. Please help me do it," not, "What shall I do?" Does this seem to you the right way to proceed?

Eliezer does the thinking and leaves it to the Lord to confirm or disconfirm. Elsewhere in the scriptures, the Lords approves of this. (See D&C 9:7–8; 58:26–29.)

Why does Eliezer address the Lord as "Lord God of my master Abraham," and not just "Lord God"? (Verse 12.)

Eliezer knows the Lord loves Abraham, so he addresses the Lord on behalf of Abraham, saying in effect that what the Lord does for Eliezer will be done for Abraham.

What does "good speed" (verse 12) mean?

"Good speed" means "a prosperous journey" or "success."

Eliezer begins and ends his prayer wanting the Lord to "shew kindness" to Abraham. (Verses 12 and 14.) What does this tell us about Eliezer's own feelings towards Abraham?

Eliezer himself feels kindly toward Abraham; perhaps he also feels protective, as he asks the Lord to show kindness to Abraham so that Abraham won't be disappointed.

Do you think Eliezer's plan for finding Isaac a wife was a good one?

There are several reasons to think it was:

1. He picks a time and place where it's likely the younger, unmarried girls will be. Apparently watering was women's work throughout the Middle East at this time, and even though Nahor's family was probably wealthy, the younger unmarried daughters, at least, retained the job, preparing perhaps for later responsibilities that would likely include the overseeing of servants who would do similar work.

2. As much as possible, Eliezer lets the Lord choose the right girl. He doesn't leave the choice up to the family—likely that would have meant getting the oldest unmarried daughter, no matter what her qualities. Nor does he feel himself adequate to the task. He is humble enough to acknowledge that it should be the Lord's decision.

3. The test Eliezer purposes is not an arbitrary one as far as the girl's character is concerned. A girl who would respond as he hopes would likely possess at least two desirable traits—generosity and vigor. After all, drawing water with a pitcher for ten thirsty camels is no easy task; this is emphasized by the repetition of "draw water," "pitcher," and "drink" up through verse 20. Even though Abraham has expressed concern only about the girl's family, Eliezer seems to know that her character is also important to Abraham, and that character is perhaps the basic reason Abraham is interested in her family.

4. If Eliezer's plan works, and a girl from Nahor's family draws the water for his camels, the event will likely be considered miraculous. And perhaps a miracle will be needed to convince Abraham's relatives to let Eliezer take the girl the Lord wants for Isaac. Eliezer is, after all, just Abraham's servant, not Abraham himself.

Did Eliezer propose too difficult a task for a young girl to perform?

The task was difficult, but it needed to be difficult to be selective. However, it may have been easier than we might think: The *New English Bible* uses the word "well" in verse 11 interchangeably with the word "spring," which means the water may have been on the surface rather than underground. This would have made the task considerably easier, though still difficult enough to be selective.

15 And it came to pass, before he had done speaking, that, behold, Rebekah came out, who was born to Bethuel, son of Milcah, the wife of Nahor, Abraham's brother, with her pitcher upon her shoulder.

16 And the damsel was very fair to look upon, a virgin, neither had any man known her: and she went down to the well, and filled her pitcher, and came up.

17 And the servant ran to meet her, and said, Let me, I pray thee, drink a little water of thy pitcher.

18 And she said, Drink, my lord: and she hasted, and let down her pitcher upon her hand, and gave him drink.

19 And when she had done giving him drink, she said, I will draw water for thy camels also, until they have done drinking.

20 And she hasted, and emptied her pitcher into the trough, and ran again unto the well to draw water, and drew for all his camels.

21 And the man wondering at her held his peace, to wit whether the Lord had made his journey prosperous or not.

22 And it came to pass, as the camels had done drinking, that the man took a golden earring of half a shekel weight, and two bracelets for her hands of ten shekels weight of gold;

23 And said, Whose daughter art thou? tell me, I pray thee: is there room in thy father's house for us to lodge in?

24 And she said unto him, I am the daughter of Bethuel the son of Milcah, which she bare unto Nahor.

25 She said moreover unto him, We have both straw and provender enough, and room to lodge in.

26 And the man bowed down his head, and worshipped the Lord.

27 And he said, Blessed be the Lord God of my master Abraham, who hath not left destitute my master of his mercy and his truth: I being in the way, the Lord led me to the house of my master's brethren.

28 And the damsel ran, and told them of her mother's house these things.

Why does the account say, "Behold, Rebekah came out" rather than just "Rebekah came out"? (Verse 15.)

The "behold" calls attention to the significance of the event, and also to Eliezer's excitement.

Rebekah's lineage is given in verse 15, and, more clearly, earlier in Genesis 22:20–23. Lineage was Abraham's main concern. What was Rebekah's relationship to Abraham?

She was the granddaughter of Abraham's brother, which would have made her a first cousin once removed to Isaac.

In Genesis 22:20–23, we find that someone told Abraham about the children and grandchildren of his brother Nahor. The only grandchild mentioned is Rebekah, except for Aram (who was significant because he was the father of the Syrians). Why do you think other grandchildren weren't mentioned?

The information may have come from Rebekah's relatives who had in mind a match with Isaac. But then, since Eliezer later tells Rebekah's family about Isaac's birth, they might not have even known about Isaac. Or perhaps Moses, who wrote Genesis, only recorded the genealogical information that seemed most relevant, omitting mention of Nahor's other grandchildren. Whatever actually happened, the message Abraham received was timely. It came after his trial at Moriah and the Lord's subsequent promise to multiply his seed (which would be through Isaac, as we find from Genesis 21:12), and before the death of Sarah—an event that probably increased Isaac's desire to take a wife. (Genesis 24:67.) It appears that for some time, the Lord had Rebekah in mind for Isaac, and events were working toward that end.

Besides family, what else about Rebekah is noted at this point?

In verse 16, her beauty and her virtue are noted, two characteristics that would be important to Isaac. Describing Rebekah's beauty, the Joseph Smith Translation says, "And the damsel being a virgin, [was] very fair to look upon, such as the servant of Abraham had not seen, neither had any man known the like unto her. (Verse 16.)

In verse 14, the servant prays, "let it come to pass." Then verse 15 begins, "It came to pass." What does the repetition emphasize?

That Eliezer's request was fulfilled. The Lord had heard him.

Rebekah gives Eliezer a drink, waits for him to finish, offers to water the camels, and then does so. Notice all the "hurry" words: in verse 17, the servant runs to meet Rebekah; in verses 18 and 20, Rebekah hastens; in verse 20 she runs again; later, in verse 28, she runs once more; and in verse 29, Laban runs out. What does all this communicate?

Everyone seems intent on their tasks, Eliezer eager to find Isaac a wife, Rebekah self-forgetful and absorbed in her work, Laban excited because such visitors were probably infrequent and welcome in Haran.

Assuming that the water source was a spring rather than a well, why don't the camels drink directly from it? Was Rebekah asked to do unnecessary work?

We don't think so. The camels, if they had drunk from the spring, would have muddied the water, which was also used by the people living in Haran.

Up until verse 21, Eliezer is referred to as "the servant." Beginning in verse 21 and for the next several verses, he is referred to as "the man." Toward the end of the story (verse 52) he once again becomes "the servant." Why the change?

Eliezer is referred to as "the man" until after he reveals his identity and mission beginning in verse 34. This gives us a feeling for the curiosity that Rebekah and her family must have felt about this "man," until he did tell them his purpose in coming.

The Joseph Smith Translation gives verse 21 as: "And the man, wondering at her, held his peace, pondering in his heart whether the Lord had made his journey prosperous or not." Rebekah's agreeing to water the camels wasn't enough; she had to do it. Eliezer may have kept quiet in order not to distract her from her task. What indicates that Rebekah did a good job watering the camels?

Rebekah doesn't just take the edge off the camels' thirst; she waits until they have "done drinking," as she says she will in verse 19.

Why does Eliezer give Rebekah only one golden earring? (Verse 22.)

The ring was a nose-ring. (See footnote 47a in the LDS edition of the Bible.) In verse 47, Eliezer says he put it on her face. This gift and the bracelets were probably generous ones, as Laban takes special note of them in verse 30.

Eliezer asks Rebekah if there's lodging for him and his men in her father's house. (Verse 23.) He is looking for lodging, but that's not the only reason he asks the question. Can you think of another?

It was a good excuse for asking whose daughter she was. Throughout this story, Eliezer is careful not to give offense.

Eliezer takes out the jewelry while Rebekah finishes watering the camels (verse 22), and then asks her who she is (verse 23). Why does he take out the jewelry before he knows who she is?

By now, Eliezer is quite certain that Rebekah is the one for Isaac, and hence from the right family. He asks only to confirm it.

In verse 47, Eliezer reports to Rebekah's family that he asked her whose daughter she was before actually putting the jewelry on her. Why does he wait to put on the jewelry until after he's asked?

By first confirming that Rebekah belongs to the right family, Eliezer shows respect to her family, avoiding even the possibility of giving offense in a situation that requires tact and courtesy.

Rebekah offers Eliezer hospitality without consulting her family. (Verse 25.) Why?

Apparently her family expects that she will act hospitably, and she does.

Rebekah answers Eliezer's questions directly, saying no more than is needed, not even giving the additional information of her own name. What does this tell us about her?

She is obliging and modest, here and in all her conversation.

What is provender?

Dry feed for animals.

What is Eliezer's reaction when he finds out that Rebekah is from Abraham's family? (Verses 26–27.) What might have been his reaction?

Eliezer doesn't pat himself on the back for his cleverness, but worships the Lord, acknowledging his guidance. He also humbly acknowledges his position as Abraham's emissary, and the fact that the Lord has done it for Abraham, not for him.

Verses 26 and 27 are worshipful and beautiful. Part of this beauty comes from the phrases bound together by repeated sounds. For example, in verse 26 the repeated ow *and* d *sounds bind together the phrase, "bowed down his head." Read verses 26 and 27 aloud and see if you can pick out other such phrases.*

Here are several we noticed: worshipped the Lord; Blessed be; Lord God; my master Abraham; not left destitute my master; Lord led; house of my master's brethren. Note also how the s sounds bind the whole of verse 27 together.

Now try rereading verses 26 and 27 aloud.
What does "I being in the way" mean? (Verse 27.)

"I, being in the vicinity" or "I, on the way here."

Instead of, "the man bowed down his head, and worshipped the Lord" (verse 26), the New English Bible *says the man "bowed down and prostrated himself to the Lord." Rebekah could not but fail to notice this. Further, it appears that Eliezer's praising of the Lord in verse 27, even though it sounds like a prayer, is intended for Rebekah's ears — the Lord is referred to in the third person, not the first. What must have been the effect of all this on Rebekah?*

It must have raised her curiosity, excitement, and anticipation.

Why doesn't Eliezer here tell Rebekah all the details of what has just happened? (Verses 26–27.)

To do so would almost be like making the proposal to Rebekah, which would put her in an awkward position. By custom, the proposal was made to the family, usually the father.

Why does Rebekah leave Eliezer standing outside? (Verse 28.)

It must have been inappropriate to bring him into her mother's house unannounced. Apparently, the tradition was for the mother's house to be separate from the father's—not a bad idea in times when polygamy was practiced. We later find Isaac bringing Rebekah to his mother Sarah's tent.

29 And Rebekah had a brother, and his name was Laban: and Laban ran out unto the man, unto the well.

30 And it came to pass, when he saw the earring and bracelets upon his sister's hands, and when he heard the words of Rebekah his sister, saying, Thus spake the man unto me; that he came unto the man; and, behold, he stood by the camels at the well.

31 And he said, Come in, thou blessed of the Lord; wherefore standest thou without? for I have prepared the house, and room for the camels.

32 And the man came into the house: and he ungirded his camels, and gave straw and provender for the camels, and water to wash his feet, and the men's feet that were with him.

33 And there was set meat before him to eat: but he said, I will not eat, until I have told mine errand. And he said, Speak on.

34 And he said, I am Abraham's servant.

35 And the Lord hath blessed my master greatly; and he is become great: and he hath given him flocks, and herds, and silver, and gold, and menservants, and maidservants, and camels, and asses.

36 And Sarah my master's wife bare a son to my master when she was old: and unto him hath he given all that he hath.

37 And my master made me swear, saying, Thou shalt not take a wife to my son of the daughters of the Canaanites, in whose land I dwell:

38 But thou shalt go unto my father's house, and to my kindred, and take a wife unto my son.

39 And I said unto my master, Peradventure the woman will not follow me.

40 And he said unto me, The Lord, before whom I walk, will send his angel with thee, and prosper thy way; and thou shalt take a wife for my son of my kindred, and of my father's house:

41 Then shalt thou be clear from this my oath, when thou comest to my kindred; and if they give not thee one, thou shalt be clear from my oath.

42 And I came this day unto the well, and said, O Lord God of my master Abraham, if now thou do prosper my way which I go:

43 Behold, I stand by the well of water; and it shall come to pass, that when the virgin cometh forth to draw water, and I say to her, Give me, I pray thee, a little water of thy pitcher to drink;

44 And she say to me, Both drink thou, and I will also draw for thy camels: let the same be the woman whom the Lord hath appointed out for my master's son.

45 And before I had done speaking in mine heart, behold, Rebekah came forth with her pitcher on her shoulder; and she went down unto the well, and drew water: and I said unto her, Let me drink, I pray thee.

46 And she made haste, and let down her pitcher from her shoulder, and said, Drink, and I will give thy camels drink also: so I drank, and she made the camels drink also.

47 And I asked her, and said, Whose daughter art thou? And she said, The daughter of Bethuel, Nahor's son, whom Milcah bare unto him: and I put the earring upon her face, and the bracelets upon her hands.

48 And I bowed down my head, and worshipped the Lord, and blessed the Lord God of my master Abraham, which had led me in the right way to take my master's brother's daughter unto his son.

The events in verses 29–30 are related out of order. Verse 29 says that "Laban ran out unto the man," but Laban didn't run out until after he'd seen and talked to Rebekah, as verse 30 points out. So why are we told about Laban's running in verse 29?

The line "Laban ran out unto the man" introduces Laban with a before-the-fact comment on how eager he was. Also, the feeling of excitement is intensified by placing Laban's running right after Rebekah's running in verse 28.

Why does Laban say, "Come in, thou blessed of the Lord," to Eliezer? (Verse 31.) How does he know Eliezer has been blessed of the Lord?

From verse 30 we learn that it was seeing the earring and bracelets on Rebekah and hearing her report that prompted Laban to go to Eliezer. Perhaps it was the earring and bracelets, signs that Eliezer had wealth, that made Laban say Eliezer was blessed of the Lord. This fits

with Eliezer's speech in verse 35, where he explains to
Laban that the Lord had blessed not him, but Abraham,
his master, with wealth. Or it may have been that
Rebekah told Laban of Eliezer's speech in verse 27, where
Eliezer said he had been blessed of the Lord. In either
case, it does seem a little strange for Laban, an idolator,
to be saying, "blessed of the Lord." He apparently is trying to assume an intimacy that doesn't exist.

*The rest of Laban's speech is also suspect. His invitation,
"Come in . . . wherefore standest thou without? for I have prepared
the house, and room for the camels" is inappropriate under the circumstances. (Verse 31.) Why?*

Eliezer is standing without because he hasn't been invited in. Further, it is unlikely that everything has been
prepared, because of Laban's hurry to get out to the man.
Laban is playing a part — that of the good host. And in doing so, he treats Rebekah unfairly, implying she should
have invited Eliezer in. Laban's showiness and back-
handedness contrast with Rebekah's modesty and directness.

Who does the first he in verse 32 refer to?

The *he* refers to Laban or, probably, his servants, who
ungirded (or unburdened) the camels and supplied water
to wash the feet of Eliezer and his men. The house Eliezer
is invited to was probably a separate guest house or tent.
Laban treats Eliezer hospitably.

Why won't Eliezer eat until he has told his errand? (Verse 33.)

By refusing to eat first, Eliezer emphasizes the importance of his errand to Rebekah's family. He's such a
diligent servant that he won't think of his own comfort
when there's work to be done.

*Eliezer begins confidently. (Verse 34.) Why is he confident
now?*

He knows that the Lord approves of his plan and will
stand behind him. He apparently speaks both to Laban
and Bethuel, Rebekah's father, although no mention is
made of Bethuel until verse 50.

How does Eliezer emphasize Abraham's wealth? (Verse 35.)

He enumerates all of Abraham's possessions, and also repeats the word "great": "And the Lord hath blessed my master *greatly;* and he is become *great . . .*" In addition, he has the evidence of the camel train to support his word. Notice that Eliezer attributes Abraham's success to the Lord, although he, as Abraham's chief servant, probably had a lot to do with the accumulation of Abraham's wealth. We've also seen him attribute his success in finding Rebekah to the Lord.

Why, after emphasizing Abraham's wealth, does Eliezer say that all of Abraham's possessions will be given to Isaac? (Verse 36.)

This is to imply that Rebekah will be well taken care of if she marries Isaac.

Eliezer further suggests that there is something special about Isaac, because Sarah bore him when she was old. How would this information affect Laban and Bethuel?

They would likely be flattered that Abraham had sent to them to find a wife for Isaac.

In verses 37–48, Eliezer recounts the preceding events of the chapter and is quite faithful to the original account. Nevertheless, there are some variations between the actual account and Eliezer's retelling of it, and these variations are quite instructive in light of Eliezer's task. Here are a list of differences. It is interesting to try to understand the reasons for each difference, saving to the last the question of whether Eliezer is being deceptive.

1. Eliezer doesn't say that Abraham made him swear "by the Lord, the God of heaven, and the God of the earth," only that Abraham made him swear (compare verse 3 and verse 37.) Why?

Mentioning "the Lord, the God of heaven, and the God of the earth" might have brought up the religious differences between Abraham and Rebekah's family.

2. While Abraham says "go unto my country and to my kindred," Eliezer says he said "go unto my father's house and to my kindred." (Compare verses 4 and 38.) Why?

Although Abraham's kindred in Haran and those of

his father's house (or father's family) were the same group of people, "father's house" brings to mind the close family ties between Abraham and his kindred, which Eliezer wants to emphasize.

3. Eliezer doesn't relate Abraham's insistence that Isaac not go to Haran. (Compare verses 6, 8 and verses 39, 41.) Why?

This insistence might easily have been taken as a negative comment on Abraham's kindred.

4. Eliezer doesn't tell of the Lord's having taken Abraham from his father's house and the Lord's subsequent covenant with Abraham. (Compare verses 7 and 40.) Why?

This information would have made Rebekah's family seem inferior to Abraham.

5. Eliezer reports that Abraham said "if they give not thee one," whereas he actually said "if the woman will not be willing to follow thee." (Compare verses 8 and 41). Why?

This change acknowledges the family's authority. It is likely that Rebekah had to consent too, but here Eliezer is trying to convince the family, and so emphasizes their authority.

6. When Eliezer recounts his prayer for a sign to know the right girl and Rebekah's subsequent fulfillment of that prayer, he mentions only the facts that show his prayer has been fulfilled in Rebekah, omitting such details as the exact manner in which Rebekah gave water to him and to the camels. (Compare verses 11-20 and verses 42-46.) Why doesn't he include more of the details?

Eliezer's retelling of the story is brief and succinct, so that the full impact of the story and the Lord's approval of Rebekah will be felt. By now Eliezer's story has almost taken the form of a ritual. It is the fourth time that the series of events in which Eliezer asks for a drink, the girl gives him a drink, and she offers also to water the camels, has been repeated. The series first occurs when Eliezer says, "Let it come to pass," second when it does come to pass, third when he says, "I said let it come to pass," and fourth when he says "it did come to pass." One can imagine people in an oral tradition enjoying this repetition, which would also help them better remember what happened.

7. Eliezer changes Rebekah's answer to the question, "Whose daughter art thou?" so that Bethuel's father instead of his mother is mentioned first. (Compare verse 24 and verse 47.) Why the difference?

It may be that Eliezer is here showing sensitivity to the patriarch's position; however the *New English Bible* and the *Jerusalem Bible* don't show this difference between Rebekah's actual answer and how Eliezer reports it.

8. In verse 27 Eliezer blessed the Lord for having led him "to the house of [his] master's brethren"; but in verse 48 he says he blessed the Lord, who had led him "in the right way to take [his] master's brother's daughter unto [Isaac]." Why this change?

In verse 48, Eliezer says in effect that it is the Lord's will that Rebekah marry Isaac. This is the strongest he's stated his case, and stating it this way prepares Rebekah's family for the question he is about to ask.

Was Eliezer being deceptive in making the above changes?

The changes were too small to say he was being deceptive. Furthermore, most of the changes were made to avoid giving offense. And since Abraham intended no offense, Eliezer was true to the spirit of Abraham's instructions. If he had been true to the letter, mechanically repeating Abraham's exact words, he might have offended Rebekah's family and been untrue to the spirit. It is a pharisaical heart that demands rigid obedience to the letter at the expense of the spirit. This doesn't mean Eliezer would have been justified in making up an untrue story to flatter Rebekah's family, but only that the changes he made were reasonable under the circumstances. Eliezer was being diplomatic — sensitive and careful not to offend, yet forcefully making his case.

Why in verse 48 is Rebekah referred to as Abraham's brother's daughter? Wasn't she his granddaughter?

In the Bible, *daughter* often means any female descendent.

49 And now if ye will deal kindly and truly with my master, tell me: and if not, tell me; that I may turn to the right hand, or to the left.

50 Then Laban and Bethuel answered and said, The thing proceedeth from the Lord: we cannot speak unto thee bad or good.

51 Behold, Rebekah is before thee, take her, and go, and let her be thy master's son's wife, as the Lord hath spoken.

52 And it came to pass, that, when Abraham's servant heard their words, he worshipped the Lord, bowing himself to the earth.

53 And the servant brought forth jewels of silver, and jewels of gold, and raiment, and gave them to Rebekah: he gave also to her brother and to her mother precious things.

54 And they did eat and drink, he and the men that were with him, and tarried all night; and they rose up in the morning, and he said, Send me away unto my master.

55 And her brother and her mother said, Let the damsel abide with us a few days, at the least ten; after that she shall go.

56 And he said unto them, Hinder me not, seeing the Lord hath prospered my way; send me away that I may go to my master.

57 And they said, We will call the damsel, and enquire at her mouth.

58 And they called Rebekah, and said unto her, Wilt thou go with this man? And she said, I will go.

59 And they sent away Rebekah their sister, and her nurse, and Abraham's servant, and his men.

60 And they blessed Rebekah, and said unto her, Thou art our sister, be thou the mother of thousands of millions, and let thy seed possess the gate of those which hate them.

Having given his account, Eliezer will not be put off. In verse 49, he asks for an answer, saying, "And now if ye will deal kindly and truly with my master, tell me . . ." The words "kindly and truly" are a figure of speech: the line means, "if ye will deal with true kindness" or "steadfast kindness." Why does Eliezer say this instead of something like, "now, if you will do the right thing, tell me"?

Eliezer's purpose has been to *convince* Laban and Bethuel that agreeing to the marriage is the right thing. He doesn't act like an authority over them, *telling* them it's the right thing; he respectfully allows them to draw their own conclusions. Notice that Eliezer wants Laban and Bethuel to show kindness to Abraham, just as he previously wanted the Lord to show kindness to him.

*What does "that I may turn to the right hand, or to the left"
mean? (Verse 49.)*

Eliezer seems to be saying that it won't matter much
which way he goes if Rebekah doesn't come with him.

*Verses 50 and 51 are the only verses in which Bethuel says
anything. His consent is necessary, but even in giving it, Laban
may have been the spokesman. (It's unlikely that they spoke in
unison.) It appears that Eliezer's story has had it's impact—Laban
and Bethuel acknowledge the hand of the Lord in what has
transpired and give their permission for Rebekah to go with
Eliezer. But they do it in an odd way, saying, "We cannot speak
unto thee bad or good" (verse 50), meaning, "We can say nothing
for or against it."* (New English Bible.) *It's as if they don't
believe they have a choice in the matter. Why do they act this way?*

Perhaps they don't want to take responsibility for
making the choice. Their situation reminds us of
Abraham's being commanded to offer up Isaac as a
sacrifice—they are being asked to give up their daughter
and sister, in all likelihood never to see her again. But,
while Abraham simply obeys, Laban and Bethuel act
superstitiously, as if they are under the influence of a
powerful god who, by the magic he has worked with
Eliezer and Rebekah, has deprived them of choice—an ir-
rational way to make a decision.

*Where was Rebekah while Eliezer was talking to Laban and
Bethuel?*

In verse 51, Laban and Bethuel say to Eliezer,
"Rebekah is before thee." Apparently, she also had been
listening to Eliezer.

*Whatever Laban and Bethuel's reasons, Eliezer is grateful
things have worked out. Once again, he worships the Lord,
acknowledging the source of his success. (Verse 52.) Then he
brings out the rest of his gifts. (Verse 53.) "Jewels of silver and
gold" means "things of silver and gold." (See the L.D.S. edition of
the Bible.) Why does Eliezer wait until Laban and Bethuel have
given their permission before bringing out the gifts?*

If given earlier, the gifts would have looked like a
bribe; as it is, they are a seal on the agreement. Laban

and Bethuel can't back down now as easily as they could have before accepting the gifts.

The gifts are given to Rebekah, her mother, and Laban. Why aren't they also given to Bethuel?

We don't know the reason, but it's not likely to have been an oversight on Eliezer's part. He's been very sensitive up to this point.

Eliezer finally gets to eat in verse 54. Then he tarries "all night." Why is this an ironic line?

During the whole of this episode, Eliezer tarries very little, amazingly little. He is in and out of Haran, with Rebekah, in less than a day, not staying even a little longer to rest from his nearly two-month journey. So, saying how long he stayed—"*all* night," actually emphasizes how short his stay was.

In the morning, Laban and Rebekah's mother are reluctant to let her go (verse 55) and ask that she be allowed to stay at least ten days. (The Scott's Bible, *a nineteenth century translation, says "days" could also have been translated "months.") Eliezer replies quite strongly, "Hinder me not." (Verse 56.) Why does he respond so sharply?*

Perhaps Eliezer would have been willing to let Rebekah stay longer if he hadn't been afraid that, given a little time for thought, Laban and Bethuel might have changed their minds, probably not an unfounded fear, remembering the way they had agreed in the first place. Future events showed Laban reluctant to let Jacob leave even after Jacob had worked fourteen years for Leah and Rachel and six additional years for flocks and herds.

In verse 58, Laban and his mother ask Rebekah, "Wilt thou go with this man?" Why do they refer rather distantly to Eliezer as "this man"?

They are probably not too happy with Eliezer's insistence on going so soon.

What does "Wilt thou go with this man?" mean? Is Rebekah just now being asked to give her consent?

Rebekah has likely already agreed to go. The purpose of the question is to see if she wants to go *now*.

What does Rebekah's willingness to go with Eliezer to a strange country, away from her family, to marry a man she has never seen, tell us about her?

Her willingness suggests a spirited disposition, an eagerness to better her position through a good marriage, and perhaps a growing faith in the Lord. It also suggests years of getting ready for the time she would consent to an arranged marriage.

Verse 60 says, "And they blessed Rebekah." Who was it that blessed her?

The referent of "they" isn't clear. From verse 55 "they" appears to refer to "her brother and her mother," but the line in the blessing, "Thou art our sister" wouldn't be appropriate coming from her mother. Laban probably blessed Rebekah because he fits both possibilities. But whoever did give the blessing, it wasn't Bethuel — this wasn't a father's blessing.

Why do you think Bethuel took such a backseat to Laban?

There are several possibilities: Bethuel was too old and infirm or was derelict in his responsibilities; Laban was just naturally more assertive or was usurping patriarchal authority; or Bethuel may even have been dead. According to some Bible scholars, Bethuel wasn't in earlier versions of this story and was put in by later scribes. (*Interpreter's Bible.*)

The blessing Rebekah is given in verse 60 is similar to the one the Lord gave Abraham: "In blessing I will bless thee, and in multiplying I will multiply thy seed as the stars of the heaven, and as the sand which is upon the sea shore; and thy seed shall possess the gate of his enemies." (Genesis 22:17.) Why the similarity?

One possibility is that Eliezer told Laban the blessing that had been given to Abraham. This seems unlikely though, given that Eliezer has already once avoided telling Laban the Lord's promise to Abraham. (Verses 7, 40.) Laban may have heard of the promise given to

Abraham from another source, but again this seems
unlikely—Abraham is not likely to have made the promise public, and communication between Abraham and his
relatives appears to have been very limited. Another suggestion is that a common nuptial wish at that time was for
a large posterity who would triumph over their enemies.
Barrenness was, after all, a cause of great sorrow. If this
latter suggestion is the correct one, then Laban's repetition to Rebekah of the Lord's blessing to Abraham is
ironic, because Laban doesn't know that the blessing has
already been given, and with much more authority than
he could possibly give it. Finally, it's possible that Laban
was, in some measure, inspired.

*Notice that in giving the blessing, the Lord is metaphorical
while Laban is not. The Lord says, "I will multiply thy seed as the
stars of heaven, and as the sand which is upon the seashore," but
Laban says, "Be thou the mother of thousands of millions." (The
Joseph Smith Translation says, "Be thou blessed of thousands—of
millions.") Is the Lord's attitude any different from Laban's?*

The Lord is serious; Laban we're not so sure about.
He appears to be exaggerating. Perhaps he's showing off.
Perhaps his exaggeration shows his reluctance to see
Rebekah go.

*What is the meaning of "Let thy seed possess the gate of those
which hate them"? (Verse 60.)*

The *New English Bible* translates this as "May your
sons possess the cities of their enemies." The connection is
that "gate" refers to the gates of the cities.

61 And Rebekah arose, and her damsels, and they rode upon
the camels, and followed the man: and the servant took Rebekah,
and went his way.

62 And Isaac came from the way of the well Lahai-roi; for he
dwelt in the south country.

63 And Isaac went out to meditate in the field at the even-
tide: and he lifted up his eyes, and saw, and, behold, the camels
were coming.

64 And Rebekah lifted up her eyes, and when she saw Isaac,
she lighted off the camel.

65 For she had said unto the servant, What man is this that
walketh in the field to meet us? And the servant had said, It is my
master: therefore she took a vail, and covered herself.

66 And the servant told Isaac all things that he had done.

67 And Isaac brought her into his mother Sarah's tent, and took Rebekah, and she became his wife; and he loved her: and Isaac was comforted after his mother's death.

Who were Rebekah's damsels? (Verse 61.)

A damsel is a young woman. These must have been Rebekah's servants. She will soon be married and with her change of status will come the need for servants.

Lahairoi (verse 62) was the well where an angel of the Lord appeared to Hagar. (Genesis 16:6–14.) It was located, according to Arab tradition, near Kadeshbarnea, south of Hebron and Beersheba, and hence was in "the south country." (Genesis 24:62; 20:1.) There are enough events occurring by wells in this chapter for the wells to be symbolic. What might they be symbolic of?

As wells were the support of life in the desert, so from the union of Isaac and Rebekah would come seed that would give spiritual life to all the nations of the earth. Christ himself, the "well of water springing up into everlasting life" (John 4:14), was a descendant of Isaac and Rebekah.

Since Isaac dwelt "in the south country," while Eliezer was coming from the northeast, Eliezer must have deliberately bypassed Abraham, taking Rebekah first to Isaac. In verse 66 we also see him giving his report to Isaac, not to Abraham. Why?

Though Isaac responsibly manages Abraham's encampment in Lahairoi, he seems, in contrast to both Abraham and Jacob, quiet and unassertive. Eliezer's actions are thoughtful, apparently intended to show respect to Isaac and to build him up in Rebekah's eyes. It is through Isaac and Rebekah now, that the Lord's promise to Abraham must be fulfilled.

The first part of verse 63 says, "Isaac went out to meditate in the field." The New English Bible *translates this as: "Isaac . . . had gone out into the open country hoping to meet them (or to relieve himself)." What if the second part of verse 63 said simply, "and he saw the camels arriving"? What more is conveyed by saying, "and he lifted up his eyes, and saw, and behold, the camels were coming"?*

As it is, verse 63 conveys Isaac's excitement. When read aloud, the excitement is intensified by pausing slightly at the commas and reading with an awareness of the repeated *c*s and *m*s in "camels" and "coming": "and he lifted up his eyes, (slight pause) and saw, (slight pause), and, (slight pause) behold, (slight pause) the *c*amels were *c*oming." When reading this line aloud, we find ourselves imagining the camels coming. Do you?

What difference would it have made if instead of saying Rebekah "lighted off the camel," verse 64 said that she "got off the camel"?

The word "lighted" suggests ease, quickness, eagerness, traits characteristic of Rebekah.

Isaac's response in verse 63 parallels Rebekah's in verse 64:
he lifted up his eyes,
and saw,
and, behold, the camels were coming.
and Rebekah lifted up her eyes,
and when she saw Isaac,
she lighted off the camel.
What does the similarity convey?

It's as if they were attuned to each other, a suggestion of the oneness that marriage brings.

Why, in verse 65, does the servant refer to Isaac as his master, when he had previously referred to Abraham as his master?

Again, the effect is to build up Isaac in Rebekah's eyes.

Why do you think Rebekah veils herself before Isaac (verse 65) when she hasn't been veiled before Eliezer and the other servants?

Apparently it was the tradition for the bride to be veiled before the bridegroom.

The story of Isaac and Rebekah is framed with references to Isaac's mother, Sarah. The previous chapter, Genesis 23, is about Sarah's death and burial; and in the last verse of this chapter, she is mentioned twice. Sarah had been dead three years when Isaac married Rebekah. (She was ten years younger than Abraham [Genesis 17:17] and would thus have been 130 when Isaac married Rebekah. However, she died when she was 127 years old [Genesis

23:1].) Her death was likely an impetus for Abraham to find Isaac a wife. In what ways does Rebekah take Sarah's place?

First, Rebekah literally takes Sarah's place, living in her tent and probably taking charge of her responsibilities at Lahairoi. (Genesis 25:11.) Rebekah also takes Sarah's place in Isaac's affection, at least as far as that is possible. Isaac and his mother were likely very fond of each other; it was Sarah who guarded Isaac's birthright and protected him from disrespectful Ishmael. (Genesis 21:8–12.) So, to say Isaac was comforted after his mother's death is to emphasize how much he loved Rebekah. There is no account of Abraham's meeting Rebekah. It is possible that he performed the marriage ceremony.

Notice the order of events in the last verse: "she became his wife" and then "he loved her," not an uncommon order then, nor at the time of the King James translation, when marriages were still arranged. Why is the line "and she became his wife; and he loved her; and Isaac was comforted after his mother's death" a fitting conclusion for this story in which Eliezer has played such a central role?

We see here the result of Eliezer's faithful service: a wife that Isaac loves.

6

I Have Trusted in Thee —
2 Nephi 4:15-35

These verses from 2 Nephi are often called the Psalm of Nephi. What is the historical setting of this psalm? What happened just before the psalm and what happens just after?

This passage occurs at a crucial point in the Book of Mormon. Lehi has just died, leaving his sons without his guidance. Under Lehi's authority, Nephi had become his brothers' "ruler" and "teacher." (2 Nephi 5:19.) But with Lehi gone, Laman and Lemuel are angry with Nephi, saying, "We will not have him to be our ruler; for it belongs unto us, who are the elder brethren, to rule over this people." (2 Nephi 5:3.) Just after Nephi's psalm, we find Laman and Lemuel becoming increasingly angry with Nephi, "insomuch that they did seek to take away [his] life." (2 Nephi 5:2.) The Lord warns Nephi to flee for his life into the wilderness, just as He earlier warned Lehi to escape from those who sought *his* life. (2 Nephi 2:1-2.) Nephi does flee, and the divided family eventually becomes two hostile nations. (See Genesis 50:15-21 for a quite different result among brothers when their father dies.)

15 And upon these I write the things of my soul, and many of the scriptures which are engraven upon the plates of brass. For

my soul delighteth in the scriptures, and my heart pondereth them, and writeth them for the learning and the profit of my children.

16 Behold, my soul delighteth in the things of the Lord; and my heart pondereth continually upon the things which I have seen and heard.

Nephi begins verse 15, "And upon these I write the things of my soul." What are "these"?

"These" are Nephi's small plates, the ones on which he was commanded to make an account of "the ministry of [his] people." (1 Nephi 9:3.)

Why, then, if these plates were for an account of his ministry, does Nephi here record on them "the things of his soul"?

The things of Nephi's soul, the things he delights in and ponders continually, are the scriptures and the things of the Lord he has seen and heard. And, of course, these he uses in teaching and ministering to his people. As you continue reading, ask yourself why Nephi thought this passage would help him minister to his people and his children. What would it teach them?

What did the plates of brass contain? (Verse 15.)

They contained the five books of Moses, a record of the Jews down to the commencement of the reign of Zedekiah, and the writings of the prophets. (1 Nephi 5:10–13.) So, Nephi must have had much of what is in our Old Testament and more besides, for he speaks of prophets whose writings we don't have. (1 Nephi 19:10.) As you read, look for the Old Testament phrases Nephi uses.

Notice how many times Nephi repeats "my soul" and "my heart" in verses 15 and 16. Why does he say "my soul" and "my heart" rather than just "I"?

These phrases emphasize his feelings instead of other aspects of his personality.

17 Nevertheless, notwithstanding the great goodness of the Lord, in showing me his great and marvelous works, my heart exclaimeth: O wretched man that I am! Yea, my heart sorroweth because of my flesh; my soul grieveth because of mine iniquities.

18 I am encompassed about, because of the temptations and the sins which do so easily beset me.

19 And when I desire to rejoice, my heart groaneth because of my sins; nevertheless, I know in whom I have trusted.

Notice the "nevertheless" at the beginning of verse 17 and the one near the end of verse 19. What do these two occurrences of "nevertheless" signal?

They signal a change of mood. In verses 15 and 16 Nephi feels delight, rejoicing, and gratitude; in verses 17 to 19 he is despondent; in the verses that follow, he once again rejoices. Nephi seems divided, torn between moods, needing to resolve and unify his feelings.

What does "wretched" mean? (Verse 17.)

The first definition the dictionary gives is "deeply afflicted." This fits with Nephi's later talk of "affliction." (Verses 26, 29.)

In verses 17 to 19, the lines "my heart sorroweth because of my flesh," "my soul grieveth because of mine iniquities," "I am encompassed about because of the temptations and the sins which do so easily beset me," and "my heart groaneth because of my sins" all repeat essentially the same idea. This repetition emphasizes Nephi's despondency. Why do you think Nephi was feeling so depressed? What might his sins have been?

Nephi must have been weighed down both with sorrow at his father's death and with the responsibility of keeping his family together. His sins probably included self-pity and anger toward his hostile brothers. We sympathize with Nephi. Who hasn't had similar feelings with less provocation? Nephi, unable to reconcile his family, must have felt anxious, knowing as he did from vision the ultimate destruction that awaited his people at the hands of his brother's people. (1 Nephi 12:1–3.) This knowledge weighs heavily on him, for he writes, "And it came to pass that I was overcome because of my afflictions, for I considered that mine afflictions were great above all, because of the destructions of my people, for I had beheld their fall." (1 Nephi 15:5.) Nephi may have hoped to avoid that terrible fall by a reconciliation. But if so, his desire to take matters into his own hands was contrary to the purposes of the Lord, as was Alma's when he wished to "speak with the trump of God, with a voice to shake the earth, and cry repentance unto every people." Alma says, "But behold, I am a man, and do sin in my wish . . . for I know that [God] granteth unto men according to their desire, whether it be unto death or unto life" (Alma 29:1-4), implying that men must be allowed their free agency. If Laman and Lemuel wanted to rebel, God would allow them that privilege, and so must Nephi.

20 My God hath been my support; he hath led me through mine afflictions in the wilderness; and he hath preserved me upon the waters of the great deep.

21 He hath filled me with his love, even unto the consuming of my flesh.

22 He hath confounded mine enemies, unto the causing of them to quake before me.

23 Behold, he hath heard my cry by day, and he hath given me knowledge by visions in the nighttime.

24 And by day have I waxed bold in mighty prayer before him; yea, my voice have I sent up on high; and angels came down and ministered unto me.

25 And upon the wings of his Spirit hath my body been carried away upon exceeding high mountains. And mine eyes have beheld great things, yea, even too great for man; therefore I was bidden that I should not write them.

26 O then if I have seen so great things, if the Lord in his condescension unto the children of men hath visited men in so much mercy, why should my heart weep and my soul linger in the valley of sorrow, and my flesh waste away, and my strength slacken, because of mine afflictions?

27 And why should I yield to sin, because of my flesh? Yea, why should I give way to temptations, that the evil one have place in my heart to destroy my peace and afflict my soul? Why am I angry because of mine enemy?

Nephi now speaks of the Lord's past goodness to him. (Verses 20-25.) Most of the events he mentions are recorded earlier in his history. He first speaks of his "afflictions in the wilderness"—the wilderness in which he wandered for eight years. (Verse 20.) Nephi uses the word "afflictions" many times in his record, and in fact begins his book saying, ". . . having seen many afflictions in the course of my days." (1 Nephi 1:1.) How did the Lord preserve Nephi "upon the waters of the great deep"?

First, the Lord guided Nephi and his family over the ocean all the way to the promised land. But more specifically, he preserved Nephi when Laman, Lemuel, and the sons of Ishmael rebelled at sea and the ship almost went under. (1 Nephi 18:9–21.)

When did the Lord fill Nephi with his love, even to the consuming of his flesh? (Verse 21.)

This may refer to the time when Nephi was so filled with the power of God that his brothers, who had wanted to throw him into the sea, couldn't even touch him. (1 Nephi 17:48.) On that occasion he said, "Touch me not, for I am filled with the power of God, even unto the consuming of my flesh." If this is the occasion referred to, it is interesting that verse 21 equates the love of God and the power of God. On that same occasion, the Lord confounded Nephi's brothers and shook them (1 Nephi 17:54)—probably the event referred to in verse 22. In this verse, Nephi calls his brothers "his enemies," which unfortunately they were, by their choice, not his.

Do you remember any times when the Lord heard Nephi's prayers? (Verse 23.)

There are several occasions Nephi specifically mentions: first, when he desired to know the truth of his father's words and the Lord softened his heart that he did believe (1 Nephi 2:16); second, when he prayed in behalf of Laman and Lemuel, and the Lord spoke to him about them (1 Nephi 2:18–19); third, when Laman and Lemuel bound him with cords intending to leave him in the desert to die and the Lord gave him strength to break his bonds (1 Nephi 7:17–18); and fourth, in the land Bountiful when the Lord showed him how to build the ship (1 Nephi 18:1–3).

When did Nephi receive "knowledge by visions in the nighttime" (verse 23), which means knowledge gained through dreams?

What this refers to isn't clear. Perhaps Nephi didn't record all of his spiritual experiences. And, in fact, he says he didn't, in verse 25.

When did angels minister to Nephi? (Verse 24.)

We know of two occasions: once to rescue him from his brothers who were beating him (1 Nephi 3:28–30), and another time to interpret a vision he had seen (1 Nephi 11:1).

These references show us Nephi remembering the Lord's past goodness to him. Do these occasions have anything in common? What does Nephi seem most grateful for?

Nephi appears particularly grateful to the Lord for protecting him from his enemies and for giving him knowledge.

In the above verses, Nephi paints a vivid picture using contrasts, for example, "wilderness" then "waters" (verse 20), and "day" then "nighttime" (verse 23). What other contrasts do you notice?

We find three others: "consuming" then "confounding" (verse 21 and 22); "voice sent up" then "angels coming down" (verse 24); "exceeding high mountains" then "valley of sorrow" (verses 25 and 26).

Now, below, read aloud Nephi's account of the Lord's goodness, taking care to breathe only at the places indicated.

20   *My God hath been my support;* (breath)
        he hath led me through mine afflictions in the wilderness;
            (breath) *and*
        he hath preserved me upon the waters of the great deep.
            (breath)
21   *He hath filled me with his love, even*
        unto the consuming of my flesh. (breath)
22   *He hath confounded mine enemies,*
        unto the causing of them to quake before me. (breath)
        Behold,
23   *He hath heard my cry by day, and*
        He hath given me knowledge by visions in the nighttime.
            (breath)
24   *And by day have I waxed bold in mighty prayer before him;*
        yea, my voice have I sent up on high; and
        angels came down and ministered unto me. (breath)
25   *And upon the wings of his Spirit hath my body been carried away upon exceeding high mountains.* (breath)

And mine eyes have beheld great things,
  yea, even too great for man; therefore
    I was bidden that I should not write them. (breath)
    O then,
26 *if I have seen so great things,*
  if the Lord in his condescension unto the children of men
    hath visited men in so much mercy, (quick breath)
  why should my heart weep and
              my soul linger in the valley of sorrow, and
              my flesh waste away, and
              my strength slacken,
    because of mine afflictions? (breath) *And*
27 *why should I yield to sin,*
    because of my flesh? (breath) *Yea,*
  why should I give way to temptations,
    that the evil one have place in my heart to destroy my peace
      and afflict my soul? (breath)
  Why am I angry
    because of mine enemy?
Now, what did you notice as you read this passage aloud?

What's most obvious is how the distance between breaths gradually increases from verse 20 to the long sentence in verse 26, then rapidly decreases again, ending with the short question, "Why am I angry because of mine enemy?"

Did you also notice that in these verses some of the clauses are similar in structure and others different?

The first few clauses are similar, most of them beginning with "he hath." Then, in verse 24, they break out of any rigid pattern. Finally, at the end of the passage, the clauses become more patterned again, most of them beginning with "why should." As the distance between breaths increases, there is more variety in structure; as it decreases, the structures become more uniform.

What is the emotional effect of all this?

Nephi's emotion seems, at first, contained; but then it gradually builds in intensity, reaching its height in verse 26, where Nephi feels the Lord's goodness so totally that his sorrow and wretchedness begin to be swept away.

Notice in verse 26, at the height of his gratitude, Nephi speaks of the Lord's condescension to the children of men. What is the condescension of God?

This question brings to mind the angel's query to Nephi: "Knowest thou the condescension of God?" (1 Nephi 11:16.) In answer, Nephi was shown the birth, ministry, and death of the Savior, the supreme manifestation of God's love.

In verses 26 and 27, Nephi questions himself. He asks, for example, "Why should I yield to sin?" rather than saying, as he did earlier, "I am encompassed about, because of the temptations and the sins which do so easily beset me." (Verse 18.) What was Nephi's attitude toward his sinning in verses 17 to 19, and what is it now in verses 26 and 27?

Earlier, Nephi felt helpless and discouraged because of his sins. He seems to have thought "they'd gotten the better of him." But now he assumes responsibility for his sins; he has given in to them, but needn't continue to do so.

What sin is Nephi describing when he says, "Why should my heart weep and my soul linger in the valley of sorrow, and my flesh waste away, and my strength slacken, because of mine afflictions"? (Verse 26.)

It seems Nephi had been feeling sorry for himself. The sin he describes is self-pity. Notice the feeling of powerlessness in the words "linger," "waste away," and "strength slacken" in verse 26 and "yield" and "give way" in verse 27.

The word "flesh" has occurred several times so far: "My heart sorroweth because of my flesh" (verse 17); "He hath filled me with his love, even unto the consuming of my flesh" (verse 21); "Why should . . . my flesh waste away, and my strength slacken" (verse 26); and "Why should I yield to sin, because of my flesh" (verse 27). What does "flesh" mean?

"Flesh" seems to mean something like "limited ability." Nephi sins because of his flesh or inability to control the situation. And, in sinning, even his limited abilities dwindle away. But when the Lord is with him, his flesh or limitations are consumed, seeming to vanish away.

*Until verse 27, Nephi says things like "my heart sorroweth,"
"my soul grieveth," "my heart weeps," and "my soul lingers," talking
about his heart and soul as if they were sorrowing more or less in-
dependently of him. Nephi seems to have a split personality. This
seems especially obvious in the line, "And when I desire to rejoice,
my heart groaneth." (Verse 19.) He wants to go one way, his
heart another. But in verse 27, we see a change: Nephi admits that
he is making the trouble for his heart and soul, saying, "Why
should I give way to temptations, that the evil one have place in my
heart to . . . afflict my soul?" What is happening in verse 27?*

Nephi's personality is beginning to come together. He
is beginning to be a whole person rather than a divided
one. He's no longer deceiving himself by saying, "I really
want to rejoice, but, you see, I have these problems."

*Nephi, up until verse 26, speaks in generalities about his sins.
But in verses 26 and 27 he acknowledges them: self-pity and anger.
Why does he wait till this point to acknowledge his sins?*

When a person acknowledges or confesses his sins, he
has begun to repent, to see his situation as the Lord sees
it. Before that, he feels frustrated but doesn't exactly know
the source of his frustration. This appears to have been
Nephi's state. And when he finally acknowledges his sins,
he is ready to change—he is, in fact, already changing.

28 Awake, my soul! No longer droop in sin. Rejoice, O my
heart, and give place no more for the enemy of my soul.

29 Do not anger again because of mine enemies. Do not
slacken my strength because of mine afflictions.

30 Rejoice, O my heart, and cry unto the Lord, and say: O
Lord, I will praise thee forever; yea, my soul will rejoice in thee,
my God, and the rock of my salvation.

*Nephi begins verse 28 saying to his soul, "Awake . . . !" Has
he been asleep?*

Nephi's "Awake!" is reminiscent of Lehi's last words to
Laman and Lemuel: "O that ye would awake; awake from
a deep sleep, yea, even from the sleep of hell, and shake
off the awful chains by which ye are bound." (2 Nephi
1:13-14.) That Nephi would use the same word in speaking to himself implies that no matter what the degree of
sin, the same processes are at work. In sinning, we lose
consciousness and perspective. To use another metaphor,

we blind ourselves; we see neither our sins nor their consequences in our lives. Recall the prodigal son. Christ described the son's repentance, saying, "When he came to himself," implying that he had been, as it were, unconscious. (Luke 15:17.)

Try to imagine a person drooping in sin. (Verse 28.) What does he look like?

We picture a person with head down, slouching, shuffling along. "Droop" means to hang or incline downward, to sink gradually, to become depressed or weakened.

Have you ever felt droopy?

We have.

In verse 28, Nephi speaks of the "enemy" of his soul; in verse 29, of his "enemies." Is he speaking of the same person or persons?

In verse 28, the enemy of Nephi's soul is "the evil one" or Satan; while in verse 29, "mine enemies" are probably Nephi's brothers.

In verses 26 and 27, Nephi confesses his self-pity and anger. He does so again in verses 28 and 29, saying he's been drooping in sin (verse 28), giving place to the enemy of his soul (verse 28), angering (verse 29), and slackening his strength (verse 29). Is it reasonable that a person would feel anger and self-pity at the same time?

It seems so to us. We feel the angriest when we're dwelling on our sense of weakness and frustration. If Nephi had felt stronger, more in control of the situation, he likely wouldn't have been angry.

Nephi begins, in verse 28, talking to his heart and soul, rather than about them. He admitted in verse 27 that he was causing their distress. Now, in verse 29, he encourages them to be strong. Finally, in verse 30, Nephi's heart and soul become one with him again; they do the same thing he does, namely, rejoice in the Lord. Nephi praises the Lord with his heart and soul, saying, "O Lord, I will praise thee forever; yea, my soul will rejoice in thee, my God, and the rock of my salvation." What has happened to Nephi?

He is no longer torn and divided, but whole again. And his wholeness comes as he prays to the Lord for the first time since he's started to ponder his wretchedness. His pondering has prepared him for prayer.

The word "rejoice" occurs a number of times in verses 28 to 30. Why is rejoicing so important to Nephi?

That is what he wants to do, as he says in verse 19. Pondering the things of the Lord makes him feel like rejoicing, but he has let his sins keep him from rejoicing.

Nephi says the Lord is the "rock" of his salvation (verse 30). In what ways is the Lord like a rock?

A rock is strong and steadfast — characteristics Nephi also finds in the Lord.

31 O Lord, wilt thou redeem my soul? Wilt thou deliver me out of the hands of mine enemies? Wilt thou make me that I may shake at the appearance of sin?

32 May the gates of hell be shut continually before me, because that my heart is broken and my spirit is contrite! O Lord, wilt thou not shut the gates of thy righteousness before me, that I may walk in the path of the low valley, that I may be strict in the plain road!

33 O Lord, wilt thou encircle me around in the robe of thy righteousness! O Lord, wilt thou make a way for mine escape before mine enemies! Wilt thou make my path straight before me! Wilt thou not place a stumbling block in my way — but that thou wouldst clear my way before me, and hedge not up my way, but the ways of mine enemy.

34 O Lord, I have trusted in thee, and I will trust in thee forever. I will not put my trust in the arm of flesh; for I know that cursed is he that putteth his trust in the arm of flesh. Yea, cursed is he that putteth his trust in man or maketh flesh his arm.

35 Yea, I know that God will give liberally to him that asketh. Yea, my God will give me, if I ask not amiss; therefore I will lift up my voice unto thee; yea, I will cry unto thee, my God, the rock of my righteousness. Behold, my voice shall forever ascend up unto thee, my rock and mine everlasting God. Amen.

From verse 31 to the end of the chapter, Nephi continues the prayer he began in verse 30. He stops praying only for a brief interlude at the end of verse 34 and the beginning of verse 35. The following chiasmus shows the form of his prayer, beginning with verse 30:

a. *I will praise thee, my God, the rock of my salvation (verse 30)*
   b. *Wilt thou redeem me (verse 31)*

     c. Deliver me from my enemies (verse 31)
       d. Make me shake at the appearance of sin (verse 31)
         e. Shut the gates of hell (verse 32)
         e. Don't shut the gates of righteousness (verse 32)
       d. Encircle me in the robe of righteousness (verse 32)
     c. Deliver me from my enemies (verse 33)
   b. I will trust thee (verse 34)
*a. I will cry unto thee, my God, the rock of my righteousness
(verse 35)*

Notice the b lines in the chiasmus: "Redemption" and "trust" are counterpointed, suggesting that they are reciprocal activities. That is, for the Lord to redeem Nephi, Nephi must trust the Lord. Nephi prays for redemption. What else does he desire of the Lord?

He prays for deliverance from his enemies and from sin. Repeatedly he asks, "O Lord, wilt thou . . . ?" realizing that he is dependent on the Lord for strength. Deliverance from sin is particularly important to him; he places his request for this at the center of the chiasmus (lines d and e). Note that while all the sentences in verses 31 to 33 are phrased as questions, the ones in verses 32 and 33 end with exclamation points rather than question marks. Question marks were used until the 1920 edition.

Nephi asks the Lord to make him shake at the appearance of sin (verse 31). Notice the rhyme of "make" and "shake," which emphasizes the word "shake." Why is the "shaking" image a vivid one for Nephi?

In all likelihood, he was remembering his brothers shaking before him when he was filled with the power of God. (1 Nephi 17:54.) He seems to want that same fear of sin.

Nephi asks, "May the gates of hell be shut continually before me, because that my heart is broken and my spirit is contrite!" (Verse 32.) What is Nephi saying? Does he mean "Since my heart is broken and my spirit contrite, will you Lord shut the gates of hell before me?", or, "Will you Lord help me to have a broken heart and a contrite spirit, so that the gates of hell will be shut before me?"

Probably the latter. Nephi also prays in these verses to be kept from sin, so it seems doubtful that he was sure his heart was broken and his spirit contrite. The latter reading also suggests that a broken heart and a contrite spirit themselves shut the gates of hell.

Nephi speaks of a broken heart and a contrite spirit. (Verse 32.) But earlier he paired "heart" with "soul." (Verses 15–17.) Why does he now put "heart" with "spirit"?

The phrases "broken heart" and "contrite spirit" occur elsewhere in the scriptures. (See Psalm 34:18.) Nephi had probably read the psalms on the plates of brass. No doubt he was also remembering the recent words of his father: "Behold, he offereth himself a sacrifice for sin, to answer the ends of the law, unto all those who have a broken heart and a contrite spirit; and unto none else can the ends of the law be answered." (2 Nephi 2:7.) A broken heart and a contrite spirit suggest a willingness to accept the will of the Lord, to lay aside one's pride and one's own desires.

What is Nephi asking of the Lord when he says, "Wilt thou not shut the gates of thy righteousness before me, that I may walk in the path of the low valley, that I may be strict in the plain road!"? (Verse 32.)

Nephi wants to walk in the "path of the low valley"—the path without rough places, not the rocky mountainous paths; he wants to be strict in the plain road—to stay in the unobstructed way. He doesn't want sin to keep him from the Lord; he desires forgiveness and mercy—an open gate.

In verse 33, Nephi asks the Lord to encircle him in the robe of his righteousness. What has Nephi been encircled in?

Earlier, Nephi said that he was "encompassed about" by temptation and sin. (Verse 18.) In contrast, Lehi earlier spoke of being "encircled about" eternally in the arms of the Lord's love. (2 Nephi 1:15.) Nephi, too, desires this. The words of his dying father seem to linger with him.

At the end of verse 33, Nephi again speaks of paths. And again he desires an unobstructed one. Is he making the same request that he did in verse 32?

Previously, Nephi didn't want sin to block off his way;

this time he doesn't want his enemies — his brothers — to
block his way.

What does "hedge" mean?

"Hedge" means to obstruct.

Nephi wants the Lord to obstruct his brothers' way. Why?

There may have been other reasons, but at least one is
obvious: his brothers were out to kill him.

*We have seen Nephi, in verses 32 and 33, compare his future
course to an actual journey, using metaphors such as "gates,"
"walk," "path," "road," "stumbling block," and "way." Why does
Nephi use journey metaphors?*

Nephi has just completed a long journey and may be
thinking it's time for another one. Indeed, in the next
chapter, the Lord warns Nephi to flee into the wilderness.
He does, and he and his company "journey in the
wilderness for the space of many days." (2 Nephi 5:7.)

*Nephi says he will trust in the Lord rather than in the arm of
flesh. (Verse 34.) What is the arm of flesh?*

An arm, like a rock, is a symbol of strength. The arm
of flesh, then, is the strength of man.

What, then, does "maketh flesh his arm" mean? (Verse 34.)

It means, "maketh man his strength."

*Nephi temporarily stops praying in verses 34 and 35 to say he
will trust in the strength of the Lord, not in the strength of man.
How will trusting in the Lord help him solve his problems?*

We in the western world like to think happiness will
come if we can just get what we want. The trouble is, we
might not have the strength or ability to get what we
want, and so we simply end up frustrated. Or, even if we
have the strength, we may find that getting what we want
doesn't really make us happy, because we may have been
wanting the wrong things. In the Orient, the idea is that
peace comes when we stop wanting. But it's hard to imagine how anyone could exist at all without wanting
something. Nephi's message seems to be neither of these:
we *should* want, but we must want what the Lord wants.

Trusting him, we'll want the right things, we won't ask "amiss," and the Lord will give liberally.

The lines, "I will lift up my voice unto thee"; "I will cry unto thee, my God, the rock of my righteousness"; and "Behold, my voice shall forever ascend up unto thee, my rock and mine everlasting God"; are successively stronger statements of the same idea. (Verse 35.) How does Nephi feel here?

We're left sensing Nephi's renewed confidence and strength in the presence of God.

Throughout this psalm, Nephi uses phrases, particularly metaphors, that have their origin in earlier scripture. Examples are: visions in the night (2 Nephi 4:23; Job 4:13, 20:8, 33:15; Isaiah 29:7); "the rock of my salvation" (2 Nephi 4:30; Psalm 89:26); "gates open or shut continually" (2 Nephi 4:32; Isaiah 60:11); "gates of righteousness" (2 Nephi 4:32; Psalm 118:19); "valley" used metaphorically (2 Nephi 4:26, 32; Psalm 23:4); "plain" way or road (2 Nephi 4:32; Isaiah 40:4); "stumbling block" (2 Nephi 4:33; Isaiah 57:14); "hedge" (2 Nephi 4:33; Proverbs 15:19; Psalm 89:40); trusting in the Lord, not in man (2 Nephi 4:34; Psalm 118:8); "arm of flesh" (2 Nephi 4:34; 2 Chronicles 32:8); "maketh flesh his arm" (2 Nephi 4:34; Jeremiah 17:5); and "my rock" (2 Nephi 4:35; 2 Samuel 22:2; Psalm 18:2). Why does Nephi so frequently use other scripture in his own writing?

Nephi began this passage, "For my soul delighteth in the scriptures." (Verse 15.) The scriptures fill him and are a part of him, so they come out in his own writing — and not mechanically; they flow from him.

There are also phrases in this passage that are not found in the Old Testament but that echo the New Testament: "gates of hell" (2 Nephi 4:32; Matthew 16:18) and God giving liberally to him that asketh (2 Nephi 4:35; James 1:5). Obviously, Nephi didn't have access to New Testament writings. Why does he then use New Testament phrases?

Perhaps Nephi and the New Testament writers shared common sources, either inspiration or Old Testament sources we no longer have. Or it may have been that New Testament phrases were used in translating Nephi's words.

Looking back over the whole twenty-one verses now, notice what has happened: Nephi has progressed from statements contrasting his joy with his sorrow (verses 15–25) to questions asking why he should be unhappy (verses 26–27) to imperatives to repent (verses 28–30) to questions calling on the Lord for help (verses 31–33) to, at the end, statements again. The statements at the end, though, express a resolution rather than a conflict. What has been resolved?

Nephi's soul. He is no longer a split person, vacillating between rejoicing and sorrowing. Now he is wholly rejoicing.

Notice also that the words I, me, my, *and* mine *have occurred over one hundred times in these twenty-one verses. This passage is a very personal entry on the small plates. How do you think it might have helped Nephi's children and thus been useful in his ministry?*

Nephi's children would undoubtedly experience some of the same frustrations that he did. They would suffer affliction in the wilderness of America and abuse by their brethren the Lamanites. Jacob, Nephi's younger brother, later records, "The time passed away with us, and also our lives passed away like as it were unto us a dream, we being a lonesome and a solemn people, wanderers, cast out from Jerusalem, born in tribulation, in a wilderness, and hated of our brethren, which caused wars and contentions; wherefore, we did mourn out our days." (Jacob 7:26.) Nephi's children would have many temptations to anger and self-pity. But Nephi here sets the example: remember the goodness of the Lord, trust in him, rejoice in him and cry to him forever; then you will be strong in him, and the weakness that gives occasion for anger and self-pity will vanish. Then there will be no need to strike out at the world or to withdraw from it out of a feeling of frustration or weakness — only the need to be patient and get on with the work of the Lord.

7

Thou Art the Man — 2 Samuel 11-12

1. And it came to pass, after the year was expired, at the time when kings go forth to battle, that David sent Joab, and his servants with him, and all Israel; and they destroyed the children of Ammon, and besieged Rabbah. But David tarried still at Jerusalem.

When does the Jewish year end?

The Jewish new year begins in September, so that "the year was expired" (verse 1) about the time the harvests were in and the cool season was coming on.

David couldn't have sent "all Israel" to war. What does this phrase mean?

David didn't literally send "all Israel," but men from all over Israel. This figurative way of speaking emphasizes that the war was a major enterprise and that David was negligent in not participating. Elsewhere in these two chapters "Israel and Judah," "the people," and "all the people" are used to refer to the army, with similar effect. (2 Samuel 11:11; 12:28, 29, 31.)

The "But" at the end of verse 1 signals a contrast. What is being contrasted?

Kings going forth to battle and King David staying home.

Why is the contrast made?

It emphasizes David's idleness, indicating that something was amiss with him from the very beginning of this story. In later chapters, we see David fighting in battle, ignoring his men's pleas that he "go no more out with us to battle" lest he be killed and "quench . . . the light of Israel." (2 Samuel 21:16–22.) But in this chapter he tarries still at Jerusalem.

Why is the historian so indirect in the way he points out David's idleness and negligence?

David is a much-loved biblical figure. Directly attacking him would no doubt arouse antagonism, perhaps making us unwilling to listen to the rest of the story. By being indirect, the historian allows us to draw our own conclusions from the facts he presents.

2 And it came to pass in an eveningtide, that David arose from off his bed, and walked upon the roof of the king's house: and from the roof he saw a woman washing herself; and the woman was very beautiful to look upon.

3 And David sent and enquired after the woman. And one said, Is not this Bath-sheba, the daughter of Eliam, the wife of Uriah the Hittite?

4 And David sent messengers, and took her; and she came in unto him, and he lay with her; for she was purified from her uncleanness: and she returned unto her house.

5 And the woman conceived, and sent and told David, and said, I am with child.

David's idleness is even further emphasized in verse 2. How?

David arises from off his bed in the "eveningtide." Although it may not have been uncommon at the palace to take an afternoon "siesta," it is certain that Joab and the army didn't have the leisure for one.

Why might David have been walking on the roof? (Verse 2.)

This probably wasn't unusual. It was a way to catch the breeze after the heat of the day.

How much might David have known about the woman he saw?

Although David didn't know who the woman was, he

must have known whose household she belonged to, as the house was close to the palace.

In verse 3, the one who was sent to inquire after the woman gives his report in the form of a question: "Is not this Bathsheba?" Why?

This was the proper way to speak to the king. For the sake of appearances, a servant wouldn't want to tell the king something the king didn't already know—hence, he asks a question. Notice this question is the first quotation in the story. The narrative of this story consists of two things: quotations and descriptions of events, the alternation between the two giving variety.

Uriah is frequently referred to as Uriah the Hittite. (Verse 3.) Why is the fact that he was a Hittite emphasized?

Because Uriah was a Hittite, a foreigner dwelling among the Israelites, David should have been especially careful not to abuse or afflict him. The Lord's commandment to Israel was, "Thou shalt neither vex a stranger, nor oppress him: for ye were strangers in the land of Egypt" (Exodus 22:21), and "The stranger that dwelleth with you shall be unto you as one born among you, and thou shalt love him as thyself." (Leviticus 19:34.) And Uriah was an especially deserving stranger. The way he shows reverence for "the ark" in verse 11 and the fact that he was fighting in Israel's army suggest that he was a convert to the Lord and probably strong in the faith, as was the convert Ruth, the Moabitess. "Uriah" means, as we learn from the LDS edition of the Bible, "Jehovah is my light." We also know that Uriah was a man of estimation in Israel. His house was close to the King's, and he is listed as one of thirty honorable men in Israel. (2 Samuel 23:39.)

David commits adultery with Bathsheba. (Verse 4.) How much choice did she have in the affair?

The historian doesn't say, though he does say several messengers were sent and "took" her. The historian's concern is with David's responsibility, not Bathsheba's.

What does it mean to be purified from uncleanness. (Verse 4.)

According to Jewish law, people and things could become "unclean" and had to be ritually purified, which usually required a waiting period and some kind of cleansing agent — sometimes fire (Numbers 31:19-24), sometimes blood (Leviticus 14:25), often water (Leviticus 15:27). A woman, after her menstrual flow, was considered unclean for seven days. (Leviticus 15:19-27.)

The fact that Bathsheba was purified from her uncleanness is given as a reason for David's lying with her. This doesn't make much sense. What sense can you make of it?

Perhaps Bathsheba had been purifying herself when David saw her washing, and the historian is telling us that the rites of purification had been completed when David took her. If this is the case, the account should probably read, ". . . *and* she was purified from her uncleanness," rather than ". . . *for* she was purified from her uncleanness." An alternative translation is found in *The New English Bible:* "When she came to him, he had intercourse with her, though she was still being purified after her period, and then she went home." If this translation is correct, the fact that she wasn't purified worsened David's sin.

Does it appear the affair was kept secret?

With several messengers having been sent to take Bathsheba, word might well have gotten around. Servants whisper among themselves, as they do later when Bathsheba's child dies. (2 Samuel 12:19.) David seems to be taking no great pains to keep the affair a secret, so we might expect Joab and Uriah to have found out about it "through the grapevine," even before David sent for Uriah. (Verse 6.) There was, for one thing, open communication between the palace and the camp of Israel. There was also enough time, since it would have taken Bathsheba about two months to know she was pregnant. Then, too, when Bathsheba found out about her condition, she "sent and told David" — via a messenger, no doubt. Once again, word was likely to get around.

Why do you think Bathsheba told David she was with child? (Verse 5.)

Her message, short and to the point, seems a plea for help. With her husband away, she was liable by Jewish law to be stoned to death for adultery. (Leviticus 20:10.)

6 And David sent to Joab, saying, Send me Uriah the Hittite. And Joab sent Uriah to David.

7 And when Uriah was come unto him, David demanded of him how Joab did, and how the people did, and how the war prospered.

8 And David said to Uriah, Go down to thy house, and wash thy feet. And Uriah departed out of the king's house, and there followed him a mess of meat from the king.

9 But Uriah slept at the door of the king's house with all the servants of his lord, and went not down to his house.

What do you think Joab thought when David sent for Uriah? (Verse 6.)

If he didn't already know, Joab must have wondered what business David had with Uriah, a subordinate. It would have been in keeping with Joab's character, as we shall see, for him to have made secret inquiries to find out.

Why does David ask Uriah about Joab and the war? (Verse 7.) After all, David was apparently in constant correspondence with Joab.

Here it seems that David, needing a pretense for calling Uriah home from the battlefield, makes small talk, pretending to check up on Joab by getting Uriah's report.

The historian makes David's speech to Uriah (verse 7) seem insincere. What makes David's speech sound that way?

David's speech seems perfunctory—he's really not interested in Joab, the people (the army), or the war, and the short phrases with the repeated *hows* and *dids* help convey this. Notice we aren't told Uriah's answers. They don't matter to David.

David tells Uriah to go down to his house and wash his feet. (Verse 8.) He dares not be more specific than this. What does he really want Uriah to do?

David's plan to cover his sin seems simple enough: get Uriah to sleep with Bathsheba so the child will appear to be Uriah's.

Why does David send a "mess of meat" after Uriah? (Verse 8.)

David's intent, it seems, isn't to feed Uriah but to make sure that he goes home. The unusual word order in the sentence points to this. The normal construction would be, "A mess of meat from the king followed him." The act of following is emphasized by placing the phrase "followed him" at the beginning of the clause "and there followed him a mess of meat from the king."

Why does Uriah spend the night with the servants of the king rather than with his wife? (Verse 9.)

Perhaps Uriah knows what's going on and doesn't want any part of it.

Verses one through eight of this chapter begin with and; *verse nine begins with* but. *What does the* but *here signal?*

It tells us that Uriah's refusal to go home is significant: David's plan has gone awry. Even Bathsheba's pregnancy seems less problematic than this turn of events.

It's unlikely that Uriah slept with all *of David's servants. Why this poetic license?*

The "all" suggests that enough of the servants were there to tell Uriah whatever David's servants might have heard about the affair and to confirm anything Uriah might have already heard. It also emphasizes that there were many witnesses to Uriah's not going home.

10 And when they had told David, saying, Uriah went not down unto his house, David said unto Uriah, Camest thou not from thy journey? why then didst thou not go down unto thine house?

11 And Uriah said unto David, The ark, and Israel, and Judah, abide in tents; and my lord Joab, and the servants of my lord, are encamped in the open fields; shall I then go into mine house, to eat and to drink, and to lie with my wife? as thou livest, and as thy soul liveth, I will not do this thing.

12 And David said to Uriah, Tarry here to day also, and to morrow I will let thee depart. So Uriah abode in Jerusalem that day, and the morrow.

13 And when David had called him, he did eat and drink before him; and he made him drunk: and at even he went out to lie on his bed with the servants of his lord, but went not down to his house.

The servants tell David that Uriah didn't go down to his house. (Verse 10.) Why do they make a point of telling David this seemingly insignificant fact?

The servants must have known what David was up to. They probably enjoyed their role in the intrigue, implying, "What are you going to do now?" when making their report to the king.

David asks Uriah why he didn't go down to his house (verse 10), thereby making too much of the fact to maintain his innocent front. What does this tell us about David's state of mind?

David is getting more desperate. The pretense isn't working. He probably suspects that Uriah knows, and asks the question to probe more deeply.

Does Uriah answer David? (Verse 11.)

Uriah doesn't confront David directly with his knowledge. But he nevertheless answers David when he says, ". . . shall I then go into mine house, to eat and to drink, and *to lie with my wife?*" This response must have shaken David.

Interesting variations on the triad, "to eat, and to drink, and to lie with my wife," recur throughout this story. In verse 13, Uriah eats and drinks before David, but lies on his bed with the servants. In 12:3, the lamb in Nathan's parable eats of the poor man's own food, drinks of his own cup, and lies in his bosom. In 12:16, David abstains from eating and drinking and lies on the earth. Then, in 12:20, David first eats (the drinking is implied) and then lies with Bathsheba. What does the repetition emphasize?

It emphasizes David's indulgence and, by contrast, Uriah's sacrifice. While Uriah is on the battlefront serving his king, David is home, not only eating, drinking and lying with *his* wives (presumably), but also with Uriah's wife. The sin is all the worse because it has been by the joint occurrence of Uriah's allegiance to David and David's neglect of duty that the adultery has so easily taken place. If Uriah had been less dutiful, he could have been home watching out for his wife.

In verse 11, Uriah says that the ark, Israel, Judah, Joab, and the servants of Joab are at the battlefront, implying, in short, that everything of importance is there. Why does he make a point of this?

David should be out there too, and this is what Uriah seems to be telling him.

Uriah doesn't say the armies are fighting, but says they "abide in tents" and "are encamped in the open fields." Why?

He seems to be drawing a contrast between where he has been sleeping and where David has been sleeping.

Why does Uriah refer twice to Joab as his lord?

It's as if he's saying that his place is with Joab, not at the palace covering up for David.

Uriah tells David, "As thou livest, and as thy soul liveth, I will not do this thing." (Verse 11.) The phrases "as thou livest" and "as thy soul liveth" mean essentially the same. Elsewhere in scripture "as thy soul liveth" is translated "as sure as you live," "as you live," "by your life," "on your life." (See the New English Bible *and* Jerusalem Bible *translations of 1 Samuel 1:26 and 1 Samuel 17:55.) Uriah's oath seems repetitious. The normal way to swear the oath seems to have been "as the Lord liveth, and as thy soul liveth." (See 1 Samuel 20:3; 1 Samuel 25:26; 2 Kings 2:2; 2 Kings 4:30.) Uriah seems to be emphasizing the sureness of David's life, perhaps even its exaltedness. Why?*

Perhaps Uriah is pointing to the difference between his own life and David's. It is probably clear to Uriah that by defying the king he has placed his own life in jeopardy, though justly, the king's life, not Uriah's, should be in jeopardy. Also, there's irony in Uriah's swearing the oath with David in place of the Lord. David has acted very unlike the Lord, and swearing the oath this way seems to emphasize that fact.

Why does David tell Uriah to "tarry"? (Verse 12.)

He apparently wants more time to make his plan work and so tells Uriah to "tarry" as he himself has been tarrying. Then, in a last-ditch effort, he gets Uriah drunk, hoping that he'll then go home to his wife.

Verse 13 says that Uriah ate and drank "before" David. Does this mean David didn't eat with him?

It's not clear. But if David did eat with Uriah, his betrayal was so much the worse, because at that time, if you had eaten with someone, you were especially obliged

to treat him as a friend. The implication of Christ's statement, "He that eateth bread with me hath lifted up his
heel against me," seems to be that Judas's betrayal was
worse because he had eaten with Christ. If David didn't
eat with Uriah, though, this wouldn't necessarily have
seemed strange. Kings frequently ate by themselves, even
at banquets, as a precaution against poisoning.

*Verse 13 says, "and at even he went out to lie on his bed with
the servants of his Lord." Does this statement seem humorous to
you?*

It's funny that Uriah's bed with the servants should be
called *his bed*. It's the historian's way of saying David's
ploys are getting a bit old in the face of Uriah's stead-
fastness. Uriah's insistence on sleeping with the servants
must have shown David that it wasn't for a whim or for an
over-zealous loyalty that he wasn't going down to his
house.

**14 And it came to pass in the morning, that David wrote a
letter to Joab, and sent it by the hand of Uriah.**

**15 And he wrote in the letter, saying, Set ye Uriah in the
forefront of the hottest battle, and retire ye from him, that he
may be smitten, and die.**

**16 And it came to pass, when Joab observed the city, that he
assigned Uriah unto a place where he knew that valiant men
were.**

**17 And the men of the city went out, and fought with Joab;
and there fell some of the people of the servants of David; and
Uriah the Hittite died also.**

*David has Uriah carry his own execution order. (Verse 14.)
Why?*

This was probably David's way of saying Uriah had
forced his hand and left him no choice. Uriah may well
have guessed the contents of the letter, but he makes no
attempt to resist or flee, and David seems almost to know
that he won't read the letter. Uriah has acted with integri-
ty, and death is the consequence. Perhaps death, especially an honorable death in battle, was an easier alternative
than facing the shame that would otherwise come upon
him and Bathsheba.

What does the letter tell you about David's attitude towards Uriah? (Verse 15.)

David appears without sympathy, vicious and vengeful. Uriah has thwarted his attempts to protect Bathsheba and himself, and Uriah must pay.

Does Joab follow David's instructions? (Verses 15–17.)

No.

Why?

To have done so would have made him obviously responsible for the death of Uriah and aroused the wrath of the army. If David had given the matter any thought, he would have realized that a commander just doesn't desert a man in the heat of battle. Perhaps David wasn't thinking, being too busy covering his sin to think clearly; perhaps he wanted Joab to take the blame to draw attention away from himself; perhaps he didn't care; perhaps all three. What Joab does is to put Uriah in a place where valiant men of the enemy are, sacrificing a number of men to make Uriah's death seem more natural. If David won't look out for Joab, Joab will look out for himself. Nevertheless, Joab does the job, helping the king cover up a sin whose evil consequences are multiplying. Joab, unlike Uriah, acts as an accomplice.

Verse 17 says, "And the men of the city went out, and fought with Joab." Does this mean Joab put himself in the same death trap that he put Uriah in?

No, only a fool would have done that. Here "Joab" must mean "some of Joab's men."

18 Then Joab sent and told David all the things concerning the war;

19 And charged the messenger, saying, When thou hast made an end of telling the matters of the war unto the king,

20 And if it so be that the king's wrath arise, and he say unto thee, Wherefore approached ye so nigh unto the city when ye did fight? knew ye not that they would shoot from the wall?

21 Who smote Abimelech the son of Jerubbesheth? did not a woman cast a piece of millstone upon him from the wall, that he

died in Thebez? why went ye nigh the wall? then say thou, Thy servant Uriah the Hittite is dead also.

22 So the messenger went, and came and shewed David all that Joab had sent him for.

23 And the messenger said unto David, Surely the men prevailed against us, and came out unto us into the field, and we were upon them even unto the entering of the gate.

24 And the shooters shot from off the wall upon thy servants; and some of the king's servants be dead, and thy servant Uriah the Hittite is dead also.

25 Then David said unto the messenger, Thus shalt thou say unto Joab, Let not this thing displease thee, for the sword devoureth one as well as another: make thy battle more strong against the city, and overthrow it: and encourage thou him.

Why does Joab instruct the messenger so elaborately in verses 20 and 21? What is he up to?

Joab is likely angry at David for having put him in an awkward position. His instructions to the messenger seem calculated to put David in his place. Joab's apparently stupid move is really David's fault, but Joab wants David first to condemn it before he lets the responsibility be known. This foreshadows Nathan's parable in chapter 12. Nathan, too, relates an incident calculated to arouse David's wrath without letting David know that he himself is the one to be condemned.

You can read the incident about Abimelech in Judges 9:50–54. Besides its similarity to the military maneuver that killed Uriah, why does this incident seem appropriate to Joab?

David's downfall, like Abimelech's, was because of a woman, and nothing, apparently, could be more disgraceful to a soldier.

Does the messenger carry out Joab's instructions? (Verses 22–23.)

It appears from the King James Version that the messenger isn't crafty enough to wait for David's angry response before telling him of Uriah's death. However, in other versions, the *New English Bible* and the *Jerusalem Bible,* for example, the servant does wait, and David repeats the anticipated questions before hearing that Uriah is dead. The effect is to emphasize David's gullibility and Joab's ability to manipulate him.

We might expect David to be angry with Joab for allowing so many soldiers to be killed. Why isn't he angry that Joab didn't carry out his specific instructions and allow only Uriah to be killed? (Verse 25.)

Perhaps he is so relieved at Uriah's death that he chooses to overlook it. He may also have felt uneasy about having put Joab in such a bad position, not because of any moral qualms, but because Joab was a person to be reckoned with—he was in charge of the army.

From what he says to the messenger (verse 25), what attitude does David take toward Joab?

David plays the magnanimous monarch, treating Joab as a well-meaning but blundering child in need of encouragement. His condescending attitude may have been calculated to arouse Joab's wrath, in return for Joab's design to arouse his.

26 And when the wife of Uriah heard that Uriah her husband was dead, she mourned for her husband.

27 And when the mourning was past, David sent and fetched her to his house, and she became his wife, and bare him a son. But the thing that David had done displeased the Lord.

Does Bathsheba really mourn for her husband, or is the mourning merely perfunctory?

There is no indication in the narrative of how she felt toward Uriah, or toward David, for that matter. Perhaps in her situation, affection was only a secondary consideration. The *New Bible Commentary* says the period of mourning would have been seven days.

David "fetches" Bathsheba to his house. (Verse 27.) What does the word "fetch" suggest?

Like the word "took," it suggests Bathsheba had little to say about the matter.

The last line of chapter 11 is: "But the thing David had done displeased the Lord." This line starts with another significant but. Why is it significant?

It indicates that David's plans are about to go awry as they did following the previous *but* when Uriah refused to go down to his house. The entire next chapter is an elaboration of just how awry David's plans go.

The Lord's displeasure in verse 27 stands in direct contrast to Joab's displeasure in verse 25. Why is the contrast drawn?

The historian seems to be saying that David should have been more concerned about displeasing the Lord than displeasing Joab.

Do you think "displeased" is the right word to describe the Lord's feelings?

"Displeased" is not a strong word, but the Lord's feelings must have been strong—the severe punishment that Nathan later pronounces upon David attests to that. The line "But the thing David had done displeased the Lord" is an ironic understatement, saying more by saying less.

1 And the Lord sent Nathan unto David. And he came unto him, and said unto him, There were two men in one city; the one rich, and the other poor.

2 The rich man had exceeding many flocks and herds:

3 But the poor man had nothing, save one little ewe lamb, which he had bought and nourished up: and it grew up together with him, and with his children; it did eat of his own meat, and drank of his own cup, and lay in his bosom, and was unto him as a daughter.

4 And there came a traveller unto the rich man, and he spared to take of his own flock and of his own herd, to dress for the wayfaring man that was come unto him; but took the poor man's lamb, and dressed it for the man that was come to him.

5 And David's anger was greatly kindled against the man; and he said to Nathan, As the Lord liveth, the man that hath done this thing shall surely die:

6 And he shall restore the lamb fourfold, because he did this thing, and because he had no pity.

The parable that Nathan tells David is a disguised version of the events of chapter 11. What parallels can you draw between the characters and circumstances of Nathan's parable and those of the David and Bathsheba story?

The rich man is David; the poor man, Uriah; the ewe lamb, Bathsheba. The rich man's many flocks and herds

are David's numerous wives and concubines. The lamb
was unto the poor man as a daughter; the father-daughter
relationship suggests the strong feelings of love and
tenderness that Uriah probably felt toward Bathsheba.
The traveler is probably a passing fancy or sexual mood
of David's. Note that the parable doesn't add that
somehow the poor man was uncooperative and so the rich
man saw to it that he was killed. That would have been
too obvious.

*What does the fact that Bathsheba is represented by a lamb im-
ply about her?*

It suggests her innocence.

Why does David respond angrily to Nathan's story? (Verse 5.)

Obviously, David takes the story as an actual case and
not as a parable. Perhaps Nathan had come in before with
stories of injustices for David to rectify. His great anger
may also have been a way to appear just before Nathan.

*In the King James Version, David says, "the man that hath
done this thing shall surely die." (Verse 5.) But, the footnote says,
"or, is worthy to die." Similarly the* New English Bible *says
"deserves to die." If the latter translations are correct, what was
David's judgment against the rich man?*

The judgment was that the man should "restore the
lamb fourfold." That the rich man also deserved to die
was David's opinion, not part of his actual judgment.

7 And Nathan said to David, Thou art the man. Thus saith
the Lord God of Israel, I anointed thee king over Israel, and I
delivered thee out of the hand of Saul;
8 And I gave thee thy master's house, and thy master's wives
into thy bosom, and gave thee the house of Israel and of Judah;
and if that had been too little, I would moreover have given unto
thee such and such things.
9 Wherefore hast thou despised the commandment of the
Lord, to do evil in his sight? thou hast killed Uriah the Hittite
with the sword, and hast taken his wife to be thy wife, and hast
slain him with the sword of the children of Ammon.
10 Now therefore the sword shall never depart from thine
house; because thou hast despised me, and hast taken the wife of
Uriah the Hittite to be thy wife.
11 Thus saith the Lord, Behold, I will raise up evil against

thee out of thine own house, and I will take thy wives before thine eyes, and give them unto thy neighbour, and he shall lie with thy wives in the sight of this sun.

12 For thou didst it secretly: but I will do this thing before all Israel, and before the sun.

13 And David said unto Nathan, I have sinned against the Lord. And Nathan said unto David, The Lord also hath put away thy sin; thou shalt not die.

14 Howbeit, because by this deed thou hast given great occasion to the enemies of the Lord to blaspheme, the child also that is born unto thee shall surely die.

"Thou art the man" is the climax of the story. (Verse 7.) How do you think David felt when Nathan uttered these words?

David must have been cut to the quick. He had condemned himself and could no longer deceive himself about the seriousness of his sin.

A very strong rebuke prefaced by "Thus saith the Lord God of Israel" follows. It is the judgment of God against David. What aspect of David's sin most concerns the Lord? (Verses 7–12.)

The Lord seems concerned, first of all, with how David has treated him, with the gross ingratitude he has shown. He reminds David of all he has done for him and then asks why David has despised him in return. "Despise" is a strong word, one the Lord uses more than once. The first time, he says David has "despised the commandment of the Lord"; the second time, he says David has despised *him.* In despising his commandments, David has despised the Lord himself.

Doesn't the Lord care about Uriah?

Part of David's ingratitude to the Lord is the ingratitude he showed to Uriah. The Lord says, "Inasmuch as ye have done it unto one of the least of these my brethren, ye have done it unto me." (Matthew 25:40.) This seems to apply here.

What does "thy master's house" in verse 8 refer to?

This refers to the house of Saul, who was king before David. Saul's house included both his family ("thy master's wives") and his kingdom ("the house of Israel and Judah").

The punishment the Lord pronounces is a fitting one. Why?

Because David has destroyed Uriah's house with murder ("thou has killed Uriah the Hittite with the sword") and adultery ("and hast taken his wife to be thy wife"), his own house will be plagued in like manner with murder ("the sword shall never depart from thine house") and adultery ("I will take thy wives before thine eyes, and give them unto thy neighbor, and he shall lie with thy wives in the sight of this sun"). Notice that the Lord says he will "take" David's wives, just as David has taken Uriah's. The words "give" and "take" recur throughout the narrative. At first the Lord gave, but when David started to take from others, the Lord took from him.

The word "sun" occurs in verse 11 and again in 12. What does the repetition emphasize?

The public nature of David's punishment.

Why is a public punishment necessary?

In all likelihood, many people had heard of David's sin, so to counteract the bad effects of his example on the people, the Lord's displeasure had to be made obvious to everyone. David had publicly shamed the Lord; the punishment is a humiliation to David in kind. The rest of David's life is a fulfillment of Nathan's judgment against him. His problems begin when his son Amnon rapes his half-sister Tamar, and Absalom, her brother, takes vengeance by killing Amnon. Then Absalom rebels against his father, David, and as part of his rebellion becomes the "neighbor" spoken of in verse 11 to lie with his father's wives in the sight of the sun. (See 2 Samuel 16:20–22.) And because David is king and ruler over the house of Israel and Judah, the damage doesn't stop at his own doorstep. The rebellion of Absalom was a political event that affected all Israel.

Did the Lord engineer all this trouble in order to punish David?

The trouble that followed David to the end of his life was according to the pronouncement of the Lord, but it was also the expected consequence of his own bad example before his children and people.

*David's condemnation is so absolute that he has nothing to say
about it. He only acknowledges his sin, saying, "I have sinned
against the Lord." (Verse 13.) How does the confession, "I have
sinned against the Lord," show a sensitivity to Nathan's pronouncement?*

Nathan emphasized David's ingratitude to the Lord.
David responds to this, saying not simply, "I have
sinned," but "I have sinned *against the Lord.*" (Compare
this with the prodigal son's confession, I have sinned
against Heaven.")

*Joseph Smith changed the line "The Lord also hath put away
thy sin" (verse 13) to "The Lord also hath not put away thy sin."
The* New English Bible *translation of this line is: "The Lord
has laid on another the consequences of your sin." These latter two
translations make more sense. Why?*

The Lord has just told David that the sword will never
leave his house, and he is about to tell him that
Bathsheba's child will die. This is inconsistent with the
Lord's having put away his sin.

*Who was the "other" on whom the Lord laid the consequences of
David's sin?*

The child. David was the one who deserved to die; the
child was the one who actually died.

*Two other translations of verse 14 are: "Because in this you
have shown your contempt for the Lord, the boy that will be born to
you shall die" (New English Bible) and "Because you have
outraged Yahweh by doing this, the child that is born to you is to
die" (Jerusalem Bible). Does it seem right that the Lord should
take the child instead of David?*

It may have been that if the child had lived, others
would have died spiritually. David himself may not have
fully realized the seriousness of his sin and begun to repent of it if the child hadn't died. Then, too, the very ex-
istence of the child would have been a painful reminder of
David's sin—a reminder that others might have used to
justify their own sins: "David did it, and he's the Lord's
chosen, so it can't be too bad if we do it too." By the child's
death, the Lord showed his displeasure with David for all
to see. As for the child, the Lord doubtless took him to his

bosom, sparing him from what might have been a very difficult life.

What are the similarities between David's pronouncement against the rich man in Nathan's parable (verses 5 and 6) and the Lord's pronouncement against David (verse 13)?

The Lord implies that David deserves to die, just as David said the rich man deserved death. And just as David's actual judgment against the rich man was in lieu of death, so is the Lord's judgment against him. Unfortunately, David cannot restore fourfold to Uriah that which he has taken, because Uriah is gone. It is interesting in this light, though, to read D&C 132:39, which says that in the next life David will lose his wives — just as the rich man did his sheep.

15 And Nathan departed unto his house. And the Lord struck the child that Uriah's wife bare unto David, and it was very sick.

16 David therefore besought God for the child; and David fasted, and went in, and lay all night upon the earth.

17 And the elders of his house arose, and went to him, to raise him up from the earth: but he would not, neither did he eat bread with them.

18 And it came to pass on the seventh day, that the child died. And the servants of David feared to tell him that the child was dead: for they said, Behold, while the child was yet alive, we spake unto him, and he would not hearken unto our voice: how will he then vex himself, if we tell him that the child is dead?

19 But when David saw that his servants whispered, David perceived that the child was dead: therefore David said unto his servants, Is the child dead? And they said, He is dead.

20 Then David arose from the earth, and washed, and anointed himself, and changed his apparel, and came into the house of the Lord, and worshipped: then he came to his own house; and when he required, they set bread before him, and he did eat.

21 Then said his servants unto him, What thing is this that thou hast done? thou didst fast and weep for the child, while it was alive; but when the child was dead, thou didst rise and eat bread.

22 And he said, "While the child was yet alive, I fasted and wept: for I said, Who can tell whether God will be gracious to me, that the child may live?

23 But now he is dead, wherefore should I fast? can I bring him back again? I shall go to him, but he shall not return to me.

24 And David comforted Bathsheba his wife, and went in unto her, and lay with her: and she bare a son, and he called his
name Solomon: and the Lord loved him.

25 And he sent by the hand of Nathan the prophet; and he
called his name Jedidiah, because of the Lord.

*Why, in verse 15, does the historian refer to Bathsheba as
Uriah's wife?*

David's responsibility in the death of the child is emphasized by doing this.

*Why is the incident of the child's death gone into at such great
length?*

The incident provides clues to David's state of mind
following Nathan's visit.

Why does David grieve so much while the child is sick?

Of course, any parent would grieve for a dying child.
But in David's case, the child was dying because of him.
Then, too, the child's imminent death foreshadowed the
ruin of his whole house. Nathan's words must have
weighed heavily on David's mind.

*David surprises his servants by apparently ceasing to grieve
after the child dies. (Verses 20 and 21.) Others in his immediate
situation might have grieved most intensely at that time. What is
behind David's actions? Has he stopped grieving?*

We don't think so. By the time the child had died,
David must have been emotionally spent. After a seven-
day fast he was probably close to death himself. His grief,
though past tears, appears to be real and particularly
poignant in the statement, "I shall go to him, but he shall
not return to me."

*The servants question David directly in verse 21 instead of cir-
cumspectly, as would be expected. What does this indicate?*

The barriers of station seem temporarily down, indicating a self-forgetfulness brought on by an exhausting
emotional experience.

*David explains in verses 22 and 23 that he stopped fasting and
weeping when the child died because, in short, there was no more*

purpose in it. Does this mean that he took a pragmatic, calculated approach to the whole situation, showing grief as long as the Lord might concede?

This seems unlikely given that one of the first things David does after the child dies is to worship. A pragmatist would have been angry that his plan had failed. Apparently, David was hoping the Lord would change his mind, but when he sees that there is no hope, he reconciles himself to the Lord's will.

Do you think that David, at this point, has repented of his sin?

David is sorrowful, but there isn't much evidence that he has repented. True, he has acknowledged his sin, but that's just a beginning. Psalm 51, written by David "when Nathan the prophet came unto him, after he had gone in to Bathsheba," contains another open acknowledgment of his sin. Verse 10 of this psalm says, "Create in me a clean heart, O God; and renew a right spirit within me," implying that, though David recognized his sin, his heart was not yet clean, nor his spirit right. In the *Teachings of the Prophet Joseph Smith* we read, "David sought repentance at the hand of God carefully with tears, for the murder of Uriah; but he could only get it through hell." (P. 339.) Part of this hell is indicated in later psalms, which show little of the optimism of Psalm 51. For example, Psalm 102:9-10 reads, "For I have eaten ashes like bread, and mingled my drink with weeping, Because of thine indignation and thy wrath: for thou hast lifted me up, and cast me down."

In verse 24, David comforts Bathsheba "his wife." Why is she here called "his wife" rather than "Uriah's wife" as she was previously called? (Verse 15.)

Comforting Bathsheba is David's first unselfish act toward her in this story. A husband should comfort his wife, and so it seems appropriate here that she be called his wife. Bathsheba must have needed comfort: she has apparently been seduced, her husband has been killed, she has been perfunctorily remarried, and she has lost the child conceived in the seduction—all in about a year's time.

Much is made of the second child's name (verse 25), but nothing was said of the first child's name. Why?

The name of a child is supposed to be an indication of its future, so it is appropriate that the first child is nameless. But Solomon is to have a great future.

Whom do the two hes in verse 25 refer to?

The first *he* refers to the Lord; the second to Nathan: *the Lord* sent by the hand of Nathan, and *Nathan* called his name Jedidiah. Solomon is called Jedidiah because the Lord loves him: *Jedidiah* means "beloved of the Lord." David also must have loved Solomon; either that or he felt guilty for all he'd done to Bathsheba, because at some time—we don't know when—he promises Bathsheba that Solomon will be his successor. (1 Kings 1:17.) Later, we find Nathan coaching Bathsheba in how to see that the promise is fulfilled. (1 Kings 1:1–14.)

26 And Joab fought against Rabbah of the children of Ammon, and took the royal city.

27 And Joab sent messengers to David, and said, I have fought against Rabbah, and have taken the city of waters.

28 Now therefore gather the rest of the people together, and encamp against the city, and take it: lest I take the city, and it be called after my name.

29 And David gathered all the people together, and went to Rabbah, and fought against it, and took it.

30 And he took their king's crown from off his head, the weight whereof was a talent of gold with the precious stones: and it was set on David's head. And he brought forth the spoil of the city in great abundance.

31 And he brought forth the people that were therein, and put them under saws, and under harrows of iron, and under axes of iron, and made them pass through the brick-kiln: and thus did he unto all the cities of the children of Ammon. So David and all the people returned unto Jerusalem.

Chapter 12 doesn't end with Nathan's second visit, though this seems a comfortable place to end. Why in the last few verses does the historian return to Joab and the war?

The war frames this story of David's sin—showing us, as we've seen, David's state of mind before he sinned, and here his state of mind after. These last events seem a reminder that the comfort David felt from Nathan's second visit wasn't to last. David's punishment, pronounced by Nathan, had just begun.

What is the city of waters Joab refers to in verse 27?

The *New English Bible* says "the King's Pool" instead of the "city of waters." This refers to the city's water supply, without which the city couldn't last long.

What is Joab's attitude toward David in verses 27 to 28?

Joab treats David like a subordinate, ordering him around. He lets David know that he [Joab] deserves the glory, but for the sake of appearances David had better get to it. Having acted as David's accomplice in sin, Joab feels entitled to lord it over David. David follows Joab's instructions, but resentfully, as the next few verses show.

Verse 30 says that David "took their king's crown from off his head, the weight whereof was a talent of gold with the precious stones: and it was set on David's head." The crown would have weighed close to 100 pounds — too much for either the Ammonite King or David to carry on his head. Several other translations say that the crown was from off the head of the Ammonite idol Milcom, and that only the precious stone from it was set on David's head. But the Lord's instructions, to the contrary, were: "Ye shall utterly destroy all the places, wherein the nations which ye shall possess served their gods, upon the high mountains, and upon the hills, and under every green tree: And ye shall overthrow their altars, and break their pillars, and burn their groves with fire; and ye shall hew down the graven images of their gods, and destroy the names of them out of that place." (Deuteronomy 12:2–3.) What do you conclude about David from this incident?

It's not clear just how blasphemous this act was. At least it shows a reckless disregard for appearances — perhaps David's way of slapping Joab (who's been so concerned about appearances) in the face, as if he were saying, "I'll do what I darn well please." David seems to be asserting himself, showing how great and exalted he is, perhaps to compensate for his lack of involvement in the war.

David then makes slaves of the conquered Ammonites. The New English Bible *clarifies the details: "He took its inhabitants and set them to work with saws and other iron tools, sharp and toothed, and made them work in the brick-kilns." Why does the historian emphasize the harsh details of David's treatment of the conquered Ammonites?*

David may not have been unusually harsh for his time, but he was harsh nevertheless, perhaps for a token of bravery to compensate for his irresponsible leadership in the war, or perhaps as a general reaction to the frustration he was feeling. David's salvation was yet to be worked out.

8

Endless Punishment — D&C 19

This revelation is addressed to Martin Harris. Martin took an early interest in Joseph Smith, financially assisting the Prophet. He certified the Book of Mormon characters with Charles Anthon and then acted as scribe for the translation of the first 116 pages, only to lose them. He didn't act as scribe again but became one of the three witnesses. Seven months before this revelation, using his farm as collateral, he contracted to pay $3,000 for the printing of 5,000 copies of the Book of Mormon, payment due eight months after the start of printing.

1 I am Alpha and Omega, Christ the Lord; yea, even I am he, the beginning and the end, the Redeemer of the world.

2 I, having accomplished and finished the will of him whose I am, even the Father, concerning me—having done this that I might subdue all things unto myself—

3 Retaining all power, even to the destroying of Satan and his works at the end of the world, and the last great day of judgment, which I shall pass upon the inhabitants thereof, judging every man according to his works and the deeds which he hath done.

4 And surely every man must repent or suffer, for I, God, am endless.

5 Wherefore, I revoke not the judgments which I shall pass, but woes shall go forth, weeping, wailing and gnashing of teeth, yea, to those who are found on my left hand.

Christ begins by introducing himself. What do "alpha" and "omega" mean? (Verse 1.)

"Alpha" and "omega" are the first and last letters of the Greek alphabet, so "alpha and omega" means "the first and the last," which is simlar to "the beginning and the end."

What does Christ mean by saying he is "the beginning and the end"? (Verse 1.) (Hint: The earlier 1833 and 1835 versions of the Doctrine and Covenants end verse 1 with a colon rather than a period, the "I" at the start of verse 2 referring back to the subject of verse 1, which is Christ. Verses 2 and 3 may be, then, an explanation of verse 1.)

First, notice all the words that relate to "end" in verses 2 and 3: "accomplished," "finished," "end of the world," "last great day of judgment." Christ is the "end," it seems, because he completed the will of the Father and because his power extends to the end of the world. We also know that he was "in the beginning" with the Father (John 1:2), the creator as well as judge of the world, though this fact isn't so much emphasized in Section 19.

Why might Christ here be emphasizing the extent of his obedience and power? (Verse 2.)

These enable Christ to redeem the world by subduing all things unto himself. And Martin Harris needs to know this; he, like each of us, is in need of repentance and redemption. Also, Christ's obedience to the Father sets the example for Martin: Martin needs to be obedient to Christ, as Christ is to the Father.

When had Christ "accomplished and finished the will" of the Father concerning him? (Verse 2.)

He seems to have done so at the time of his crucifixion. John says that on Calvary, Christ knew "that all things were now *accomplished,* that the scripture might be fulfilled." (John 19:28.) And before he died, Christ said, "It is *finished.*" (John 19:30.)

What does "subdue" in verse 2 mean?

There are two meanings that seem relevant: first, to conquer and bring into subjection; second, to bring under cultivation, as in "subdue the earth"—more generally, to tame. Elsewhere in the scriptures we read that Christ shall subdue "all enemies under his feet." (D&C 76:106.) This is consistent with "conquering"; and so is verse 3 of this section, where we read that Christ will destroy Satan and his works at the end of the world. Satan is, of course, the enemy of all righteousness. The second meaning, "to tame," also seems appropriate, as "taming" is what Christ does to Martin Harris in this section. The prophet Micah says that God "will turn again, he will have compassion upon us; he will *subdue* our iniquities; and thou wilt cast all their sins into the depths of the sea." (Micah 7:19.) Christ subdues each of us by working with us to bring about our repentance. He is our Redeemer from sin.

What are "the works" of Satan? (Verse 3.)

In Section 76 we read, "And this is the gospel, the glad tidings, which the voice out of the heavens bore record unto us—That he came into the world, even Jesus, to be crucified for the world, and to bear the sins of the world, and to sanctify the world, and to cleanse it from all unrighteousness; That through him all might be saved whom the Father had put into his power and made by him; *Who glorifies the Father, and saves all the works of his hands, except those sons of perdition who deny the Son after the Father has revealed him.*" (D&C 76:40-43.) Apparently, then, the works of Satan, the things Satan has fashioned, are the sons of perdition, who suffer destruction with Satan, everyone else being finally redeemed. Of their punishment and destruction Christ says, "And the end thereof, neither the place thereof, nor their torment, no man knows." (D&C 76:45.) The works of Satan are also destroyed, in another sense, when men repent—which all but the sons of perdition will do by the end of the world, for Christ will deliver his kingdom "spotless" to the Father. (D&C 76:107.)

Notice in verses 2 and 3 all the words ending in -ing: having, concerning, having, retaining, destroying, judging, according. What is conveyed by all these "ing" words?

They make us aware of Christ's power to act and to fulfill his words.

In verse 1, Christ says that he is the beginning and the end, and then in verse 4 he says that he is endless. How might this paradox be resolved?

End seems to be used in two different ways. "End" in verse 1 has to do with the end of Christ's work. Presumably "endless" in verse 4 means unchanging, since it is used in the explanation of why men must repent or suffer: repentance or suffering has been previously decreed. Since the Lord is endless and will not revoke that decree, men *must* repent or suffer.

Why does the Lord use this paradox?

Paradoxes get our attention, making us realize we don't understand as much as we thought we did. The Lord is subduing us with this paradox, helping us become teachable.

What sounds are prominent in verse 5's description of the torment of the unrepentant?

The *w, o, e,* and *ing* sounds emphasize the groans of those in torment: "*Wo*es shall *go* forth, *wee*ping, *wa*il*ing* and gnash*ing* of teeth."

Who will be found on Christ's left hand? (Verse 5.)

Recall the parable of the sheep and the goats. (Matthew 25:31–46.) The goats—those who will be found on Christ's left hand—are those who haven't cared for the needy. More generally, they are the unrepentant.

6 Nevertheless, it is not written that there shall be no end to this torment, but it is written *endless torment.*

7 Again, it is written *eternal damnation;* wherefore it is more express than other scriptures, that it might work upon the hearts of the children of men, altogether for my name's glory.

8 Wherefore, I will explain unto you this mystery, for it is meet unto you to know even as mine apostles.

9 I speak unto you that are chosen in this thing, even as one, that you may enter into my rest.

10 For, behold, the mystery of godliness, how great is it! For, behold, I am endless, and the punishment which is given from my hand is endless punishment, for Endless is my name. Wherefore—

11 Eternal punishment is God's punishment.

12 Endless punishment is God's punishment.

Verses 6 through 12 continue the discussion of the word endless. *We are told that "endless punishment" doesn't mean "punishment without end," which initially seems as odd as saying that a meatless diet isn't a diet without meat. The effect is again an intellectual dislocation, a feeling that we cannot be very sure of ourselves and that we'd better listen. What is the meaning of endless punishment?*

The Lord says that endless punishment is his kind of punishment and not necessarily punishment that doesn't end. This doctrine shouldn't surprise us, for in the Book of Mormon we find that Alma the Younger was "racked with *eternal* torment" and "encircled about by the *everlasting* chains of death" for three days. (Alma 36:12, 18.) But the Lord's explanation resolves any confusion we might have had and we feel rewarded for having listened. Something has happened here that we'll see again at the end of the section: after listening to the Lord, we have cause to be glad and to rejoice.

Do the meanings of "endless" and "eternal" differ? (Verses 6, 7, 11, 12.) If not, why are both words used?

Both words are used interchangeably in this section; at least they seem to be in verses 6 and 7, which say, ". . . it is written endless torment. Again, it is written eternal damnation"; and in verses 11 and 12, which say, "Eternal punishment is God's punishment. Endless punishment is God's punishment." In each case the thought is repeated and the feeling builds because of the repetition. Having two words similar in meaning allows a thought to be repeated and thus emphasized without having to use exactly the same words.

In verse 7, what does "express" mean?

Here, "express" seems to mean "designed for or adapted to its purpose." The Lord uses the words "eternal" and "endless" to describe his punishment, even though the punishment is not "eternal" and "endless" in the familiar sense. He does this so that "it might work upon the hearts of the children of men." (Verse 7.)

Isn't this a little deceptive?

Perhaps for those who haven't experienced God's punishment, mistakenly believing that it will last forever gives them a better idea of how terrible it is than if the punishment were just called God's punishment, an incorrect idea in this case being closer to the truth than no idea at all. Nevertheless, those who believe incorrectly are not "one" with the Lord; that is, they need to have a different belief than the Lord about how long the punishment lasts in order to have a similar belief about how terrible it is.

In verse 8, what does "this mystery" refer to?

It refers to "the mystery of godliness" (verse 10), which includes the mystery of why Christ calls his punishment endless.

What is a religious mystery?

It is a religious truth that men can only know through revelation or that cannot be fully understood by men. The Lord says, "For, behold, the mystery of godliness, how great is it!" He means that it is a great mystery — one not easily understood by men. *Mystery* also refers to the specialized practices and knowledge peculiar to a group of people. Only those who are "chosen in this thing" will have the mystery revealed to them.

Do we know when Christ explained "the mystery of godliness" to his Apostles? (Verse 8.)

When the Twelve asked Christ why he spoke in parables, he answered, "Unto you it is given to know the mystery of the kingdom of God: but unto them that are without, all these things are done in parables." (Mark 4:11; see also Matthew 13:10–11, Luke 8:9–10.) Perhaps he explained "the mystery of godliness" on an occasion like this one.

What does the Lord mean when he says he speaks to those chosen "even as one"? (Verse 9.)

This probably means that he speaks "even as one *with them.*" He speaks directly to their understanding, that they may enter into his rest or have peace in him (verse 23) and no longer be confused or unsettled. Christ must unsettle the wicked in order to subdue them, but to the righteous he brings peace.

Why is Martin Harris one of the chosen? Hadn't he been pretty bad?

Though disobedient, Martin was apparently still righteous enough to have this mystery explained to him without it being to his detriment; he could receive it in the way the Lord intended.

At this point, how much do we know about the nature of endless punishment?

We know only its source, not what it's like, though we certainly feel it must be terrible.

13 Wherefore, I command you to repent, and keep the commandments which you have received by the hand of my servant Joseph Smith, Jun., in my name;

14 And it is by my almighty power that you have received them;

15 Therefore I command you to repent — repent, lest I smite you by the rod of my mouth, and by my wrath, and by my anger, and your sufferings be sore — how sore you know not, how exquisite you know not, yea, how hard to bear you know not.

16 For behold, I, God, have suffered these things for all, that they might not suffer if they would repent;

17 But if they would not repent they must suffer even as I;

18 Which suffering caused myself, even God, the greatest of all, to tremble because of pain, and to bleed at every pore, and to suffer both body and spirit — and would that I might not drink the bitter cup, and shrink —

19 Nevertheless, glory be to the Father, and I partook and finished my preparations unto the children of men.

20 Wherefore, I command you again to repent, lest I humble you with my almighty power; and that you confess your sins, lest you suffer these punishments of which I have spoken, of which in the smallest, yea, even in the least degree you have tasted at the time I withdrew my Spirit.

21 And I command you that you preach naught but repentance, and show not these things unto the world until it is wisdom in me.

22 For they cannot bear meat now, but milk they must receive; wherefore, they must not know these things, lest they perish.

In verse 13, the Lord tells Martin to keep the commandments he has received from the hand of Joseph Smith. What commandments were these?

It seems likely that these were commandments given in earlier revelations written "by the hand" of Joseph and received by the "almighty power" of God. (See Sections 5 and 17.)

In the first half of Section 19 there are twenty-one occurrences of the words repent, suffer, *and* punishment, *besides several occurrences of* judgment *and* torment. *In addition, three times the Lord tells Martin, "I command you to repent." (Verses 13, 15, 20.) Apparently, like many of us, Martin was slow to listen, so the Lord emphasizes his instructions by repeating them. In verses 13–22, he uses parallel phrases to emphasize just how bad the Lord's punishment is, for example, in verse 15, the phrases "by the rod of my mouth," "by my wrath," and "by my anger." Can you find other groups of such phrases?*

Also in verse 15, we find the phrases "how sore you know not," "how exquisite you know not," "how hard to bear you know not"; then, in verse 18, "to tremble because of pain," "to bleed at every pore," and "to suffer both body and spirit"; finally in verse 20, "repent, lest I humble you with my almighty power," and "confess your sins, lest you suffer these punishments of which I have spoken."

All of this leaves no doubt about the intensity of the suffering. We are also given clues to the kind of punishment the Lord administers. What kind of punishment is suggested by the phrase, "the rod of my mouth"? (Verse 15.)

This phrase suggests a rebuke. Remembering childhood, people sometimes say a deserved rebuke from their parents was worse than a spanking. In the Book of Mormon, Alma the Younger was "racked with eternal torment" at the angel's rebuke. (Alma 36:12.) Apparently, the suffering can also result from the Lord playing a more passive role — withdrawing his Spirit and leaving us to our own devices. The time the Lord withdrew his Spirit from Martin may have been sometime after he had lost the 116 manuscript pages of the Book of Mormon.

In verse 16, we feel the compassion of the Lord. He suffered these things that we might not suffer if we repent. But we must suffer even as Christ, if we do not repent. The inevitability of suffering for the unrepentant is emphasized by the chiasmus in verses 16 and 17:

a.   I, God, have suffered these things for all,
  b.   *that* they might not suffer
    c.   if they would repent;
    c.   *But* if they would not repent,
  b.   they must suffer
a.   *even as* I

Which ideas are similar and which contrasting in this chiasmus?

The *a* lines are similar; the *b* lines and the *c* lines are opposites and tell us our alternatives. Christ has already suffered for us; whether or not we suffer is up to us.

Notice the repeated short i *sounds in the phrase: "to suffer both body and spirit — and would that I might not drink the bitter cup, and shrink." (Verse 18.) The sound almost leaves a bitter taste in one's mouth. Notice also the rhyme of "drink" and "shrink." What does "shrink" here describe, and why after this word is the sentence cut off with a dash?*

At the time Christ drank from the cup of suffering, he shrank from doing it. The cut-off sentence suggests that the suffering was beyond what Christ here wishes to reveal, which makes it all the more forbidding.

Christ gives glory to the Father that he was able to partake of the bitter cup and thereby finish his preparations unto the children of men. (Verse 19.) What did his preparations prepare him to do? (See verse 2.)

To subdue all things unto himself and thereby redeem mankind.

The Lord says he will "humble" Martin Harris with his "almighty power" if he doesn't repent. (Verse 20.) A year earlier, the Lord said of Martin, "Behold, I say unto him, he exalts himself and does not humble himself sufficiently before me; but if he will bow down before me, and humble himself in mighty prayer and faith, in the sincerity of his heart, then will I grant unto him a view of the things which he desires to see." (D&C 5:24.) At that time, Martin desired to be one of the three witnesses. Now the Lord is telling Martin that if he doesn't humble himself, the Lord will humble him. Why is humility emphasized here? Could Martin repent without it?

A proud man will not confess or acknowledge his sins and so can't even begin to repent. Humility and confession are associated in verse 20 and also in Section 6, where the Lord says of Martin, "Except he humble himself and acknowledge unto me the things that he has done which are wrong . . . he shall have no such views." (D&C 5:28.)

The Lord tells Martin to "preach naught but repentance." (Verse 21.) Wasn't he supposed to talk about the Book of Mormon or Joseph Smith?

In preaching the gospel, the aim is crucial. Nothing should be taught that doesn't aim at bringing about repentance. Though the topics may vary, the aim should not. The Lord seems to be setting the example in this section; he speaks of endless punishment to bring about Martin's repentance.

The Lord tells Martin to "show not these things unto the world." (Verse 21.) What "things" is he talking about?

Earlier, the Lord spoke of those who were chosen to have the mysteries explained to them. (Verse 9.) It's likely that the things the world mustn't know are those same mysteries—specifically, the mystery of godliness, which includes the Lord's explanation of "endless punishment."

If, then, the mysteries shouldn't be shown to the world, but only repentance should be preached, why does the Lord speak of the mysteries to Martin when calling him to repentance?

Those of the world are not likely to see the mysteries in the context of the first principles of the gospel—particularly repentance—while those of the kingdom should be able to see them in the correct perspective.

In verse 22, the Lord says, "For they cannot bear meat now, but milk they must receive." In verse 8, he says, "Wherefore, I will explain unto you this mystery, for it is meet unto you to know even as mine apostles." What is the purpose of this word play between "meat" and "meet"?

It calls attention to the fact that for some it is both meat (not milk) and meet (appropriate rather than inappropriate) that they learn about endless punishment, while for others it is not.

Why might those of the world perish on hearing the doctrine of endless punishment? (Verse 22.)

Perhaps there are people who, on learning that God's punishment will not last forever, would say, "Eat, drink, and be merry; nevertheless, fear God—he will justify in committing a little sin; yea, lie a little, take the advantage of one because of his words, dig a pit for thy neighbor; there is no harm in this; and do all these things, for tomorrow we die; and if it so be that we are guilty, God will beat us with a few stripes, and at last we shall be saved in the kingdom of God." (2 Nephi 28:8.) This kind of attitude is hardly conducive to repentance.

23 Learn of me, and listen to my words; walk in the meekness of my Spirit, and you shall have peace in me.

24 I am Jesus Christ; I came by the will of the Father, and I do his will.

25 And again, I command thee that thou shalt not covet thy neighbor's wife; nor seek thy neighbor's life.

26 And again, I command thee that thou shalt not covet thine own property, but impart it freely to the printing of the Book of Mormon, which contains the truth and the word of God—

27 Which is my word to the Gentile, that soon it may go to the Jew, of whom the Lamanites are a remnant, that they may believe the gospel, and look not for a Messiah to come who has already come.

28 And again, I command thee that thou shalt pray vocally as well as in thy heart; yea, before the world as well as in secret, in public as well as in private.

29 And thou shalt declare glad tidings, yea, publish it upon the mountains, and upon every high place, and among every people that thou shalt be permitted to see.

30 And thou shalt do it with all humility, trusting in me, reviling not against revilers.

31 And of tenets thou shalt not talk, but thou shalt declare repentance and faith on the Savior, and remission of sins by baptism, and by fire, yea, even the Holy Ghost.

Beginning with verse 23, the feeling of this section changes. How?

We no longer find a preponderance of words like *repent, suffer* and *punishment.* Instead we find words like *meekness, humility, gladness, rejoicing,* and *free.*

Verse 23 is beautiful. What sounds do you notice in this verse?

The *m, s, l,* and *e* sounds are prominent: "*l*earn of *m*e, and *l*isten to *m*y words; walk in the *m*ee*k*ne*s*s of *m*y *S*pirit, and you sha*ll* have p*e*a*c*e in *m*e.

How does this verse make you feel?

It makes us feel peaceful and inclined to turn to the Lord.

In verse 24, why does Jesus talk about his own obedience to the Father?

He seems again to be reminding Martin and us of the example he set, implying that just as he obeys the Father, we should obey him.

The Lord prefaces his commandments to Martin in verses 25, 26, and 28 with "And again, I command thee. . ." Why?

This repetition is continuous with the three "I command you to repent" imperatives in verses 13, 15, and 20, and also with the imperative, "I command you that you preach naught but repentance" in verse 21. The repetition of "command" emphasizes the importance of obedience.

The Lord tells Martin not to covet his neighbor's wife or seek his neighbor's life. (Verse 25.) From what you know of Martin, did he have any reason to commit such sins?

Martin's unbelieving wife had nagged and harrassed him while he helped with the translation of the first 116 pages of the Book of Mormon and may have conspired in their eventual loss. There must have been others involved in the loss too. It's likely that Martin was at least angry with his wife and possibly with others he may have suspected. He may also have been using their wickedness as an excuse for his own, maintaining his anger against them to avoid fully confessing his own sins. (See verse 20.) However, it may be that the Lord is simply telling Martin, "Just as you know that you shouldn't covet your neighbor's wife nor seek his life, I now tell you not to covet your own property," the point being to show the continuity between previous commandments like the Ten Commandments and the present one about his property.

The Lord commands Martin not to covet his own property. (Verse 26.) How can a person covet his own property?

You covet something when you want what you don't own and shouldn't own. But you also covet when you want to hold on to something you feel you should let go of. That must have been Martin's situation. He apparently wanted to hold back property he felt he should impart for the printing of the Book of Mormon. (See verses 34–35.) Martin was to impart the property "freely," not begrudgingly, not wanting to hold onto it.

Why, in verse 27, does the Lord talk about the mission of the Book of Mormon?

To inspire Martin so he'll "freely" assist in its publication. The Lord explains how important the Book of Mormon is: it contains the truth and the word of God; and its influence will be far-reaching—it will go to the Gentiles, the Jews, and the Lamanites. Martin's privilege will be to help bring it forth. The line ". . . and look not for a Messiah to come who has already come" touches us as it must have Martin.

We learn from the Book of Mormon that the Lamanites were descendants of Joseph, not Judah. (1 Nephi 5:14.) Why, then, does the Lord in verse 27 call them a remnant of the Jews?

One definition of *Jew* is "a member of the tribe of Judah"; but another is "an Israelite." In this case, the appropriate definition must be the second one; the Lamanites are a remnant of the Israelites, Israel being Joseph's father.

In verse 28, the Lord tells Martin, "Pray vocally as well as in thy heart"; then he reiterates, "before the world as well as in secret, in public as well as in private." Why do you think the Lord repeats these instructions to Martin?

Martin probably hesitated to pray in public, perhaps because of fear or pride.

There is a feeling of rejoicing in verse 29. The sentence builds from "declare" to "yea, publish" to "upon the mountains, and upon every high place, and among every people." How does the Lord want Martin to feel about missionary work?

He wants Martin to feel eager and joyful about publishing the good tidings, to act not just from a sense of duty but from a love of the work. Notice that the Lord talks about the people Martin will be "permitted" to see. Preaching the gospel to these people will be a privilege.

After the Lord tells Martin to publish the glad tidings upon the mountains and high places, he then tells him to be humble. (Verse 30.) There is a contrast here between the high and the low. What is the point of the contrast?

In exalting the gospel of Jesus Christ, we shouldn't also exalt ourselves. A sense of self-importance will get in our way, perhaps leading us into the next two sins the Lord speaks of: reviling and talking of tenets.

What are tenets? (Verse 31.)

These are the beliefs or doctrines peculiar to various churches or other organizations. The doctrine of endless punishment is a tenet.

Why shouldn't tenets be discussed?

As every missionary knows, discussing tenets leads too easily to contention, giving occasion for revilers to revile, especially when there is no agreement on even fundamental principles. The first principles — faith, repentance, baptism by immersion, and the Holy Ghost — must be the foundation on which all else is built.

32 Behold, this is a great and the last commandment which I shall give unto you concerning this matter; for this shall suffice for thy daily walk, even unto the end of thy life.

33 And misery thou shalt receive if thou wilt slight these counsels, yea, even the destruction of thyself and property.

34 Impart a portion of thy property, yea, even part of thy lands, and all save the support of thy family.

35 Pay the debt thou hast contracted with the printer. Release thyself from bondage.

36 Leave thy house and home, except when thou shalt desire to see thy family;

37 And speak freely to all; yea, preach, exhort, declare the truth, even with a loud voice, with a sound of rejoicing, crying—Hosanna, hosanna, blessed be the name of the Lord God!

38 Pray always, and I will pour out my Spirit upon you, and great shall be your blessing—yea, even more than if you should obtain treasures of earth and corruptibleness to the extent thereof.

39 Behold, canst thou read this without rejoicing and lifting up thy heart for gladness?

40 Or canst thou run about longer as a blind guide?

41 Or canst thou be humble and meek, and conduct thyself wisely before me? Yea, come unto me thy Savior. Amen.

In verse 32, what does the "great and last commandment" refer to? What does "this matter" refer to?

Apparently, the "great and last commandment" is the whole of this revelation, including the specific counsel in the next verses. However, the referent of "this matter" isn't clear; the specific events that led to this revelation are not known.

Why might the Lord have told Martin "This shall suffice for thy daily walk, even unto the end of thy life"? (Verse 32.)

Perhaps Martin was too quick to ask Joseph for revelations from the Lord and not diligent enough in keeping the commandments he had already received through Joseph. The Lord here tells Martin that he doesn't need to ask for more revelation "concerning this matter."

The Lord tells Martin that misery and destruction await him if he slights the counsels he has received. (Verse 33.) Where else in this section has the Lord talked about destruction, and what light does the former verse shed on this one?

In verse 3, the Lord spoke of his power to destroy Satan and his works at the end of the world. Here, the Lord seems to be telling Martin that he may be destroyed with Satan at the last day if he isn't obedient.

How was Martin to pay the debt he had contracted with the printer? (Verse 35.)

Verse 34 suggests that he was to pay the debt by selling a portion of his property. Shortly after this revelation, Martin sold 151 acres of his farm and paid the printer.

Why is Martin told to sell all save the support of his family, assuming he didn't need to sell this much to pay the printer? (Verse 34.)

Without excess property, Martin could devote more time to preaching the gospel.

Why is he told to leave his house and home? (Verse 36.)

So he can preach the gospel.

How is verse 37 like verse 29?

Both verses are a joyful call to declare the glad tidings, meant to inspire Martin with a love of the Lord's work. Both verses build in emotional intensity, the high point of verse 37 being, "Hosanna, hosanna, blessed be the name of the Lord God!" The word "hosanna" is what Martin shouted when, as one of the three witnesses, he beheld the angel and the plates. The Lord apparently wants him to preach with the same excitement he felt then. Both verses also build by using the word *yea* ("Speak freely to all; *Yea,* preach . . ." and "declare glad tidings, *yea,* publish . . ."), and by using triads ("preach, exhort, declare" and "upon the mountains, and upon every high place, and among every people").

How does saying "We should be engaged in missionary work" compare to these two verses?

Not very well. Next to the words of the Lord, this line sounds dull and lifeless.

The Lord promises to bless Martin with his Spirit if he is prayerful. (Verse 38.) Where else in this section has the Lord spoken of his Spirit?

In verse 20, the Lord spoke of the punishment Martin suffered when the Lord withdrew his Spirit. The Lord's blessing is an abundance of the Spirit; his punishment, withdrawal of the Spirit.

What is the Lord's attitude toward the treasures of the earth in verse 38, and what is he telling Martin about them?

The Lord equates the treasures of the earth with corruptibleness, in effect telling Martin that they really aren't important, likely because Martin attaches too much significance to them. The Spirit of the Lord is the great blessing, not the treasures of the earth. "Corruptibleness" is reminiscent of the Lord's instructions to his disciples, "Lay not up for yourselves treasures upon earth, where moth and rust doth corrupt, and where thieves break through and steal." (Matthew 6:19.)

What does "to the extent thereof" mean? (Verse 38.)

"To the extent of the earth," as many corruptible things as can be gotten.

The Lord ends by asking Martin three questions that Martin must answer in his own heart. With what attitude is each question asked? (Verses 39, 40, 41.)

The first question seems to be asked hopefully: "Behold, canst thou read this without rejoicing, and lifting up thy heart for gladness?" True, the Lord has given Martin a stiff warning, but he doesn't want him to be gloomy about it; the promise in verse 38 is a glorious one. The second question seems pointed and sharp: "Or canst thou run about longer as a blind guide?" meaning "Are you still going to run about as a blind guide?" Christ called the scribes and Pharisees blind guides during his earthly ministry. They were supposed to be the spiritual leaders, but didn't know the way themselves. The final question seems to be entreating: "Or canst thou be humble and meek, and conduct thyself wisely before me?"

Try reading each of these three questions in a way that reflects the Lord's attitude.

The Lord ends, "Yea, come unto me thy Savior." Why do you think "Savior" is used here instead of another of the Lord's names?

The Lord will *save* Martin if Martin will allow it. He has suffered for all men and has the power to save them from all their sins and follies. We're left thinking of the Lord as our Savior, and ourselves as needing a savior.

9

When Shall the Earth Rest? —
Moses 7:20-69

20 And it came to pass that Enoch talked with the Lord; and
he said unto the Lord: Surely Zion shall dwell in safety forever.
But the Lord said unto Enoch: Zion have I blessed, but the
residue of the people have I cursed.

21 And it came to pass that the Lord showed unto Enoch all
the inhabitants of the earth; and he beheld, and lo, Zion, in process of time, was taken up into heaven. And the Lord said unto
Enoch: Behold mine abode forever.

22 And Enoch also beheld the residue of the people which
were the sons of Adam; and they were a mixture of all the seed of
Adam save it was the seed of Cain, for the seed of Cain were
black, and had not place among them.

23 And after that Zion was taken up into heaven, Enoch
beheld, and lo, all the nations of the earth were before him;

*Enoch says, "Surely Zion shall dwell in safety forever." (Verse
20.) Is he making a statement or asking a question?*

The Lord responds as if Enoch had asked a question,
answering, "Zion have I blessed."

*Why does the Lord then add, ". . . but the residue of the people
have I cursed?"*

Enoch's heart seems to be with Zion. By the power of
his righteousness and the righteousness of his people, and
the great mercy of the Lord, Zion has been built, de-

fended, and made glorious. We read that "the fear of the Lord was upon all nations, so great was the glory of the Lord, which was upon his people." (Moses 7:17.) By saying, ". . . the residue of the people have I cursed," the Lord is drawing Enoch's attention to the people Enoch must not have sufficiently considered: those not part of Zion.

The Lord uses the word residue *several times, also* mixture. *(Verses 20 and 22.) What do these words suggest about the people they refer to?*

They suggest that these people are the dross, the impurities; and in fact, they are the "leftovers" from Enoch's great missionary efforts. Yet, as the unfolding vision shows, they are greatly loved by the Lord.

How does the Lord's answer, "Zion have I blessed, but the residue of the people have I cursed" (verse 20), relate to what Enoch sees in the next three verses?

Enoch sees what he has just heard: first, Zion blessed by being taken up to heaven, where it becomes the "abode" of the Lord, to dwell in safety forever (verse 21), as Enoch desired; and then the residue, "all the nations of the earth" (verses 22 and 23).

24 And there came generation upon generation; and Enoch was high and lifted up, even in the bosom of the Father, and of the Son of Man; and behold, the power of Satan was upon all the face of the earth.

25 And he saw angels descending out of heaven; and he heard a loud voice saying: Wo, wo be unto the inhabitants of the earth.

26 And he beheld Satan; and he had a great chain in his hand, and it veiled the whole face of the earth with darkness; and he looked up and laughed, and his angels rejoiced.

27 And Enoch beheld angels descending out of heaven, bearing testimony of the Father and Son; and the Holy Ghost fell on many, and they were caught up by the powers of heaven into Zion.

What does it mean that Enoch was in the bosom of the Father and of the Son of Man? (Verse 24.)

The bosom of the Father is mentioned six times in Enoch's account (verses 24, 30, 31, 47, 63, 69), usually in

the context of something being taken to the Father's
bosom. In this context, the meaning of bosom that seems
most appropriate is "a close relationship marked by affection and protectiveness." Taken to the bosom of the
Father and of the Son of Man, Enoch is taken into their
inner circle; he becomes on intimate terms with them,
seeing into their hearts, coming to better understand how
they think and feel, and eventually coming to think and
feel that way himself.

*What thing is most obvious to Enoch from the vantage point of
eternity, and what does this imply about the way the Lord sees
things?*

Enoch sees the power of Satan upon all the face of the
earth. Even a hopeful sign, angels descending out of
heaven, is quickly followed by a portent of evil, a loud
voice saying, "Wo, wo be unto the inhabitants of the
earth." (Verse 25.) The Lord sees Satan as a great threat
to the welfare of his children.

What is Satan's chain symbolic of? (Verse 26.)

A chain is a symbol of slavery and bondage. Satan is
still about the business he began before the creation: to
destroy the agency of man. (Moses 4:3.)

*Try and picture the great chain in the hand of Satan veiling the
earth with darkness. Why does the chain make the earth dark?*

It blocks the light of the sun, casting a shadow on the
earth.

*What does this suggest about the way Satan destroys man's
agency?*

Satan tries to block the source of light, or the Lord's
influence with his children, and by cutting off the source
of light, limit the choices of those under his influence.

What is the significance of Satan's looking up *and laughing?*
(Verse 26.)

He laughs with derision in the face of God, as if to say,
"You thought these were your children, but now you see
they are mine."

What people do the angels bear testimony to? (Verse 27.)

Speaking of these people, the Lord later says to Enoch, "These which thine eyes are upon shall perish in the floods." (Verse 38.) This tells us that the angels were bearing testimony to Noah's wicked contemporaries, so that not only did they reject Noah's testimony, but even the testimony of angels.

What must these people have been like?

They must have been a very hard-hearted people, entrenched in their wickedness, to reject the Lord's heavenly ministers as well as his earthly one.

28 And it came to pass that the God of heaven looked upon the residue of the people, and he wept; and Enoch bore record of it, saying: How is it that the heavens weep, and shed forth their tears as the rain upon the mountains?

29 And Enoch said unto the Lord: How is it that thou canst weep, seeing thou art holy, and from all eternity to all eternity?

30 And were it possible that man could number the particles of the earth, yea, millions of earths like this, it would not be a beginning to the number of thy creations; and thy curtains are stretched out still; and yet thou art there, and thy bosom is there; and also thou art just; thou art merciful and kind forever;

31 And thou hast taken Zion to thine own bosom, from all thy creations, from all eternity to all eternity; and naught but peace, justice, and truth is the habitation of thy throne; and mercy shall go before thy face and have no end; how is it thou canst weep?

Enoch sees the God of heaven weep over these hardened people. (Verse 28.) And three times Enoch asks variations of the question, "How is it thou canst weep?" (Verses 28, 29, 31.) What does this tell us about Enoch's reaction to the Lord's sorrow?

He is amazed.

Enoch exclaims, "How is it that the heavens weep, and shed forth their tears as the rain upon the mountains?" (Verse 28.) Why, at this time, is the comparison "as rain upon the mountains" particularly appropriate?

It is as if the flood of rain soon to fall in torrents upon the earth was literally tears of sorrow shed by the heavens over unrepentant mankind.

In verse 29, Enoch asks the Lord, "How is it thou canst weep?" and without waiting for an answer, proceeds into a lengthy speech about why he is so puzzled. (Verses 29–30.) Why does he feel the need to explain himself?

Apparently he wants the Father to know that his question isn't a matter of idle curiosity. He shows respect to the Father, approaching him only about his real concerns. It reminds us of Joseph Smith saying, "It is a great thing to inquire at the hands of God, or to come into His presence; and we feel fearful to approach Him on subjects that are of little or no consequence." (*Teachings*, p. 22.)

The formality of Enoch's speech also shows his respect for the Father. How is the speech formal?

First, it is a chiasmus:

a. How is it that thou canst weep? (Verse 29.)
   b. Thou art holy. (Verse 29.)
      c. Thou art from all eternity to all eternity. (Verse 29.)
         d. Thy creations are great. (Verse 30.)
            e. Thy curtains are stretched out *still*. (Verse 30.)
               f. Thou art there. (Verse 30.)
               f. Thy bosom is there. (Verse 30.)
            e. Thou art just, merciful and kind *forever*. (Verse 30.)
         d. Thou has taken Zion from all thy creations. (Verse 31.)
      c. Thy creations are from all eternity to all eternity. (Verse 31.)
   b. Peace, justice, truth, and mercy are thine abode. (Verse 31.)
a. How is it thou canst weep? (Verse 31.)

Second, much of his speech is cast in scriptural language. The phrase "all eternity to all eternity," which occurs twice in Enoch's speech (verses 29 and 31), also appears several times in the Book of Mormon and the Doctrine and Covenants. (Mosiah 3:5; Alma 13:7; Moroni 8:18; D&C 39:1.) It probably means something similar to the phrase "without beginning of days or end of years." (See Moses 6:67.) And Enoch's statement "And were it possible that man could number the particles of the earth, yea, millions of earths like this, it would not be a beginning to the number of thy creations" (verse 30) is reminiscent of the Lord's statement earlier in the book of Moses, "Worlds without number have I created." (Moses 1:33.) Much of the scriptural language is figurative. The line "thy curtains are stretched out still" (verse 30) is a metaphor, one that occurs in the Old Testament. David says, "O Lord my God, thou art very great . . . who stretchest out the heavens like a curtain." (Psalm 104:1-2.) And Isaiah asks, "To whom then will ye liken God? or what likeness will ye compare unto him? . . . It is he . . . that stretcheth out the heavens as a curtain, and spreadeth them out as a tent to dwell in." (Isaiah 40:18, 22.) A curtain in Biblical times was a panel of cloth that tents were made from.

So what does "thy curtains are stretched out still" mean?

Enoch appears to be saying that the heavens and all the Lord's creations are still as he made them; things haven't fallen into chaos because the Lord packed up his tent and moved on.

The statement ". . . and naught but peace, justice, and truth is the habitation of thy throne; and mercy shall go before thy face and have no end" (verse 31) is very similar to a verse from the psalms of David: "Justice and judgment are the habitation of thy throne: mercy and truth shall go before thy face." (Psalm 89:14.) Notice the figures of speech: Enoch treats "peace, justice, and truth" as if they were a location, the habitation of the Lord's throne; and "mercy" he personifies, treating it as if it were a person going before the Lord's face.

Enoch, in his speech, points out the Lord's greatness and his goodness. Why should these characteristics of the Lord make Enoch surprised at his sorrow?

Enoch seems to imply, "How can you feel so sorry for these creatures when they are only an infinitesimal part of your creation and you've given them every chance they deserve and more besides, and they've still rejected you?" Enoch is baffled but open about showing his confusion. He doesn't feel like weeping, so why does the Father?

32 The Lord said unto Enoch: Behold these thy brethren; they are the workmanship of mine own hands, and I gave unto

them their knowledge, in the day I created them; and in the Garden of Eden, gave I unto man his agency;

33 And unto thy brethren have I said, and also given commandment, that they should love one another, and that they should choose me, their Father; but behold, they are without affection, and they hate their own blood;

34 And the fire of mine indignation is kindled against them; and in my hot displeasure will I send in the floods upon them, for my fierce anger is kindled against them.

35 Behold, I am God; Man of Holiness is my name; Man of Counsel is my name; and Endless and Eternal is my name, also.

36 Wherefore, I can stretch forth mine hands and hold all the creations which I have made; and mine eye can pierce them also, and among all the workmanship of mine hands there has not been so great wickedness as among thy brethren.

37 But behold, their sins shall be upon the heads of their fathers; Satan shall be their father, and misery shall be their doom; and the whole heavens shall weep over them, even all the workmanship of mine hands; wherefore should not the heavens weep, seeing these shall suffer?

38 But behold, these which thine eyes are upon shall perish in the floods; and behold, I will shut them up; a prison have I prepared for them.

39 And that which I have chosen hath plead before my face. Wherefore, he suffereth for their sins; inasmuch as they will repent in the day that my Chosen shall return unto me, and until that day they shall be in torment;

40 Wherefore, for this shall the heavens weep, yea, and all the workmanship of mine hands.

The Lord begins his answer to Enoch, saying, "these thy brethren." (Verse 32.) Why does he choose to say this rather than "these people" or "these my children"?

The Lord seems to be gently reminding Enoch, "These, too, are your brothers, Enoch, not just those in Zion." The repeated *th* sounds in this phrase slow it down and thus emphasize it: "*th*ese *th*y bre*th*ren."

We might expect the Lord next to say something like, "They are also my children." But he doesn't. He speaks instead of the relationship between a creator and his creation, saying, "They are the workmanship of mine own hands." (Verse 32.) Why does he do this?

The Lord speaks in terms Enoch will respond to. Ap-

parently the thing most dear to Enoch at this time was
Zion—a city Enoch helped create.

*The Lord next emphasizes that man is an agent, using the
parallel sentences, "I gave unto them their knowledge, in the day I
created them" and "In the Garden of Eden, gave I unto man his
agency." (Verse 32.) Why does the Lord talk here about man's
agency?*

Knowledge and agency have made the current
wickedness possible. It's not that man was created wrong,
but that he went wrong of his own accord.

*The Lord continues, "Unto thy brethren have I said, and also
given commandment. . ." (Verse 33.) In other words, "I not only
told them, but I also commanded them." Why does the Lord here
make a point of telling Enoch that he instructed men in
righteousness?*

The Lord is again telling Enoch that men are responsible for their own wickedness. They were shown the right
way.

*The two commandments that the Lord gives men are: "That
they should love one another" and "that they should choose me their
Father." (Verse 33.) Notice the similarities in form between the
two commandments: both are simple sentences beginning with "they
should," both have the same number of syllables, and both end with
the same sound (another, Father). What does the form help convey about the commandments?*

The similarity and simplicity of form helps convey the
simplicity, directness, and reasonableness of the commandments—traits that make worse the wickedness of
transgressing them.

*Particularly reasonable is the commandment "that they should
choose me their Father"; the Lord, after all, is their Father. How
do you think the Lord feels here?*

The Lord doesn't say that being rejected by his
children has hurt him, but his grief is apparent, perhaps
all the more because it is understated.

*Continuing, the Lord says, "But behold, they are without af-
fection, and they hate their own blood." (Verse 33.) The implica-*

*tion is, "they are even without affection and hate their own blood."
What's the difference between affection and love?*

Affection brings to mind feelings of warmth and
tenderness, though it is a more moderate, less intense at-
tachment than love. The Lord grieves because his
children don't even feel the natural affection toward each
other that we often see animals showing toward their
kind.

What does "they hate their own blood" mean?

It could mean either that they hate their own kindred
or that they hate their own lives. If the latter interpretation is correct, it brings to mind Mormon's description of
his fallen people: "They did curse God, and wish to die."
(Mormon 2:14.)

*It is the Lord's sadness that Enoch, up to this point, has seen.
Now he sees his anger, conveyed by the image of "burning." How
many words related to burning do you find in verse 34?*

The word *fire* occurs once, *kindled* twice, and *hot* once.
And the anger is pointed: note the phrases "against them,"
"upon them," and "against them" at the end of the three
successive lines in verse 34.

*In the context of the "burning" image, what might the purpose
of the floods have been?*

To extinguish the fire or wrath of God. The image of
the floods quenching the fire parallels the image of the
rain as tears of sorrow. Sorrow and anger are both there,
the sorrow intensifying the anger and the anger the sorrow. The Lord at this point seems very human, the most
human, in fact, that he will appear for the remainder of
the vision.

*After seeing the Lord's humanity, Enoch next sees his
godliness. (Verse 35.) Why does the Lord here want Enoch to see
his godliness?*

Earthly parents, when they see their children go
astray, often feel helpless and torn between sorrow and
anger. Not the Lord. Though he feels these emotions, he
isn't at their mercy. He will not be swept into unrighteous
anger or self-pitying sorrow; "Man of *Holiness*" is his

name. He knows what to do with his children when they sin; "Man of *Counsel*" is his name. His righteousness and purpose are constant and unchanging; "Endless and Eternal" is his name also. Note that the Lord says, "*Man* of Holiness," "*Man* of Counsel." God is not so different from man that we cannot eventually learn to think and feel as he does.

How does the repetition of "is my name" make you feel about the Lord?

It makes us feel his power and authority and makes us inclined to reverence him.

The Lord says that because he is God, he can "hold" all his creations. (Verse 36.) What does this mean to you?

To us it means that the Lord can still "work upon" the workmanship of his hands. The image of a fine craftsman comes to mind. The shaping of human souls didn't end in the Garden of Eden, but continues through all of man's wickedness.

What does "mine eye can pierce them also" mean? (Verse 36.)

This suggests that the Lord can see into the minds and hearts of his children. He knows them with a perfect knowledge, far better than they know themselves. And because he knows them, he states there has not been so great wickedness among all the workmanship of his hands as among Enoch's brethren. What a damning judgment, especially remembering Enoch's statement that "were it possible that man could number the particles of the earth, yea, millions of earths like this, it would not be a beginning to the number of thy creations." (Verse 30.) The phrase "so great wickedness" is emphatic; each word is stressed and each successive word stressed more.

What does the phrase "their sins shall be upon the heads of their fathers" mean? (Verse 37.)

We have seen the Father feeling sorrow for his wicked children. But he hasn't felt guilty, because he has given his children agency and taught them righteousness. Not so with the earthly fathers of Enoch's wicked brethren. These fathers must have contributed to their children's sinning, and so bear guilt and responsibility for the sins of their children. Perhaps they will have to repent for their children's sins, as if those sins were their own.

Does this mean the children won't have to repent?

Even those who die without law or who ignorantly sin must repent before they can be heirs of salvation. (See D&C 138:32–33.) Still, repentance must be easier for those who have sinned ignorantly than for those who have sinned knowingly.

In what way will Satan be the father of the wicked? (Verse 37.)

Children tend to follow their parents and to become like them. Similarly, the wicked follow Satan and become like him. "Misery shall be their doom" because Satan teaches them to live miserably, so that "all men might be miserable like unto himself." (2 Nephi 2:27.)

The Lord uses the word father *two different ways in verse 37, first literally in "their sins shall be upon the heads of their fathers" and then figuratively in "Satan shall be their father." Why?*

For one thing, it helps us see that earthly fathers are like Satan when they lead their children into sin and misery. It also sharpens the contrast between God as the true father and Satan as the usurper who takes his place.

The Lord, in verse 37, says "The whole heavens shall weep over them, even all the workmanship of mine hands." Does he mean that all his workmanship will be wept over, or that all his workmanship will weep?

Not all are wicked, so all won't be wept over. The line must mean that all will weep—the wicked because they suffer and the righteous because they see the wicked suffer. Verse 40 makes it clear that all will weep: "For this shall the heavens weep, yea, and all the workmanship of mine hands." Shortly after this, Enoch weeps, and later, even the earth mourns.

After the emotion of verse 37, verse 38 seems calm and matter-of-fact. The Lord will do what has to be done; he will cut the wicked off and shut them up in prison. But feeling is still there, a feeling of deep sadness, of resignation to what must be done. The feeling comes through in part because of the sounds. What repeated sounds bind this verse together?

"But behold, these which th*i*ne *ey*es are u*p*on *sh*all *p*er*i*sh in the floods, and behold, *I* will *sh*ut them *up*; a *p*rison have *I pre*p*a*red for them."

Why does the Father cut off his sinful children? Isn't he merciful?

He is, but "no unclean thing can dwell . . . in his presence." (Moses 6:57.) Moroni gives us some insight into this when he says, "Behold, I say unto you that ye would be more miserable to dwell with a holy and just God, under a consciousness of your filthiness before him, than ye would to dwell with the damned souls in hell. For behold, when ye shall be brought to see your nakedness before God, and also the glory of God, and the holiness of Jesus Christ, it will kindle a flame of unquenchable fire upon you." (Mormon 9:4–5.) The Lord acts mercifully in cutting the wicked off; otherwise they would be in greater torment.

The Lord says, "a prison have I prepared for them." (Verse 38.) What does the word "prepared" tell you about the prison? For what purpose might it have been prepared?

"Prepared" suggests that the prison isn't just some place that the Father happened to find convenient at the time. Rather, it seems to be a place or condition especially suited to the prisoners. In the Doctrine and Covenants we read, "And after this another angel shall sound, which is the second trump; and then cometh the redemption of those who are Christ's at his coming; who have received their part in that prison which is prepared for them, *that they might receive the gospel,* and be judged according to men in the flesh." (D&C 88:99.) Their experience in prison helps prepare the wicked to receive the gospel.

Why does the Lord say, "that which" I have chosen, rather than "he whom" I have chosen? (Verse 39.)

By saying "that which" instead of "he whom" the

Father distances himself from the Son and the cause he is pleading—the cause of sinful mankind. He will not grant the Son's request just because he loves him, though he will listen to Christ, because Christ is his "Chosen."

What does "plead" mean? (Verse 39.)

"Plead" here probably doesn't mean "beg," but instead something like "to argue a case or cause in a court of law." Christ is our "advocate" with the Father. (D&C 29:5.)

What is the relationship between Christ's pleading and his suffering? (Verse 39.)

"Wherefore" is similar to "therefore." Christ has pled for them; therefore he suffers for them. It's as if he suffers in order to strengthen his case. In the Doctrine and Covenants, Christ says, "I am Christ, and in mine own name, and by virtue of the blood which I have spilt, have I pleaded before the Father for them." (D&C 38:4.)

Verse 39 reads more easily if the last sentence is punctuated as follows: "Wherefore, he suffereth for their sins, inasmuch as they will repent in the day that my Chosen shall return unto me; and until that day they shall be in torment . . ." What does "inasmuch" mean?

The definition that best fits is "to the degree that." Christ's suffering for their sins is efficacious "to the degree that" those sins are repented of.

When did the Chosen return to the Father, and what happened "the day" he returned? (Verse 39.)

This must have been the time of Christ's ascension. Shortly before that time, between his crucifixion and resurrection, Christ went to the spirit world and sent the righteous spirits to preach to the wicked who had been destroyed in the flood. (See D&C 138.) Because of the suffering of Christ for the wicked, those who repented were released from prison and torment. We later learn that these repentant spirits "came forth, and stood on the right hand of God." (Verse 57.)

41 And it came to pass that the Lord spake unto Enoch, and told Enoch all the doings of the children of men; wherefore Enoch

knew, and looked upon their wickedness, and their misery, and wept and stretched forth his arms, and his heart swelled wide as eternity; and his bowels yearned; and all eternity shook.

42 And Enoch also saw Noah, and his family; that the posterity of all the sons of Noah should be saved with a temporal salvation;

43 Wherefore Enoch saw that Noah built an ark; and that the Lord smiled upon it, and held it in his own hand; but upon the residue of the wicked the floods came and swallowed them up.

44 And as Enoch saw this, he had bitterness of soul, and wept over his brethren, and said unto the heavens: I will refuse to be comforted; but the Lord said unto Enoch: Lift up your heart, and be glad; and look.

45 And it came to pass that Enoch looked; and from Noah, he beheld all the families of the earth; and he cried unto the Lord saying: When shall the day of the Lord come? When shall the blood of the Righteous be shed, that all they that mourn may be sanctified and have eternal life?

46 And the Lord said: It shall be in the meridian of time, in the days of wickedness and vengeance.

47 And behold, Enoch saw the day of the coming of the Son of Man, even in the flesh; and his soul rejoiced, saying: The Righteous is lifted up, and the Lamb is slain from the foundation of the world; and through faith I am in the bosom of the Father, and behold, Zion is with me.

Enoch began by asking, "how is it thou canst weep?" (Verse 29.) How has the Lord answered his question? (Verse 41.)

By getting Enoch to weep.

Verse 41, the description of Enoch's sorrow, is beautiful and powerful. What makes us feel so keenly Enoch's sorrow?

We notice several things. First, the words "arms," "heart," and "bowels" convey a sorrow so intense that it is actually physical; second, the words "stretched" and "swelled," show the sorrow to be so great that Enoch's body can't contain it; third, the feeling builds in intensity through the verse as short, descriptive phrases follow each other. Particularly descriptive are the verbs "looked," "wept," "stretched," "swelled," "yearned." Next, the repetition of *eternity* emphasizes the vastness of the sorrow. Then, in the line "all eternity shook," the emotion reaches its height as Enoch's sorrow becomes one with the sorrow of the heavens, his sorrow reverberating with theirs until all creation shakes. Finally, repeated sounds throughout the verse bind the passage together, emphasizing Enoch's sorrow:

"And it came to pass that the Lord spa*k*e unto Eno*ch*, and told Eno*ch* all the do*i*ngs of the *ch*ild*re*n of m*e*n; wherefore Eno*ch* kn*ew*, and *l*oo*k*ed upon their *w*i*ck*ed*ness, and their m*i*se*r*y, and *w*e*p*t and *str*e*tch*e*d* forth h*i*s a*r*ms, h*i*s hea*rt* s*w*e*lle*d *w*i*d*e as e*t*e*r*ni*t*y; and h*i*s bowels yea*r*ne*d*; and all e*t*e*r*ni*t*y shoo*k*."

Try reading the phrase "all eternity shook," emphasizing the word "eternity." Now try reading it again, emphasizing "all" and "shook." Which way is better?

"Eternity" was emphasized in the line "his heart swelled wide as eternity," so it shouldn't be emphasized again here. The phrase should be read "*all* eternity *shook*," with "shook" emphasized even more than "all." Note the sound repetition in "looked" and "shook," which further emphasizes "shook." We are left with a vivid image of shaking.

The last line of verse 41 doesn't read "all eternity shook with great sobs." Would that have been a better way of putting it?

That would have been sentimental. Deep emotion is felt most intensely when it is conveyed through well-chosen words and form — not through over-done description.

The account next says that Enoch saw Noah (verse 42), but Noah hasn't yet been introduced in this vision. How did Enoch learn about Noah?

We don't know. Perhaps the Lord told Enoch more about Noah in this vision than is recorded. Or perhaps Enoch learned about Noah previous to this vision, though there is no record of it in the Book of Moses.

Why does the Lord show Enoch Noah's salvation (verse 42) before showing him the destruction of the wicked (verse 43)?

We can't help but think the Lord wanted to soften the blow, giving Enoch hope in Noah before showing him the end of the wicked.

How else has the Lord helped to soften Enoch's grief?

The Lord *told* Enoch the wicked would perish (verse 38) before actually showing him their destruction (verse 43), thus giving the bitter medicine in small doses. He also told Enoch that Christ would redeem the wicked if they repented. (Verse 39.)

What does it mean that the posterity of Noah "should be saved with a temporal salvation"? (Verse 42.)

In context, this means they would escape death in the flood. Notice, though, the "a"; it is just "a" temporal salvation; they wouldn't escape death forever.

What earlier line does the line "the Lord . . . held it in his own hand" (verse 43) remind you of?

Earlier the Lord said, "I can . . . hold all the creations I have made." (Verse 36.) One way the Lord "holds" his creations is by protecting the righteous like Noah.

Imagine the Lord holding the ark in his hand and smiling upon it. Do the words "smile" and "hold" bring any other images to your mind?

We picture a parent holding and smiling upon his child.

Earlier, the Lord said he would shut the wicked up. (Verse 38.) Now Enoch sees the floods swallow them up. (Verse 43.) What is conveyed by the phrases "shut them up" and "swallowed them up"?

The awful, final state of the wicked, cut off from the presence of God.

What is "bitterness of soul?" (Verse 44.)

In the scriptures, bitterness of soul comes from sin. Alma the Younger, realizing his guilt, cried out in his heart, "O Jesus, thou Son of God, have mercy on me, who am in the *gall of bitterness,* and am encircled about by the everlasting chains of death." (Alma 36:18.) Alma later tells his son Corianton, "Behold, an awful death cometh upon the wicked; for they die as to things pertaining to things of righteousness; for they are unclean, and no unclean thing can inherit the kingdom of God; but they are cast out, and consigned to partake of the fruits of their labors or their works, which have been evil; and *they drink the dregs of a bitter cup.*" (Alma 40:26.) And when Moses encountered Satan, he "began to fear exceedingly; and as he began to fear, he saw the *bitterness of hell.*" (Moses 1:20.) Notice that just as Enoch understands the Lord's sorrow by feeling it himself (verse 41), he understands the misery of the wicked by feeling it himself (verse 41), he understands the misery of the wicked by feeling their bitterness of soul (verse 44).

Enoch isn't a wicked man, though. Why does he feel bitterness of soul as the wicked do?

Enoch now sees the wicked as "his brethren." (Verse 44.) He suffers, it seems, because he takes their burden — the burden of sin — upon himself. Out of love, Christ took our sins upon himself, and in so doing, partook of the "bitter cup." (D&C 19:18.)

Is Enoch's expression, "I will refuse to be comforted" (verse 44) an expression of weakness or of strength?

Of both, really. Of weakness, because Enoch, unlike Christ, couldn't bear the misery of the wicked and doubts he'll ever find comfort again. The burden just seems too heavy. But also of strength, because Enoch is feeling the love of God for his brothers.

In the depths of Enoch's sorrow, the Lord tells him to lift up his heart and be glad. (Verse 44.) Then the Lord shows Enoch all the families of the earth. (Verse 45.) Why should this make Enoch glad?

After death, there is comfort in new life, just as there is in spring's renewal of life after winter.

Enoch doesn't respond to the scene by being comforted, but instead asks, "When shall the day of the Lord come?" (Verse 45.) Why is he anxious for Christ to come?

Enoch has just said he will refuse to be comforted, and though he eventually is comforted, it seems to take more than the vision of Noah's children to do it. He is still mourning, but apparently in the midst of suffering, he recalls the redemptive power of Christ. He had earlier taught his people of Christ, saying, "Ye must be born again into the kingdom of heaven, of water, and of the Spirit, and be cleansed by blood, even the blood of mine Only Begotten; that ye might be sanctified from all sin, and enjoy the words of eternal life in this world, and eternal life in the world to come, even immortal glory." (Moses 6:59.) But now that he knows the depth of suffering that sin brings, Christ's coming seems more urgent to Enoch.

Wicked people can mourn, but in their sins they can't be sanctified and have eternal life, so who are "all they that mourn"? (Verse 45.)

A mourner sorrows because a loved one has died. Maybe for Enoch "they that mourn" are the righteous who sorrow over the spiritual destruction of their loved ones.

What does it mean to be sanctified? (Verse 45.)

The phrase "sanctified from all sin" suggests that *sanctified* means something like *cleansed.*

If "all they that mourn" are righteous, why must they be sanctified from sin?

The easy answer is that no one is righteous — except Christ. Enoch refers to Christ as "the" Righteous. (Verse 45.) But there appears to be more going on here. Enoch has been troubled over the sins of the wicked, not his own sins. Here he seems to feel in need of cleansing, as if the sins of the wicked have somehow tainted him. To one degree or another, we all share in the blood and sins of our own generation and need to be sanctified or cleansed from those sins.

Christ is to come in "the days of wickedness and vengeance." (Verse 46.) Whose vengeance?

In verse 60, the "last days" are also called "the days of wickedness and vengeance." The vengeance spoken of, in both cases, may be the vengeance of Christ on the wicked. In the meridian of time, vengeance was clearly taken on the wicked in America. It appears that in the last days, it will be universal. Christ says, "And it shall come to pass, because of the wickedness of the world, that I will take

vengeance upon the wicked, for they will not repent."
(D&C 29:17.)

*In verse 45, Enoch asks, "When shall the blood of the
Righteous be shed?" Then in verse 47 he says, "The Righteous is
lifted up . . ."—this must mean "lifted up on the cross"—and "the
Lamb is slain from the foundation of the world." Why this emphasis on blood and death instead of the resurrection?*

Enoch is interested in sanctification (verse 45), and
from the Book of Remembrance kept by Adam, he learned
that sanctification was made possible through the shed-
ding of blood—Christ's blood. (Moses 6:59–60.)

*How is it that Christ was slain "from the foundation of the
world"? (Verse 47.) What does this mean?*

It must mean that Christ's atonement was ordained
from the foundation, or beginning, of the world.

*Enoch speaks of future events as if they were present, saying,
"The Righteous is lifted up," "the Lamb is slain," "through faith I
am in the bosom of the Father," and "Zion is with me." (Verse
47.) Why does he speak this way?*

Using the present tense to describe future events must
have seemed appropriate to Enoch; he was, after all, seeing future events as if they were present.

*Enoch says that he is in the bosom of the Father "through
faith." What does this mean? Wasn't he actually with the Father
right then?*

Here, Enoch may be distinguishing between his present state, which actually is in the bosom of the Father,
and the future state he looks forward to in faith, in which
he will again be in the bosom of the Father.

48 And it came to pass that Enoch looked upon the earth; and
he heard a voice from the bowels thereof, saying: Wo, wo is me,
the mother of men; I am pained, I am weary, because of the
wickedness of my children. When shall I rest, and be cleansed
from the filthiness which is gone forth out of me? When will my
Creator sanctify me, that I may rest, and righteousness for a
season abide upon my face?

49 And when Enoch heard the earth mourn, he wept, and
cried unto the Lord, saying: O Lord, wilt thou not have compas-

sion upon the earth? Wilt thou not bless the children of Noah?

50 And it came to pass that Enoch continued his cry unto the Lord, saying: I ask thee, O Lord, in the name of thine Only Begotten, even Jesus Christ, that thou wilt have mercy upon Noah and his seed, that the earth might never more be covered by the floods.

51 And the Lord could not withhold; and he covenanted with Enoch, and sware unto him with an oath, that he would stay the floods; that he would call upon the children of Noah;

52 And he sent forth an unalterable decree, that a remnant of his seed should always be found among all nations, while the earth should stand;

53 And the Lord said: Blessed is he through whose seed Messiah shall come; for he saith—I am Messiah, the King of Zion, the Rock of Heaven, which is broad as eternity; whoso cometh in at the gate and climbeth up by me shall never fall; wherefore, blessed are they of whom I have spoken, for they shall come forth with songs of everlasting joy.

Why, just when Enoch is feeling comforted, does the Lord show him something else that makes him sorrowful: the earth mourning? (Verse 48.)

It seems there is still more for Enoch to see. His moment of comfort and rejoicing was apparently a needed break from the sorrow he had been feeling, but not an end to it. Having seen the suffering of the wicked and the sorrow of the heavens, he now must see the suffering earth. Experiencing this "fulness of sorrow" seems to prepare him for the "fulness of joy" that will come at the end of the vision.

Does the earth really speak, or is this all figurative? (Verse 48.)

We once heard a lively Sunday School class discussion about this question. One sister said the earth has intelligence and so is capable of thought and speech. A brother replied, "But how can rocks and dirt talk?" There may be both a literal and figurative interpretation of this passage. The scriptures make it clear that the earth literally has intelligence: "And again, verily I say unto you, the earth abideth the law of a celestial kingdom, for it filleth the measure of its creation, and transgresseth not the law—Wherefore, it shall be sanctified; yea, not-

withstanding it shall die, it shall be quickened again, and
shall abide the power by which it is quickened, and the
righteous shall inherit it." (D&C 88:25–26.) But whether
the earth has the kind of intelligence needed to think and
speak is hard to say. Figuratively, the mourning earth, in
need of sanctification, seems a symbol of "all they that
mourn." Earlier, Enoch asked, "When shall . . . all they
that *mourn* be *sanctified* and have eternal life?" (Verse 45.)
Now Enoch hears "the earth *mourn*" and ask, "When will
my Creator *sanctify* me?" (Verse 48.) The repetition points
to the symbolism. Notice also the similarity between the
weeping heavens and the mourning earth. Just as the
heavens wept when torrents of rain fell on the earth, so
also the earth mourns, shaking, when Christ is crucified
and again before his second coming. (Verses 56, 61.) And
while the weeping heavens (verse 37) seemed to stand for
"the weeping hosts of heaven," the mourning earth
similarly seems symbolic of "the mourning inhabitants of
the earth."

*Why does the earth call herself the "mother of men" and speak of
the filthiness which is "gone forth" out of her, as if in birth?*

This reminds us of the creation: "And the Lord God
formed man of the dust of the ground." (Genesis 2:7.)
The earth is the mother of men, it seems, because they
were formed from her elements. Also, the mourning of a
righteous mother over the wickedness of her children suggests the deepest kind of grief experienced by any
righteous mourner. And the need to be sanctified seems
clearer in a family context than in any other; family
members share more in each other's sins and are more
burdened by them than any other group of people.

*Enoch hears the voice from the bowels of the earth, as if from
the very core of her being, and is grieved at her sorrow. (Verse 48.)
What repeated words, sounds, and ideas give the earth's speech its
emotional effect?*

Here are the repeated words and sounds;
Wo, wo is *me*, the *m*other of *m*en;
 I am pained,
 I am weary,
   because of the *w*icked*ness* of my children.

When shall I *rest,*
    and be cleansed *from* the *fil*thiness which is
    gone *forth* out of *me,*
When will *my* Creator *s*anctif*y me,*
    that *I* may *rest,* and
    *r*ighteou*sness* for a *s*eason ab*i*de upon m*y* face?

The repeated ideas are: the need for rest ("I am weary," "When shall I rest," "that I may rest"), the need for cleansing ("When shall I . . . be cleansed," "When will my Creator sanctify me"), and the wickedness of men ("the wickedness of my children," "the filthiness which is gone forth out of me").

Can you sympathize with the earth's need for rest?

We once saw a television series about the personal lives of several of the Roman emperors. Each succeeding episode showed more murder, treachery, and infidelity, until we began to feel weary just watching. No doubt only God could come away still clean, pure, and alive from a hundred million such real-life episodes, knowing more than we could the tragedy of each one. Notice how little the earth asks: only for "a season" of rest, like a parent of young children hoping for one good night's sleep.

Now Enoch weeps again. (Verse 49.) By this time he must be sorely in need of rest himself. He asks two questions: "O Lord, wilt thou not have compassion upon the earth?" and "Wilt thou not bless the children of Noah?" He asks about the earth because he's been weeping over her, but why does he ask about the children of Noah, whom he hasn't said anything about since he first saw them in verse 45?

Now that the flood has destroyed everyone but Noah and his children, they are the only ones left to give the earth grief. Enoch wants the Lord to bless Noah's children, it seems, so that the earth won't have so much to grieve over.

How, specifically, does Enoch want the Lord to bless Noah's children?

He asks the Lord to bless them by staying the floods. (Verse 50.)

Why does the way they die matter to Enoch? Aren't there worse ways to die?

Enoch may not be worried so much about drowning as about wholesale destruction. Perhaps drowning to him was the only conceivable way for everyone to be destroyed at once. The Lord responds as if total destruction were Enoch's concern, promising him that "a remnant of his seed should always be found among all nations, while the earth should stand." (Verse 52.) This promise should comfort a generation that lives with nuclear nightmares; the Lord will not let us utterly blow ourselves off the face of the earth.

Why would it be worse for everyone to die at once, in a flood, for example, than for them to die separately?

Total destruction means "the end of all flesh" (Moses 8:30), not just the end of various individuals. Gone is any hope for mankind — no new life, no rising generation to redeem the old.

How is it that staying the floods will comfort the earth, who mourns over the wickedness of her children?

Staying the floods and calling upon the children of Noah seem to go hand in hand. That is, the alternative to destruction is repentance, brought about by God calling on men to repent. If the Lord never gives up calling on the children of Noah, then there is hope they will eventually repent and righteousness for a season will abide upon the face of the earth. But if the Creator destroys men, then hope for them in the flesh is gone — and of course the flesh is what the earth is mother of. She would be left desolate, mourning that the great wickedness of her children led to their total annihilation.

Why is it that "the Lord could not withhold" granting Enoch's request? (Verse 51.)

One reason is found earlier in the Book of Moses where the Lord says, "If thou wilt turn unto me, and hearken unto my voice, and believe, and repent of all thy transgressions, and be baptized, even in water, in the name of mine Only Begotten Son, who is full of grace and truth, which is Jesus Christ, the only name which shall be given under heaven, whereby salvation shall come unto the children of men, *ye shall receive the gift of the Holy Ghost,* *asking all things in his name, and whatsoever ye shall ask, it shall be given you." (*Moses 6:52.) Enoch has asked in the name of the Son and presumably filled the other conditions of the promise, so the Lord cannot withhold. We don't think this was necessarily perfunctory, though; we picture the Lord moved with compassion at Enoch's request.

What phrases emphasize that the Lord really will stay the floods and call upon the children of Noah? (Verse 51.)

The phrases, "He covenanted with Enoch" (verse 51), "[he] sware unto him with an oath" (verse 51), and "he sent forth an unalterable decree" (verse 52). There can be no mistake that the Lord will fulfill his oath.

How does the Lord's statement "Blessed is he through whose seed Messiah shall come" (verse 53) relate to what's gone before?

The Lord appears to be saying that one reason he will bless Noah, preserving his children, is that he, Jesus Christ, will be of Noah's seed.

Who does the "he" refer to in the phrase "for he saith"? (Verse 53.)

This must refer to Christ.

Read aloud the line "I am Messiah, the King of Zion, the Rock of Heaven." (Verse 53.) What creates the rhythm of this line?

Several things: each of the phrases is five syllables in length; the last two phrases have the same number of words, with the same number of syllables in corresponding words; the last two phrases end in the same sound: Zion, Heaven,; finally, the pattern of emphasis is the same at the end of each of the three phrases:

I am Mes͢siah
the Kín͢g of Zión
the Róck of Héaven

The phrase "broad as eternity" (verse 53) reminds us of the earlier line "his heart swelled wide as eternity" (verse 41). Does this similarity suggest anything to you?

To us it suggests that Christ's power is great enough to heal Enoch's sorrow. And indeed, as the next metaphor shows, it's great enough to heal any sorrow: "Whoso com-

eth in at the gate and climbeth up by me shall never fall."
(Verse 53.)

What is "the gate"? (Verse 53.)

We remember what Nephi said: "For the gate by
which ye should enter is repentance and baptism by
water; and then cometh a remission of your sins by fire
and by the Holy Ghost." (2 Nephi 31:17.)

Who are "they of whom I have spoken"? (Verse 53.)

Apparently, these are they who come in at the gate
and climb up by Christ.

*Do you know of other scriptures that might tell you why the
righteous "shall come forth with songs of everlasting joy." (Verse
53.)*

This phrase and similar ones are found in scriptures
that describe the joy of the righteous coming to Zion. One
scripture is in Isaiah: "And the ransomed of the Lord shall
return, and come to Zion with songs and everlasting joy
upon their heads: they shall obtain joy and gladness, and
sorrow and sighing shall flee away." (Isaiah 35:10.) Try to
imagine how you would feel coming to Zion, a society
that encourages rather than discourages righteousness.
What would it be like? No depressing headlines, locked
doors, or fear of violence, no poverty, no guilt because
you eat while others don't.

54 And it came to pass that Enoch cried unto the Lord, saying: When the Son of Man cometh in the flesh, shall the earth
rest? I pray thee, show me these things.

55 And the Lord said unto Enoch: Look, and he looked and
beheld the Son of Man lifted up on the cross, after the manner of
men;

56 And he heard a loud voice; and the heavens were veiled;
and all the creations of God mourned; and the earth groaned; and
the rocks were rent; and the saints arose, and were crowned at
the right hand of the Son of Man, with crowns of glory;

57 And as many of the spirits as were in prison came forth,
and stood on the right hand of God; and the remainder were
reserved in chains of darkness until the judgment of the great
day.

*The Lord makes some glorious promises to Enoch in verses 51
to 53. But again, Enoch isn't immediately comforted. He asks,*

"When the Son of Man cometh in the flesh, shall the earth rest?"
(Verse 54.) The Lord's promise to stay the floods must have given
Enoch hope that some day the earth would rest. We know also he
had faith that through the "blood of the Righteous" "all they that
mourn" would be "sanctified and have eternal life." (Verse 45.)
What more does Enoch want here?

Enoch seems to want firsthand knowledge. He asks, "I
pray thee, *show* me these things." (Verse 54.) It appears
that Enoch can't or won't be comforted until he sees the
earth at rest.

Why does Enoch think the earth might rest when Christ comes?

Enoch knows that the earth must be sanctified before
she can rest (verse 48), that sanctification will come
through Christ (verse 45), and that Christ will come in
the flesh (verse 47). So perhaps he wonders if the earth
will rest when Christ does come in the flesh.

How does the Lord answer Enoch? (Verse 55.)

He shows Enoch Christ's crucifixion, at which the
earth groans and all the creations of God mourn. No rest
for the earth then!

What is it that occurs "after the manner of men"? (Verse 55.)

The lifting up is after the manner of men. Men don't
lift up like God does. Men lift up to destroy, God to heal.

Enoch hears a loud voice and sees the heavens veiled. (Verse
56.) Earlier in his vision, before the flood, he also heard a loud
voice and saw the heavens veiled. (Verses 25 and 26.) At that time
a loud voice said, "Wo, wo be unto the inhabitants of the earth"
(verse 25), and the heavens were veiled with darkness (verse 26).
How might Enoch have reacted to the similarity between these two
occasions?

The earlier portents were signs of impending doom
for Noah's contemporaries. Now Enoch sees the ominous
signs for Noah's children as well. He must have been glad
for the Lord's promise that he would stay the floods and
call upon the children of Noah, but also more anxious to
know when the promise would be fulfilled. And in fact,
shortly after this, he asks the Lord, "Wilt thou not come
again upon the earth?" (Verse 59.)

At the time of Christ's crucifixion, was the loud voice actually heard and the veil seen, or were these only spiritually discerned?

At least in America, the signs were seen by all: "And it came to pass that there was thick darkness upon all the face of the land . . . And . . . there was a voice heard among all the inhabitants of the earth, upon all the face of this land, crying: Wo, wo, wo unto this people; wo unto the inhabitants of the whole earth except they shall repent." (3 Nephi 8:20, 9:1,2.)

What makes verse 56 so powerful?

We think it's partly the short descriptive phrases, which have the most effect when punctuated with breaths as follows:

> And he heard a loud voice; (breath)
> and the heavens were veiled; (breath)
> and all the creations of God mourned; (breath)
> and the earth groaned; (breath)
> and the rocks rent; (breath)
> and the saints arose, and were crowned at the right
> hand of the Son of Man, with crowns of glory
> (breath).

This way of breathing emphasizes the last and longest line, which describes the rising of the Saints. The power also comes from the pervasive feeling of mourning. Besides "mourned" and "groaned," the words "loud voice," "veiled," and "rent" also suggest mourning. In the Old Testament, mourners often cried with loud voices, covered themselves, and rent their clothes. For example, during a time of "great mourning among the Jews" (Esther 4:3), "Mordecai rent his clothes, and put on sackcloth with ashes, and went out into the midst of the city, and cried with a loud and a bitter cry" (Esther 4:1). (See also Ezekiel 24:17; 2 Samuel 15:30, 32; 2 Samuel 19:4.) In verse 56, the heavens and the earth mourn, sharing in a grief so pervasive that it extends even to inanimate creation. Sound repetitions are also important in this verse. You might want to try picking out the repeated sounds. Notice the image created by placing the line "the saints arose" after the line "the rocks were rent." It seems the rocks rend in order to deliver up the saints from the earth.

What are "crowns of glory"? (Verse 56.)

In the Doctrine and Covenants, the Lord, speaking of the earth, says, "For after it hath filled the measure of its creation, it shall be crowned with glory, *even with the presence of God the Father;* That bodies who are of the celestial kingdom may possess it forever and ever." (D&C 88:19–20.) It appears that the Saints are crowned with the presence of God the Father, implying that they inherit the celestial kingdom.

"And as many of the spirits as were in prison came forth, and stood on the right hand of God." (Verse 57.) What does this line mean?

This line must mean that there were as many prisoners that came forth as there were Saints. It couldn't mean that all the spirits in prison came forth, because we next read that some were reserved in chains of darkness. (Verse 57.)

How are the Saints who arise like and unlike the prisoners who come forth?

Both Saints and former prisoners end up at the right hand of Christ, which means they have all been cleansed by Christ and have taken upon themselves his name. (Mosiah 5:8–10; Alma 5:58.) However, the prisoners who rejected Christ in the flesh, though they afterward received him, are heirs of a terrestrial glory, while the Saints receive a celestial glory. (D&C 76:71–74.)

What's the difference between those who come forth out of prison and those who are reserved in chains of darkness? (Verse 57.)

In Joseph F. Smith's Vision of the Redemption of the Dead, we read, "And the chosen messengers went forth to declare the acceptable day of the Lord and proclaim *liberty* to the captives who were bound, *even unto all who would repent of their sins and receive the gospel."* (D&C 138:31.) The prisoners who came forth were the repentant ones. (See also Moses 7:39.)

When is "the judgment of the great day"? (Verse 57.)

In the Doctrine and Covenants, the Lord says, "The

residue of the wicked have I kept in chains of darkness until the judgment of the great day, *which shall come at the end
of the earth.*" (D&C 38:5.)

58 And again Enoch wept and cried unto the Lord, saying:
When shall the earth rest?

59 And Enoch beheld the Son of Man ascend up unto the
Father; and he called unto the Lord, saying: Wilt thou not come
again upon the earth? Forasmuch as thou art God, and I know
thee, and thou hast sworn unto me, and commanded me that I
should ask in the name of thine Only Begotten; thou hast made
me, and given unto me a right to thy throne, and not of myself,
but through thine own grace; wherefore, I ask thee if thou wilt
not come again on the earth.

60 And the Lord said unto Enoch: As I live, even so will I
come in the last days, in the days of wickedness and vengeance,
to fulfil the oath which I have made unto you concerning the
children of Noah;

61 And the day shall come that the earth shall rest, but before
that day the heavens shall be darkened, and a veil of darkness
shall cover the earth; and the heavens shall shake, and also the
earth; and great tribulations shall be among the children of men,
but my people will I preserve;

62 And righteousness will I send down out of heaven; and
truth will I send forth out of the earth, to bear testimony of mine
Only Begotten; his resurrection from the dead; yea, and also the
resurrection of all men; and righteousness and truth will I cause
to sweep the earth as with a flood, to gather out mine elect from
the four quarters of the earth, unto a place which I shall prepare,
an Holy City, that my people may gird up their loins, and be
looking forth for the time of my coming; for there shall be my
tabernacle, and it shall be called Zion, a New Jerusalem.

63 And the Lord said unto Enoch: Then shalt thou and all
thy city meet them there, and we will receive them into our
bosom, and they shall see us; and we will fall upon their necks,
and they shall fall upon our necks, and we will kiss each other;

64 And there shall be mine abode, and it shall be Zion,
which shall come forth out of all the creations which I have made;
and for the space of a thousand years the earth shall rest.

*Now knowing that the earth won't rest when Christ comes in
the flesh, Enoch persistently asks again, "When shall the earth
rest?" (Verse 58.) Does his persistence resemble that of anyone else
you are familiar with in the scriptures?*

We think of Joseph Smith deciding to ask God which

church was right, remembering what to ask when the Lord appeared and telling his mother the answer. Joseph and Enoch weren't easily distracted when they wanted answers. It's interesting that in Section 78 the Lord calls Joseph Smith by the name Enoch.

Up until verse 59, "the Lord" appears to be "the Father." (See verses 33, 39, 47, 50.) But beginning in verse 59, when Enoch asks if he will come again upon the earth, "the Lord" appears also to be the Son. How do you explain this?

Probably this is and has been Jesus speaking for the Father. We think of Section 29, which begins with Jesus introducing himself, saying, "Listen to the voice of Jesus Christ, your Redeemer, the Great I am" (verse 1), but later has Jesus speaking for the Father, saying, "I, the Lord God, gave unto Adam and unto his seed, that they should not die as to the temporal death, until I, the Lord God, should send forth angels to declare unto them repentance and redemption, through faith on the name of *mine Only Begotten Son.*" (Verse 42.) The son speaks for the Father because they are one, and his doing so helps us sense their oneness. (See also Revelations 22:6–9 for an example of an angel speaking for Christ.)

In verse 59, to whom does Enoch call, the Son of Man he sees ascending, the Father, who is also in the vision, or "the Lord" he has been talking to?

The question "Wilt thou not come again upon the earth?" suggests that this is the Son, as does the fact that Enoch calls as if the person were going away from him. But then Enoch says, "Thou hast . . . commanded me that I should ask in the name of *thine Only Begotten,*" which suggests he is talking to the Father. Then again, the account says he calls to "the Lord" — the person he's been talking with all along. Again, this blurring of individuals is probably intentional. Here Enoch seems almost to step into the vision, no longer a passive witness but an active participant who encourages Christ to come again upon the earth. Previously, he asked, "When the Son of Man cometh in the flesh, shall the earth rest?" talking *about* Christ. (Verse 54.) Now he talks *to* Christ, saying, "Wilt *thou* not come again upon the earth?" (Verse 59.)

Why does Enoch ask the Lord if he will come again? Hasn't the Lord already promised that he would call on the children of Noah?

Enoch may be wondering if the promise was fulfilled when Christ came in the flesh and if men had lost their chance because they rejected him when he came.

Looking at Enoch's speech to the Lord in verse 59, how does Enoch feel about asking the Lord to come again upon the earth?

Just as in verses 29 to 31, Enoch here seems hesitant to ask the Lord his question without explaining himself. He tells the Lord why he asks and why he feels it's right for him to ask, not wanting to be disrespectful.

Notice how he softens his request in verse 59: he says, "thou hast sworn unto me," omitting what it is the Lord has sworn, instead of saying, "thou hast sworn unto me that thou would call upon the children of Noah"; and he says, "thou hast . . . given unto me a right to thy throne, and not of myself, but through thine own grace," instead of just, "thou hast . . . given unto me a right to thy throne." Why doesn't he speak more to the point?

We think he doesn't want to be demanding. He's not trying to browbeat the Lord with the equivalent of the child's "But you promised."

Enoch seems to feel he's asking a great favor of the Lord. Why?

He's just seen what happened to the Lord the first time he came. Asking him to come back after an experience like that must have taken a lot of courage! Still, Enoch appears to feel justified in asking.

The Lord promises Enoch that he will come in the last days and swears it, saying, "as I live." (Verse 60.) Why does he so strongly state the promise?

The Lord's firmness seems a response to Enoch's uncertainty. He reassures Enoch: he will not cease calling on men; his oath is for all time.

In verse 61 and again in verse 64, Enoch is told, finally, that the earth shall rest. This must have been a great comfort to him. But he also sees the great tribulation that will precede the coming of

Christ. A picture of this tribulation is created in the following lines from verse 61:

> *the heavens shall be darkened, and*
> *a veil of darkness shall cover the earth; and*
> *the heavens shall shake, and also*
> *the earth [shall shake];*

What repetition do you find in these lines, and what does the repetition emphasize?

Heavens and *earth* are repeated, as are the images of darkness and shaking. The repetition of *heavens* and *earth* emphasizes the extent of the tribulation; the repetition of *darkness* and *shaking* emphasizes the fearfulness of it.

Verse 61 seems an abbreviated version of other accounts of the last days. What other accounts are you reminded of?

We think of Christ teaching his disciples what the signs of his second coming would be. (Matthew 24; Mark 13; Luke 21; Joseph Smith 1.) In the various accounts, we read of "great tribulation" (Matthew 24:21), of "great earthquakes" (Luke 21:11), and that the sun shall be "darkened, and the moon shall not give her light, and the stars shall fall from heaven, and the powers of the heavens shall be shaken" (Matthew 24:29). Verse 66 of Moses 7 also describes the tribulation of the last days, and is the only other verse in Moses 7 that does. This verse describes the sea being troubled and men's hearts failing them, reminding us most of Luke's account of the last days, in which we read about "the sea and the waves roaring" (Luke 21:25) and "men's hearts failing them for fear" (Luke 21:26).

In earlier verses of Moses 7, much was said about the suffering of the wicked at the time of the flood. Why is so little said about the suffering of the wicked in the last days?

Perhaps by now Enoch has learned what the Lord wanted him to learn about the suffering that sin brings, so there is no need to go into more detail. Like Christ, Enoch's bowels are filled with compassion for the wicked and for the righteous who mourn because of them, and he is now ready for the Lord to show him what he has to look forward to and rejoice about. The suffering, it seems, has prepared him to receive the joy.

What is emphasized by saying "My people will I preserve" (verse 61) instead of "I will preserve my people"?

What is emphasized is that the people of the Lord, not the wicked, will be preserved.

From what verse 62 says, how will the Lord call on the children of Noah?

To us, the line "righteousness will I send down out of heaven" suggests heavenly messengers, and the line "truth will I send forth out of the earth" suggests the Book of Mormon, which did come forth from the earth. The Book of Mormon bears testimony of Christ, his resurrection, and the resurrection of all men; heavenly messengers at the time of the Restoration also bore testimony of these things.

The feeling in verse 62 builds in intensity with the repetition of "righteousness" and "truth"; these the Lord will cause to sweep the earth "as with a flood." Try reading verse 62 and notice how the feeling builds. (Breathe according to the punctuation — at the semi-colons and, if needed, after "an Holy City.") Why is the simile "as with a flood" particularly appropriate here?

Instead of a flood of waters, the Lord will send a flood of "righteousness and truth." The two are alternatives, reminding us of the Lord's earlier promise to Enoch that he would stay the floods and call upon the children of Noah. (Verse 51.)

Who are the elect of God? (Verse 62.)

The elect of God are those who hear his voice, believe in him, and harden not their hearts. (D&C 29:7, 33:6.) Christ says, "They . . . shall see me, and shall not be asleep, and shall abide the day of my coming; for they shall be purified, even as I am pure." (D&C 35:21.)

What are the four quarters of the earth? (Verse 62.)

Elsewhere in the scriptures, we read about "the four *corners* of the earth." (2 Nephi 21:12.) In reference to the earth, "quarters" and "corners" seem to mean the same.

Both words refer to the extremities or ends of the earth — its remotest parts. The four quarters are the four ends or directions from which the wind blows. Some scriptures say the gathering will be "from the four *winds,* from one end of heaven to the other." (D&C 133:7; Joseph Smith 1:37.) The gospel, in other words, will be preached in all the earth. We are reminded of another scripture: "And this gospel of the kingdom shall be preached in all the world for a witness unto all nations; and then shall the end come." (Matthew 24:14.)

What does "gird up their loins" mean? (Verse 62.)

One reference book tells us that the Hebrews wore girdles when traveling or working, girding or fastening their clothes about them to ensure free movement of their limbs. To "gird up their loins" means, then, to prepare for action. Apparently, coming to Zion won't mean rest. In the Doctrine and Covenants we read, "They shall be gathered in unto one place upon the face of this land, to *prepare* their hearts and be *prepared* in all things against the day when tribulation and desolation are sent forth upon the wicked." (D&C 29:8.) The emphasis here on preparation also suggests action.

In the following lines of verse 62, what do "there" and "it" refer to: ". . . for there shall be my tabernacle, and it shall be called Zion, a New Jerusalem"?

Both "there" and "it" apparently refer to the Holy City. Christ's tabernacle will be in the Holy City, and the City will be called Zion, a New Jerusalem.

What is Christ's tabernacle? (Verse 62.)

We see two possibilities: (1) his temple; in the Holy City shall be his temple; and (2) his dwelling place; the Holy City shall be his dwelling place. Both statements are true.

Enoch lived a long time before Old Jerusalem was built. What meaning would the phrase "a New Jerusalem" have for him? (Verse 62.)

It may be that Enoch had seen Old Jerusalem in vision and knew it by name. Or it may be that Enoch knew the Holy City by another name, which was translated "New Jerusalem" for our benefit.

Why, like Enoch's city, is the Holy City to be called Zion? (Verse 62.)

Both cities are cities of holiness. The earlier Zion was called "the City of Holiness" (Moses 7:19); this Zion is called "the Holy City" (verse 62.)

Verse 63 is another verse expressing deep emotion. A scene of joyful reunion is vividly described. Does this scene remind you of any others in the scriptures?

Strikingly similar are the reunion scenes of the father and the prodigal son, and of Jacob and Esau. The first reads, "But when he was yet a great way off, his father saw him, and had compassion, and ran, and fell on his neck, and kissed him" (Luke 15:20); and the second, "And Esau ran to meet him, and embraced him, and fell on his neck, and kissed him: and they wept" (Genesis 33:4).

Why do you think the emotion is so strong when the two cities meet? What is the bond between them?

For the father and the prodigal son, and for Jacob and Esau, the bond was kinship. For the two Zions, the bond is spiritual brotherhood. Though separated by millennia, by language and custom, the two Zions are fundamentally one—one in Christ.

Why is the line "and they shall see us" (verse 63) significant?

The account doesn't say "and we shall see them" because "we" have been seeing "them," behind the veil, for a long time, eagerly awaiting the day "which was sought for by all holy men." (D&C 45:12.) What's new is that "they," their brothers in Christ, shall see "us." Try to imagine yourself in that scene, weeping for joy, that the long-awaited day has finally come.

The first lines of verse 64 are quite similar to the last lines of verse 62. Verse 62 says, ". . . for there shall be my tabernacle, and it shall be called Zion"; verse 64 says, "And there shall be mine abode, and it shall be Zion." Why does Christ emphasize the fact that he will dwell in Zion?

This is Christ's fulfillment of his promise to Enoch that he would come again upon the earth and call upon the children of Noah. With the Restoration, the promise began to be fulfilled; with the establishment of Zion and the millennial reign of Christ, it comes to glorious fruition.

The Lord tells Enoch, "and it shall be Zion, which shall come forth out of all the creations which I have made," (verse 64) echoing an earlier line of Enoch's, "And thou hast taken Zion to thine own bosom, from all thy creations." (Verse 31.) What's the significance of Zion's coming forth out of all the creations the Lord has made?

The idea seems to be that Zion is one of the creations, out of *all* the creations, that will come forth and be an abode of the Lord. Out of the millions of seeds that were planted, Zion is one that grows, and in fact grows in rather barren soil, coming forth clean out of greater wickedness than the wickedness of any other of the Lord's creations. Remember that the Lord said to Enoch, "Among all the workmanship of mine hands there has not been so great wickedness as among thy brethren." (Verse 36.) Just as there is great joy when the lost sheep is found, there is great joy when a pure people comes forth from a lost world like ours.

65 And it came to pass that Enoch saw the day of the coming of the Son of Man, in the last days, to dwell on the earth in righteousness for the space of a thousand years;

66 But before that day he saw great tribulations among the wicked; and he also saw the sea, that it was troubled, and men's hearts failing them, looking forth with fear for the judgments of the Almighty God, which should come upon the wicked.

67 And the Lord showed Enoch all things, even unto the end of the world; and he saw the day of the righteous, the hour of their redemption; and received a fulness of joy;

68 And all the days of Zion, in the days of Enoch, were three hundred and sixty-five years.

69 And Enoch and all his people walked with God, and he dwelt in the midst of Zion; and it came to pass that Zion was not, for God received it up into his own bosom; and from thence went forth the saying, Zion is Fled.

Just as Enoch was first told about the flood (verse 38) and then shown it (verse 43), he now sees what he has just been told about the last days (verse 65). Why do you think the Lord first tells Enoch about these events, then shows them to him?

The Lord, by first telling, seems to prepare Enoch for the things he will be shown, interpreting what he will see, directing his attention to the things most important for him to understand, and helping him not to be overwhelmed.

The fact that the earth will finally have a season of rest is emphasized by the two lines "for the space of a thousand years the earth shall rest" (verse 64) and "to dwell on the earth in righteousness for the space of a thousand years" (verse 65). What this will be like for the earth is beautifully described in D&C 84:101:

> *The earth hath travailed and brought forth her strength;*
> *And truth is established in her bowels;*
> *And the heavens have smiled upon her;*
> *And she is clothed with the glory of her God;*
> *For he stands in the midst of his people.*

How does the earth's state here compare to what it was in verse 48?

Here the earth has brought forth her strength—her righteous children; earlier the filthiness of her children weighed her down. Earlier the voice from the bowels of the earth was one of pain and fatigue; now truth is established in her bowels. Before, she desired sanctification; now she is clothed with the glory of her God. Then she wished righteousness for a season to abide upon her face; now it does.

In verse 67, we read of "the end of the world," "the day of the righteous," and "the hour of their redemption"? When do each of these events take place?

Apparently, "the end of the world" is at the end of the Millennium. (D&C 43:30–31.) The "day of the righteous" must be the Millennium. (We know that "one day is with the Lord as a thousand years" [2 Peter 3:8], and that during the Millennium Christ's people shall be redeemed and reign with him on earth [D&C 43:29–30].) The "hour of their redemption," we are told, will be the time of the first resurrection, which comes at the beginning of the Millennium. (D&C 88:95–99.)

Like the earth, Enoch comes from deep grief to a fulness of joy. (Verse 67.) But we are told no more about his joy. The sorrow Enoch earlier experienced was described in detail (verse 41), so why isn't his joy?

Perhaps the intent of Moses 7 is to give us a better understanding of the misery that wickedness brings and a greater compassion for those who suffer under the burden of sin. Joseph Smith said, "The nearer we get to our heavenly Father, the more we are disposed to look with compassion on perishing souls; we feel that we want to take them upon our shoulders, and cast their sins behind our backs." (*Teachings,* p. 241.) Perhaps only with that compassion can we really know "good and evil" and consequently "the joy of our redemption" (Moses 5:11), and no amount of description can otherwise communicate it.

10

Let No Man Think Me a Fool —
2 Corinthians 11:16–33

Alleged ministers of Christ had begun to corrupt the minds of the Corinthian Saints. (2 Corinthians 10; 11:3.) These false apostles, as Paul calls them (11:13), were commending themselves by criticizing Paul (10:12). Granted, they say, Paul's letters are "weighty and powerful" (10:10), still "his bodily presence is weak" (10:10) — *Paulus* means little — and his "speech contemptible" (10:10). Joseph Smith confirms this description of Paul: "He is about five feet high; very dark hair; dark complexion; dark skin; large Roman nose; sharp face; small black eyes, penetrating as eternity; round shoulders; a whining voice, except when elevated, and then it almost resembled the roaring of a lion." (*Teachings,* p. 180.) Besides his contemptible appearance and speech, Paul, they say, has offended the Corinthians; he wouldn't accept money from them when he was there and in need, but instead accepted money from brethren who came up from the church in Macedonia. (11:9.) No doubt the false apostles were practiced orators, fine in voice, speech, and appearance and *quite willing* to accept money.

How might Paul respond to this criticism? How do you think he should respond?

Paul, though living among worldly ways, won't try to

defend himself after the ways of the world (10:3) by commending himself or boasting: "He that glorieth, let him glory in the Lord. For not he that commendeth himself is approved, but whom the Lord commendeth." (10:17–18.) He writes, "The weapons of our warfare are not carnal, but mighty through God to the pulling down of strong holds; Casting down imaginations, and every high thing that exalteth itself against the knowledge of God, and bringing into captivity every thought to the obedience of Christ." (10:4–5.) The weapon he then uses is irony; he parodies the false apostles, parrots them, imitates them, showing by his example how foolish it is to blow one's own trumpet. He writes that he refused to accept the money so as to cut off "those superlative apostles" (*New English Bible* 11:5) who desired occasion (11:12) to "boast" that they were "no different from" Paul (Knox translation) in receiving money and he ironically asks "What is it wherein ye were inferior to other churches, except it be that I myself was not burdensome to you? forgive me this wrong." (12:13.)

16 I say again, Let no man think me a fool; if otherwise, yet as a fool receive me, that I may boast myself a little.

17 That which I speak, I speak it not after the Lord, but as it were foolishly, in this confidence of boasting.

18 Seeing that many glory after the flesh, I will glory also.

19 For ye suffer fools gladly, seeing ye yourselves are wise.

20 For ye suffer, if a man bring you into bondage, if a man devour you, if a man take of you, if a man exalt himself, if a man smite you on the face.

21 I speak as concerning reproach, as though we had been weak. Howbeit whereinsoever any is bold, (I speak foolishly,) I am bold also.

Paul says he's going to boast a little. (Verse 16.) Does he? Is his boasting sinful?

Paul begins by asking the Saints not to think of him as a fool, as weak and contemptible; but he quickly adds that if they insist on it, then they should allow him to play the part of the fool and boast a little as other fools do, the other fools being the false apostles who had been foolishly criticizing him. He proceeds as it were to speak foolishly, boasting, reminding us in verse 17 that such speaking, taken at face value, isn't of the Lord. But Paul isn't really boasting; he's pretending to boast, using irony to teach a lesson. And because he's teaching a lesson, he *is* speaking after the Lord, as he explicitly states he is in 12:19: "We speak before God in Christ: but we do all things, dearly beloved, for your edifying."

What does suffer *mean in verses 19 and 20?*

In verse 19, "suffer" means "allow." Paul is saying that the Corinthian Saints willingly allow or tolerate fools, since they are so wise that they don't need to worry about being wronged by them. But then in verse 20, "suffer" can have either of two meanings. If "suffer" is taken in its ordinary sense, then Paul is saying in verse 20 that the Saints endure hardships if a man brings them into bondage, devours them, takes of them, exalts himself, or smites them on the face — an obvious truth. But if taken in the sense of "allow," as in verse 19, verse 20 says that they allow or tolerate men bringing them into bondage, devouring them, taking their money, and so on — the kinds of things the false apostles are doing to them. Thus, verse 20 can be taken in two ways and is an ironic statement of just how "wise" they are in tolerating the fools.

Paul says, "I speak as concerning reproach, as though we had been weak." (Verse 21.) Other translations of this line are: "And we, you say, have been weak! I admit the reproach" (New English Bible)*; and "I am quite ashamed to say that I was not equal to that sort of thing!" (Moffatt). What is the sort of thing Paul is not equal to?*

He isn't equal to the Corinthian's endurance; they tolerate much more readily than he would all the abuse of the false apostles. Given all the things the Corinthians endure, Paul is willing to admit he is weak — he wouldn't endure them!

Paul then begins his parody, saying that in terms of boldness, he is as bold as the best. Parenthetically, he again reminds us that speaking so is speaking foolishly. (Verse 21.) Why the reminder?

He wants us to remember that this is pretended boasting, not serious boasting.

22 Are they Hebrews? so am I. Are they Israelites? so am I. Are they the seed of Abraham? so am I.

23 Are they ministers of Christ? (I speak as a fool) I am more; in labours more abundant, in stripes above measure, in prisons more frequent, in deaths oft.

24 Of the Jews five times received I forty stripes save one.

25 Thrice was I beaten with rods, once was I stoned, thrice I suffered shipwreck, a night and a day I have been in the deep;

26 In journeyings often, in perils of waters, in perils of robbers, in perils by mine own countrymen, in perils by the heathen, in perils in the city, in perils in the wilderness, in perils in the sea, in perils among false brethren;

27 In weariness and painfulness, in watchings often, in hunger and thirst, in fastings often, in cold and nakedness.

28 Beside those things that are without, that which cometh upon me daily, the care of all the churches.

Who does the pronoun "they" in verses 22 and 23 refer to?

Paul is speaking of the false apostles.

How, in verse 22, does Paul make his "boasting" seem ridiculous?

Apparently, the false apostles made much of their lineage, so Paul, as they, claims descent from Abraham, but he overdoes it, three times saying, "so am I," showing how silly such boasting is. The Joseph Smith translation adds a fourth "so am I" instead of the "I am more" in verse 23, making the speech seem even more ridiculous.

Paul's "boastful" speech is excessively repetitious. What other overdone repetition do you find?

The repetitiveness begins in verse 22 and reaches its peak in verse 26, where "in perils" is repeated eight times. His speech was probably not unlike the false apostles' boastful speeches, labored and excessive. By imitating their overworked rhetoric, he shows how foolish their boasting is.

Paul says that he's been "in deaths oft." (Verse 23.) Obviously, he hadn't died more times than the false apostles, though he was more than once near death, and once, after being stoned, was even left for dead. Why does he say this?

The phrase is an ironic exaggeration, used to show what extremes such boasting leads to.

Why do you think Paul says "forty stripes save one" instead of "thirty-nine stripes" in verse 24?

The Jews were allowed to give only forty lashes (Deuteronomy 25:3), and so to be quite sure they didn't exceed the limit, they always stopped at thirty-nine.

Paul says he suffered shipwreck three times. (Verse 25.) How many shipwreck accounts do we know of?

We only have the account of one. (Acts 27.) The record must be incomplete.

Paul melodramatically tells about all the perils he has been in, saving for last, the position of most importance, the peril of being among false brethren. (Verse 26.) Is he still being ironic when he mentions false brethren?

He is and he isn't. While maintaining the ironic tone, he points here to his real concern — the harm false brethren are doing to the church at Corinth. In verse 28, he generalizes this expression of concern to "all the churches."

29 Who is weak, and I am not weak? who is offended, and I burn not?
30 If I must needs glory, I will glory of the things which concern mine infirmities.
31 The God and Father of our Lord Jesus Christ, which is blessed for evermore, knoweth that I lie not.

A modern translation of verse 29 is: "Who is weak, but I share his weakness? Who is caused to fall, but I burn with indignation? (Conybeare.) The Joseph Smith Translation reads, "Who is weak, and I am not weak? who is offended, and I anger not?" What is Paul "boasting" of here?

Paul is probably saying that he had felt anger toward those false ministers who were causing the Saints in Corinth to fall, his reaction being, "Are they leading you astray? Then I am furious!" This is the kind of boasting some might engage in, vaunting their sympathy for others. But in verse 30, we see that Paul regards his anger as a real weakness; by glorying in it, he has been glorying in an infirmity or weakness. A Christian shouldn't suffer offense when others suffer offense. To feel the wrong way for someone else is as wrong as feeling it for oneself. In becoming upset at wrongs suffered by others, one is not being virtuous. You might compare Nephi's sorrow over *his* anger in 2 Nephi 4:15–35.

In verse 31, Paul says he has been telling the truth and the Lord knows it. What has he been telling the truth about?

One possibility is that he has been telling the truth about all the hardships he has suffered. But perhaps verse 31 refers more specifically to what he has just indirectly admitted in verses 29 and 30, namely, that he wrongfully got upset. He is then saying that the Lord knows he regards his reaction as a weakness, probably because his anger has been a matter of concern he has been taking to the Lord.

32 In Damascus the governor under Aretas the king kept the city of the Damascenes with a garrison, desirous to apprehend me:

33 And through a window in a basket was I let down by the wall, and escaped his hands.

The incident in verses 32 and 33 goes back to Paul's idea of glorying in his infirmities. How is it an example of glorying in infirmity?

In these verses, we're given an example of Paul being saved in a very unheroic way. It was a great thing that the Lord rescued him, but the rescue itself was humiliating; he was let down from a wall in a basket. The sort of thing to be put in a basket is an ape, not a man. The Corinthians had been saying that Paul shouldn't be so humble, so weak, so little, and here Paul is showing that with just those attributes he was able to be saved. If that is the way the Lord will take care of Paul, it is fine with him. And if Paul has to play the part of a fool to save the Corinthians from the garrison of false apostles, he is willing to do that too. Thus, even while he plays the fool, we still see the truth about Paul—his humility, as well as the great number of hardships he has suffered for Christ. And in this we see that the false apostles, in trying to compare themselves favorably to Paul, were doubly foolish—first because boasting is foolish in itself, and second because they couldn't hope to compete with Paul.

Do you know anyone else who, out of love, has parodied sinful behavior in a way that shows how foolish it is?

Like Paul, Joseph Smith used parody as a means of

instruction. Here are two incidents that occurred during Zion's camp.

We crossed the Embarras river and encamped on a small branch of the same about one mile west. In pitching my tent we found three massasaugas or prairie rattlesnakes, which the brethren were about to kill, but I said, "Let them alone — don't hurt them! How will the serpent ever lose his venom, while the servants of God possess the same disposition, and continue to make war upon it? Men must become harmless, before the brute creation; and when men lose their vicious dispositions and cease to destroy the animal race, the lion and the lamb can dwell together, and the sucking child can play with the serpent in safety." The brethren took the serpents carefully on sticks and carried them across the creek. I exhorted the brethren not to kill a serpent, bird, or an animal of any kind during our journey unless it became necessary in order to preserve ourselves from hunger.

I had frequently spoken on this subject, when on a certain occasion I came up to the brethren who were watching a squirrel in a tree, and to prove them and to know if they would heed my counsel, I took one of their guns, shot the squirrel and passed on, leaving the squirrel on the ground. Brother Orson Hyde, who was just behind, picked up the squirrel, and said, "We will cook this, that nothing may be lost." I perceived that the brethren understood what I did it for, and in their practice gave more heed to my precept than to my example, which was right. (*History of the Church,* vol. 2, pp. 71-72.)

The following is from Heber C. Kimball's journal:

When we had all got over [the Mississippi], we camped about one mile back from the little town of Louisiana, in a beautiful oak grove, which is immediately on the bank of the river. At this place there were some feelings of hostility manifested again by Sylvester Smith, in consequence of a dog growling at him while he was marching his company up to the camp, he being the last that came over the river. The next morning Brother Joseph told the camp that he would descend to the spirit that was manifested by some of the brethren, to let them see the folly of their wickedness. He rose up and commenced speaking by saying, "If any man insults me, or abuses me, I will stand in my own defense at the expense of my life; and if a dog growls at me, I will let him know that I am his master." At this moment, Sylvester Smith, who had just returned from where he had turned out his horses to feed, came up, and hearing Brother Joseph make those remarks, said "If that dog bites me, I'll kill him." Brother Joseph turned to Sylvester and said, "If you kill that dog, I'll whip you," and then went on to show the brethren how wicked and unchristianlike such conduct appeared before the eyes of truth and justice. (*History of the Church,* vol. 2, p. 83.)

What was Joseph showing to be foolish in these two stories?

In the first, killing animals for sport; in the second, hostility.

Now try reading 2 Corinthians 11:16–33 aloud again, this time with the tone of voice you think Paul would use.

Reflections and Refinements

As a result of science and technology, we are continually learning more about ourselves and the world around us. Unfortunately, at the same time we are also forgetting more and more. With the decline of classical education and the emphasis on scientific and pseudo-scientific jargon, we are losing our sensitivity to the language that is our common heritage. We don't understand the scriptures, largely because we don't understand the language of the scriptures, a language as suited to the Lord's purposes as the language of mathematics is to science.

When the Lord speaks, he doesn't intend merely to inform us, but to change us, to open our minds and hearts, to unstop our ears and to break down our pride. Consequently, when we understand how scriptural language serves these purposes, we don't read solely for information, combing the pages for doctrine, settling for simple paraphrases, missing altogether the power of the scriptures to change our attitudes and soften our hearts. Nor do we become sentimental and read into the scriptures our own emotional preconceptions. An understanding of scriptural language helps us develop a more disciplined, sensitive response to the scriptures.

11

Reading the Word

Dennis Jay Packard

I can't remember when I started reading the scriptures, though I'm sure I began with the Book of Mormon, which is still probably my favorite book of scripture. No doubt I read much like my seven-year-old nephew, whom I watched in the midst of food, toys, cousins, and general chaos reading the Book of Mormon, one word at a time, the cloth marker laid across the page indicating the line he was on, his eyes and finger aiming at the exact word he was reading.

During my seminary years, I read the scriptures, not very diligently, but with some interest. I tried getting straight about who was who in the scriptures and struggled with such puzzles as why Mormon, who wasn't supposed to come until the end of the book, put those Words of Mormon just before King Benjamin's speech.

In the mission field, my interest increased. I enjoyed reading for doctrine, which seemed to us missionaries, even in the Language Training Mission, the most exciting thing in the scriptures to talk about. We felt like initiates into the higher mysteries as we spoke with subdued voices about the Second Comforter and the more sure word of prophecy. I can remember studying for an hour or so with my companion at lunchtime in Florence, Italy, while people took their naps. We sat at opposite ends of a

long table, our books stacked in the middle, and read the
Doctrine and Covenants, a section a day. We would read
individually and then share the doctrinal insights we had
discovered. The idea was to read so thoroughly that you
found everything the other found, and hopefully more. It
was great fun. And I think of that elder with affection,
especially because we studied the scriptures together in
that way. I recall wishing, as foolish as it seems to me
now, that I could read the Doctrine and Covenants so
completely that I would never need to read it again.

Then, not surprisingly, a period of boredom set in.
The scriptures seemed without new doctrine for me. I
had, as it were, exhausted them. Several years passed.
Then, fortunately, I began to recover. I began noticing a
beauty and a power in the scriptures, and I found that
Church leaders would frequently quote the passages that
to me were particularly poignant. I concluded that their
love for the scriptures was based on more than just doctrine. I began reading aloud beautiful passages of scripture, several verses at a time, to a priesthood group I was
teaching. The class's reaction was like mine. It was as if
each passage was directed to us individually, so that just
hearing the words — the sounds, the repetitions, the whole
message — seemed to increase our love for the Lord and
our desire to serve. When I started teaching the Doctrine
and Covenants in Sunday School, I found I was reading a
new book. Section 19, for instance, is not, as it seemed to
me before, simply a doctrinal exposition on the nature of
suffering. It is a call to repentance, directed to Martin
Harris and to us. It is skillfully constructed. The first half
is harsh and repetitious to sober Martin up — the words *repent, suffer,* and *punishment* occur over twenty times. The
second half is gentle sounding and assuring, to show Martin the Lord's love.

It seems obvious to me now that if the scriptures were
written just for the doctrine, they were written rather
poorly — too much stuff to wade through to get to the nug-
gets. It would have been better to lay out the doctrine in
treatise form. That begins to sound rather cold. And it
would be. Besides informing, the scriptures entreat. They
aim to change us, to bring us to repentance.

Now, almost starting over again, I've been trying to

learn how to read the scriptures. My family and I will be reading them for years to come, and so if I learn even a little, it will go a long way. I've read "the scriptures on the scriptures" and modern prophets on the scriptures. I've studied Shakespearean English—the language of the King James translators. I've read Bible scholars. Even in a ward choir, I've learned something about the scriptures.

In a choir, you have to get the notes right. There is no way around that. You need to get the vowels full and rich, not shrill and nasal; and the consonants articulated, particularly at the ends, to make words intelligible. And there are dynamics to learn: pianissimo at this point, forte at that, a crescendo and then a diminuendo. And perhaps the most difficult at first, you have to breathe right or you'll break sentences in the wrong places and end up with bits and pieces, unexpressive and nonsensical. Then, of course, beyond that, beyond all technique comes the spirit, sincerity, and testimony, singing to praise God, to declare his glory—not ours.

It sounds complicated and it can be. Those notes can be hard to find; the vowels and consonants, obstinate; the dynamics, easy to forget. And those phrases best not interrupted by a breath can be long, and only a deep breath at the beginning and a slightly quickened pace get you to the end before you turn blue. But with practice it all comes together more and more easily, more and more naturally. And it is worth it. Anyone who has been in a choir knows that singing fine religious music enlarges the soul.

One morning, after having thought about such things at a choir practice the night before, I was reading the scriptures aloud to myself—aloud, because I didn't want to miss anything. Scripture, I believe, is best appreciated when heard, just as music is. Some few people, not I, can appreciate music by reading it to themselves. But even they must appreciate it more when they hear it. According to one Bible scholar, ancient writers, including biblical writers, designed their material "to be heard," "to be read in public," "to reach the audience through hearing," "to appeal through the ear."[1] He cites as an example Jeremiah, who, unable to go to the house of the Lord himself, commands his scribe Baruch, "Therefore go thou, and read in the roll, which thou hast written from my mouth, the words of the Lord *in the ears* of the people in the Lord's house upon the fasting day: and also thou shalt read them *in the ears* of all Judah that come out of their cities." (Jeremiah 36:6.) When Baruch does so, some of the princes get word of it and summon Baruch. "And they said unto him, Sit down now, and read it *in our ears.* So Baruch read it *in their ears.* Now it came to pass, when they had heard all the words, they were afraid both one and other, and said unto Baruch, We will surely tell the king of all these words." (Verses 15-16.) They do, and "the king sent Jehudi to fetch the roll. . . . And Jehudi read it *in the ears* of the king, and *in the ears* of all the princes which stood beside the king." (Verse 21.) It seems crucial to everyone involved that they *hear* Jeremiah's words, *in their ears.*

Another example is Ezra, who "brought the law before the congregation both of men and women, and all that could hear with understanding . . . [and] the ears of all the people were attentive unto the book of the law . . . And he read therein . . . from the morning until midday . . . [and] read in the book in the law of God distinctly, and gave the sense, and caused [the people] to understand the reading . . . [and] all the people wept, when they heard the words of the law." (Nehemiah 8.) Even letters were read aloud, as we find in Jeremiah 29:29.

According to another scholar, "in Greek, all literature was written to be heard, and even when reading to himself a Greek read aloud."[2] Augustine remarked that when his friend Ambrose read "his voice and tongue were at rest," and he offers several possible explanations for such *strange* behavior.[3] Perhaps Ambrose had learned to read "aloud" silently, like those musicians who can "hear" music just by reading it.

Now, as I was reading the scriptures aloud, I had no trouble with each word, with getting the notes right, as it were. I knew I'd hear repeated vowels and consonants, like the repeated *s* sound in the Lord's description of the serpent: "And now the *s*erpent was more *s*ubtle than any bea*s*t of the field which I, the Lord God, had made" (Moses 4:5); or the *ou* and *i* sounds in the Lord's rebuke to Martin Harris: "Or canst th*ou* run ab*ou*t longer as a bl*i*nd guide?" (D&C 19:40). And I knew not to read in a monotone; some syllables in a phrase want to come out with more force, with more emphasis, as in this passage from the Doctrine and Covenants: "And *all* saints who remember to *keep* and *do* these sayings, walking in *obe*dience to the commandments, shall receive *health* in their navel and *mar*row to their bones; And shall find *wis*dom and great *trea*sures of knowledge, even *hid*den treasures." (D&C 89:18-19.)

But when it came to breathing, I noticed I was taking breaths when I felt like it, at quite regular intervals, a luxury I had learned to forgo when singing in a choir. Then I remembered reading about punctuation; our modern method of punctuation "has been in use for about eighty years, and anyone who reads books written before the First World War will come across classics of our century punctuated in the earlier way. The old mode was "oratorical," that is, based on the needs of a speaker reading the text aloud. It [the punctuation] indicated pauses in the sentence more than it did the relation of its parts; it was therefore abundant. Ours is spare; it is—or tries to be—logical, cares nothing about speech pauses, and forever strives to avoid punctuating at all."[4] The scriptures, the modern ones as well, are quite clearly punctuated "abundantly" and in the older tradition. So, thinking about breathing in music, I began taking breaths at periods, exclamation marks, and question marks nearly always; at dashes, colons, and semi-colons usually; and rarely at commas.

And, to my delight, what I was reading became more interesting, not at all like the writing one author called "Tedious. Lifeless. Just plain boring to read."[5] He was thinking of the predominant "Official Style" in education, business, and government, prose like the following, which, as he points out, cannot be read aloud naturally: "It is the totality of the interrelation of the various components of language and the other communication systems which is the basis of referential memory."[6] The passages of scripture I was reading ceased sounding mechanical, like notes barely learned. The phrases differed in length. I could hear the variety and change that makes one say, "A living voice!"[7]

Two examples:

And his fame went throughout all Syria: *(breath)* **and they brought unto him all sick people that were taken with divers diseases and torments, and those which were possessed with devils, and those which were lunatick, and those that had the palsy;** *(breath)* **and he healed them.** *(breath)* **(Matthew 4:24.)**

And when the Jews heard these things they were angry with him; *(breath)* **yea, even as with the prophets of old, whom they had cast out, and stoned, and slain;** *(breath)* **and they also sought his life, that they might take it away.** *(breath)* **But behold, I, Nephi, will show unto you that the tender mercies of the Lord are over all those whom he hath chosen, because of their faith, to make them mighty even unto the power of deliverance.** *(breath)* **(1 Nephi 1:20.)**

The ancients managed without punctuation; manuscripts like the Gospels and the Acts were written with no punctuation, with no spaces between the words, and all in capital letters.[8] And I find it interesting that Joseph Smith translated the Book of Mormon into English with "absolutely no punctuation."[9] It was the printer who added the commas, the periods, and the rest. As he said, "I punctuated it to make it read as I supposed the Author intended, and but very little punctuation was altered in proof-reading."[10] Apparently, punctuating the Book of Mormon was quite a routine matter; the language itself made clear the correct punctuation. What is not routine, at least for moderns like me who rarely read aloud, is using the punctuation as a guide to reading aloud.

That evening, I told my wife about punctuation and breathing, and she spent almost an hour reading aloud her favorite passages. At dinner, I read a passage to the family, as usual just before dessert — this time, by request, Joseph Smith's prayer in Liberty jail. I took breaths according to the punctuation, and I do believe they heard more of what I said. They seemed to listen more attentively. At their ages, six and under, I'm never sure what they understand of the scriptures. But they frequently surprise me, they remember so much. One home evening I was reading about the beggar Lazarus who "died, and was carried by the angels into Abraham's *bosom.*" My boy

said, "Oh, like Joseph Smith." It turned out he was
remembering the hymn "Oh, How Lovely Was the
Morning," the last two lines of which are "Oh, what rap-
ture filled his *bosom,* For he saw the living God." That's a
nice line for him to be remembering. And then, too, even
before my children know what is said, they seem acutely
aware of how it is said; they sense the intonation, the tone
of voice. They like to hear about Jesus entering
Jerusalem and the multitude saying "Hosanna to the Son
of David; Blessed is he that cometh in the name of the
Lord; Hosanna in the highest." They like the "Hosanna,"
"Blessed," "Hosanna." Children, I believe, have an ear for
what shows life. That's important. Faith comes by *hearing*
the word, the words of eternal life.

The following Sunday I listened to how the scriptures
were being read aloud during the priesthood lesson. And
the one brother who followed the punctuation was the
choir director.

Of course, there is more to reading the scriptures than
just reading them aloud. There is discussing them, thinking about them, pondering over them, posing questions,
asking, knocking. And, not surprisingly, knocking is
more than I thought it was. I've found it goes hand in
hand with reading aloud. The better the reading aloud,
the better the pondering, and the better the pondering,
the better the rereading aloud.

In the past, the scriptures had to answer the questions
I happened to be interested in. When Nephi was talking
about rebirth or atonement or some other favorite subject
of mine, he was worth reading carefully. Otherwise he
was not. I was, in effect, telling the prophets what was
and wasn't important for me to hear. It seems to me now
so much more sensible to let Nephi say whatever he has to
say and not to miss his message simply because it doesn't
appear among my current top ten topics.

I now try to read the scriptures on *their* terms. I still try
to answer questions, but those of a different kind: questions that arise naturally from what I'm reading, those
prompted by the actual words on the page. Just as the
Spirit can guide us in what to ask for as we pray, the
words of the scriptures can guide us in what to ask about
as we read. The best questions, I have found, are not the

sophisticated, clever, learned ones, but the plain, naive ones asked with a childlike curiosity and a simple faith that there is a reasonable forthcoming answer.

Obviously, not every question that comes up in reading the scriptures and the prophets leads to a simple answer. Some questions may even be so ill-conceived as not to have any answer at all—questions as strange to the Lord as the child's asking his father in all earnestness, "Where does your lap go when you stand up?" Still, I am convinced that one will receive if one asks "not amiss." (2 Nephi 4:35.) And that conviction grows the more I go back to the actual words of the scriptures, reading them carefully and patiently like my young nephew.

1. Yehoshya Gitay, "Deutero-Isaiah: Oral or Written?" *Journal of Biblical Literature,* 99/2, 1980, pp. 185–97.

2. G. A. Kennedy, *The Art of Persuasion in Greece* (Princeton: Princeton University Press, 1963), p. 4.

3. Augustine, *Confessions,* VI, par. 3.

4. Jacque Barzun, *Simple and Direct* (New York: Harper and Row, 1975), pp. 188–89.

5. Richard A. Lanham, *Revising Prose* (New York: Charles Scribner's Sons, 1979), p. 12.

6. Ibid., p. 4.

7. Ibid., p. 112.

8. Joseph Robertson, *An Essay on Punctuation* (Scolar Press, 1969), pp. 1–2.

9. Stan Larson, "A Most Sacred Possession": The Original Manuscript of the Book of Mormon, *Ensign,* Sept. 1977, p. 89.

10. Wilford C. Wood, *Joseph Smith Begins His Work* (Salt Lake City: Deseret News Press, 1958).

12

Reading Scriptures to Children

Sometimes brothers and sisters, parents and children, even husbands and wives live together for years without ever getting to know each other. That's been our experience with the scriptures; we've been acquainted for a long time, but friends only recently. Our earliest memories are of Sunday School and Primary classes where we learned stories from the scriptures, stories most often retold in someone else's words. We had scripture books for children — books with stories again told in someone else's words. They were interesting, but without, as we see now, the life, the power, the richness of the scriptures themselves. Later, we learned principles abstracted from the scriptures, doctrines from this verse and that, here and there a verse used to support someone's point, and more stories, again all told in someone else's words. We grew up pretty much at arm's length from the scriptures.

As adults, married, with several children, we came to love the scriptures. And the more we did, the more we wanted our children to hear the scriptures and come to love them too. Our first attempt at scripture reading, though, wasn't very promising. We started somewhere in the Book of Mormon, reading a few verses each day.

Nobody seemed to enjoy it much, particularly us — it took such an effort just to keep everyone quiet. We let our attempt simply fade away, and it was some time before we tried again. We had to learn a few things first.

Now, at last, we're reading the scriptures to our children and enjoying it. We're not, mind you, reading simplified scriptures (can anyone enjoy thistles after they've had figs?). Nor have we gone to playing them a stranger's voice on a tape. We are reading to them the standard works, the real thing. And, fortunately, our children are still young, six and under, still like sponges, absorbing everything they hear.

Our children, like most, enjoy choosing — meals, clothes, even punishments — whether they'll go to their room for ten minutes or clean up for their brother or sister they've hurt. So, we let our children choose the scriptures they want to hear. For our family, the best time to read the scriptures is at dinner, right before dessert. (Before dinner, everyone is too hungry to be patient. After dessert, they're all too eager to go back to work or play.) We go around the table, everyone getting their turn to choose the passage of scripture they want to hear. The children choose their favorites, and when it comes time for dad or mom to choose, we introduce new passages. Our children look forward to their turn.

One of their favorite passages is "David and Goliath," and our children know it so well that they've memorized a good deal of it. We've seen our two-year-old (who often chooses "David and Goliath") sitting by herself, playing with her toys, repeating in a taunting tone of voice, "Come to *me*," Goliath's "come-on" to David. Our oldest son, six years old, sometimes likes to say the words along with us as we read. And all the children like to fill in the words if we stop reading in mid-sentence. They may not have breadth of scriptural understanding, but at least in places they'll have the beginnings of a depth, and this, to us, seems important, especially when they're ready for that understanding. Our children are no different from us. They learn line upon line, precept upon precept, and they know, often better than we, the line or precept they're ready for. We think of our six-year-old saying

along with his father, "Then said David to the Philistine,
Thou comest to me with a sword, and with a spear, and
with a shield: but I come to thee in the name of the Lord
of hosts, the God of the armies of Israel, whom thou hast
defied. This day will the Lord deliver thee into mine
hand; and I will smite thee, and take thine head from
thee; and I will give the carcases of the host of the Phil-
istines this day unto the fowls of the air, and to the wild
beasts of the earth; that all the earth may know that
there is a God in Israel. And all this assembly shall know
that the Lord saveth not with sword and spear: for the
battle is the Lord's, and he will give you into our hands."
(1 Samuel 17:45–47.) The more he chooses that story, the
more those words become a part of him, almost as if he
senses that on some unknown battlefield of the future,
he'll be facing a Goliath.

Knowing that our children are likely to choose a
passage several times keeps us from anxiously trying to do
the impossible: we don't have to "make sure they understand it all" the first time they hear it. The passage will
come up again, so we can talk about it a little at a time,
letting them (and us) discover gradually what all the
words mean and what the passage is saying. One night,
for instance, we might tell them what "fowls of the air"
and "beasts of the field" are, and on another night how a
sling works; on still another, one of them might ask,
"What's a shield?"

Most often, our children pick familiar passages.
Sometimes, though, they want to hear about something
new we've talked about during the day. For example, all
our children, at one time or another, worry about
"naughty people," from neighborhood bullies to witches,
monsters, and babysnatchers (especially babysnatchers!).
One day when "naughty people" seemed to be their concern, we told them about Zion — the place where the wicked won't dare come. It had great appeal to them, and
when it came time for scripture reading, they insisted we
read to them about Zion.

These days, we're choosing fairly short passages of
scripture, passages a minute or two long. When our
children are older and their sense of continuity is

stronger, we'll no doubt choose longer ones, maybe a whole book, like the book of Mosiah, reading a portion each night. We'll continue, of course, letting our children take turns choosing. And, for now, we are doing all the reading. As soon as they're able, we'll let them take turns doing that, too.

We keep several things in mind as we choose what to read. We select passages we particularly like, ones that say something to us. We look for passages we can give easily remembered names to, often stories and sometimes passages on particular topics, especially those topics we want our children to learn about at their ages. We pick stories that have elements children enjoy, such as animals, children, and repetition.

We try not to let preconceptions about what children should or shouldn't hear get in our way. Many "experts" think children shouldn't be exposed to violence. We agree about TV violence, but violence in the scriptures is there for a reason, for us and our children to learn something from. How can our children understand goodness without understanding evil? What can faith and courage mean to them if we don't let them see how good men face danger? — "David *hasted,* and *ran* toward the army to meet the Philistine." (1 Samuel 17:48.) How can they desire righteousness without seeing the effects of sin, or feel compassion without witnessing suffering? — "Then Herod . . . was exceeding wroth, and sent forth, and slew all the children that were in Bethlehem, and in all the coasts thereof, from two years old and under. . . . Then . . . was there a voice heard, lamentation, and weeping, and great mourning, Rachel weeping for her children, and would not be comforted, because they are not." (Matthew 2:16-18.) Children can understand these things, and they need to understand them.

Here are some of our children's favorite passages with the names we use:

A Time for Everything	Ecclesiastes 3:1-8
Baby Jesus	Luke 2:1-19
David and Goliath	1 Samuel 17:44-51
Enos	Enos 1-8
Hosanna	Mark 11:1-10
Jesus and the Children	3 Nephi 17:11-25

Joseph Smith in Jail	D&C 121:1-11
King Benjamin	Mosiah 4:9-15
King Herod	Matthew 2:1-18
Mary	Luke 1:26-38
Samuel, the Boy Prophet	1 Samuel 3:1-18
The Boy Who Ran Away	Luke 15:11-32
The Good Samaritan	Luke 10:25-37
The Loaves and the Fishes	Matthew 15:29-38
The Sheep and the Goats	Matthew 25:31-46
Zion	D&C 45:64-71

When one of our children chooses "Mary" or "Baby Jesus" or "King Benjamin" or "Joseph Smith in Jail" and is sitting there listening, we want to read the passage well, never stumblingly or haltingly or in a way that will be confusing. We want our children to hear what the passage is saying. So we're trying to learn how to read the scriptures aloud. And, as we see it, that means simply listening to how we read and trying to do better the next time. It's like repentance; there is no repentance until we finally see our behavior as not good enough. We must see that what we have been doing is less than what we could be doing.

So, we ask ourselves after we've read a passage of scripture whether or not we like the way we read it. Usually we like some things and not others—there are many things to listen for. For example, when we read aloud, we try to read in phrases, not like a robot, one word at a time. We say a phrase, pause and take a breath, and then say another phrase, maybe longer, maybe shorter. That means we have to consider where we take breaths. For example, how does the following passage sound, taking breaths at these places?

O then despise not, and wonder not, but hearken unto the words of the Lord, *(breath)* and ask the Father in the name of Jesus for what things soever ye shall stand in need. *(breath)* Doubt not, but be believing, and begin as in times of old, and come unto the Lord with all your heart, *(breath)* and work out your salvation with fear and trembling before him. *(breath)* Be wise in the days of your probation; strip yourselves of all uncleanness; *(breath)* ask not, that ye may consume it on your lusts, but ask with a firmness unshaken, *(breath)* that ye will yield to no temptation, but that ye will serve the true and living God. *(breath)* See that ye are not baptized unworthily; see that ye partake not of the sacrament of Christ unworthily; *(breath)* but see that ye do all things in wor-

thiness, and do it in the name of Jesus Christ, the Son of the living God; *(breath)* and if ye do this, and endure to the end, ye will
in nowise be cast out. *(breath)* Behold, I speak unto you as though
I spake from the dead; for I know that ye shall hear my words.
(breath) (Mormon 9:27-30.)

Or how does the passage sound read this way?

O then despise not, and wonder not, but hearken unto the
words of the Lord, and ask the Father in the name of Jesus for
what things soever ye shall stand in need. *(breath)* Doubt not, but
be believing, and begin as in times of old, and come unto the
Lord with all your heart, and work out your own salvation with
fear and trembling before him. *(breath)* Be wise in the days of
your probation; *(breath)* strip yourselves of all uncleanness;
(breath) ask not, that ye may consume it on your lusts, but ask
with a firmness unshaken, that ye will yield to no temptation,
but that ye will serve the true and living God. *(breath)* See that ye
are not baptized unworthily; *(breath)* see that ye partake not of
the sacrament of Christ unworthily; *(breath)* but see that ye do all
things in worthiness, and do it in the name of Jesus Christ, the
Son of the living God; *(breath)* and if ye do this, and endure to the
end, ye will in nowise be cast out. *(breath)* Behold, I speak unto
you as though I spake from the dead; *(breath)* for I know that ye
shall hear my words. *(breath)* (Mormon 9:27-30.)

Which sounds better? Which makes more sense?
Read the first way, the passage seems rather boring, the
distances between breaths too close to the same, no long
ones, no short ones. Without long distances, long
thoughts get broken up; and without short ones, short,
important thoughts go unemphasized. Read the second
way, we begin to *hear* Moroni's words, almost as if he were
here speaking to us now. Notice how this second way
follows the punctuation; breaths come at all punctuation
marks except commas (which is a rule-of-thumb we
generally like to follow). There is more variety and more
interest this way. Long thoughts cohere so we understand
them easier. And there's time to savor the short ones.

It's a simple thing to read in phrases according to the
punctuation. And for us, it has made the scriptures much
more understandable and enjoyable.

Besides phrasing, we also listen for words we emphasize more than others. Our voices resist sounding
monotone. English is a "stress" language, and our voices

are always varying, a heavy stress on one syllable, a light stress on another. And as we read, we're constantly choosing words to emphasize, some possibilities equally good (each one showing something about what the passage is saying), but some possibilities definitely worse.

For example, how do you say ". . . great treasures of knowledge, even hidden treasures"? Which of these two sounds better?

> ". . . great *treasures* of knowledge, even hidden *treasures*."
> ". . . great *treasures* of knowledge, even *hidden* treasures."

(Note that we use italics to indicate emphasis, which is quite common. In the Bible, though, italics are used to indicate uncertainty in translation rather than emphasis.) Now, which sounds better? We like the second. Having emphasized *treasures* once, it needn't be emphasized again. What's new should be emphasized—the new word is *hidden*. Similarly, in the verse "I say unto you, be *one;* and if ye are *not* one ye are not *mine*," we'd emphasize *one* and *not* the first time they occur, but not the second.

Here is a longer example—the Beatitudes. How do you say these verses?

> **Blessed are the poor in spirit: for theirs is the kingdom of heaven. Blessed are they that mourn: for they shall be comforted. Blessed are the meek: for they shall inherit the earth. Blessed are they which do hunger and thirst after righteousness: for they shall be filled. Blessed are the merciful: for they shall obtain mercy. Blessed are the pure in heart: for they shall see God. Blessed are the peacemakers: for they shall be called the children of God. Blessed are they which are persecuted for righteousness' sake: for theirs is the kingdom of heaven. Blessed are ye, when men shall revile you, and persecute you, and shall say all manner of evil against you falsely, for my sake. Rejoice, and be exceeding glad: for great is your reward in heaven: for so persecuted they the prophets which were before you. (Matthew 5:3–12.)**

Some people, various clergymen for example, would begin like this, emphasizing key repeated words over and over: "*Blessed* are the *poor* in *spirit:* for *theirs* is the *kingdom* of *heaven*. *Blessed* are *they* that *mourn:* for *they* shall be *comforted*. *Blessed* are the *meek:* for *they* shall *inherit* the *earth*. . ." That reading illustrates the so-called frozen style, a very high register of language. We prefer a more natural reading emphasizing the new words and phrases so the sense of the passage comes through:

Blessed are the *poor* in *spirit:* for theirs is the *kingdom* of *heaven.* Blessed are they that *mourn:* for they shall be *comforted.* Blessed are the *meek:* for they shall *inherit* the *earth.* Blessed are they which do *hunger* and *thirst* after *righteousness:* for they shall be *filled.* Blessed are the *merciful;* for they shall *obtain* mercy. Blessed are the *pure* in *heart:* for they shall see *God.* Blessed are the *peacemakers:* for they shall be called the *children* of God. Blessed are they which are *persecuted* for righteousness' sake: for *theirs* is the kingdom of heaven. Blessed are ye, when men shall *revile* you, and persecute you, and shall say *all* manner of *evil* against you falsely, for my sake. *Rejoice,* and be exceeding *glad:* for *great* is your *reward* in heaven: for so persecuted they the *prophets* which were before you. (Matthew 5:3-12.)

There is a lot to be understood in that passage. But even young children can begin to understand a passage like this if it's read often and well, with the new words and phrases emphasized. Then the passage becomes stirring to them, and hopefully becomes something they'll want to think about and talk about.

Proper phrasing and reasonable emphasis—these are some of the things we listen for as we read the scriptures aloud. We also watch for other, more obvious things, like whether we're reading too fast or too slow. And all these details are parts of a whole we listen for—the Spirit with which we read.

In the Doctrine and Covenants, the Lord tells us, "These words . . . are given by my Spirit unto you, and by my power you can read them one to another . . . Wherefore, you can testify that you have heard my voice, and know my words." (D&C 18:34-36.) When we read the scriptures aloud by his power, it "shall be the voice of the Lord, and the power of God unto salvation." (D&C 68:4.)

That is a sobering thought. Our voices, as we read with inspiration, become the voice of the Lord. That means, of course, that we'll do more than read "correctly." Our spirit will be right. We'll avoid the condescending, sing-song, baby-talk tone of voice common in reading to children. We won't speak theatrically, trying to show off our reading ability. We'll have to ask ourselves, how would this sound if the Lord were saying it to us for the first time? How would Jesus say it? When would his voice be "a voice of warning" (D&C 1:4), when "a voice of gladness" (D&C 128:19), a voice of "rebuke" (D&C 112:9) or a "voice of mercy" (D&C 43:25).

This sounds almost impossible. It isn't. There have been times when we're reading a familiar passage, one we've read frequently enough that we don't have to worry about the phrasing or the emphasis, times when we're relaxed and peaceful inside, when we're self-forgetful, not trying to be fancy or trying to impress anyone, when we're filled with the desire to hear what the Lord wants to say. It is then that we open our mouths to read and out comes the voice of the Lord. Everyone becomes very quiet, eyes wide, ears open, listening to the voice speaking to us.

Those times should come more often. They don't because we're not humble enough, not thoughtful enough, not prayerful enough. And we don't listen carefully enough to each other, telling each other what we hear, helping each other improve. But the promise is there, and we know it.

13

Language, Scripture, and the Heart

Sandra Bradford Packard

Most people who know me would undoubtedly say, if given a choice, that I'm more "harmless as a dove" than "wise as a serpent." And as far as I can tell, they'd be right. I can only be grateful that the Lord has blessed my well-intentioned ignorance; I've had good friends and now an eternal companion with whom I am very happy. But I know others less fortunate, who, influenced by so-called friends, have suffered intensely. Now I am a mother. I'm responsible, with my husband, for four of our Father's children, and I'd like to teach them while they are young to be discerning. Then perhaps they won't suffer needlessly when they are older. I want them to live their lives less haphazardly, with more awareness, than, to this point, it seems I have lived mine.

But you can hardly teach something you don't understand yourself. And so I have turned to the scriptures. What I have found is that, according to the scriptures, you can see into a person's heart by the language he uses.

After some rather foolish but wicked criticism from the Pharisees, Jesus rebuked them, saying, "O generation of vipers, how can ye, being evil, speak good things? for out of the abundance of the heart the mouth speaketh. A good man out of the good treasure of the heart bringeth forth good things: and an evil man out of the evil treasure bringeth forth evil things. But I say unto you, That every idle word that men shall speak, they shall give account thereof in the day of judgment. For by thy words thou shalt be justified, and by thy words thou shalt be condemned." (Matthew 12:34-37.) What this scripture says to me is that a person's character will always be manifest in his language, at least to those with ears to hear. An evil heart can never be concealed beneath a flawless exterior; it always shows, one way or another, in one's language. James puts it this way: "If any man offend not in word, the same is a perfect man, and able also to bridle the whole body." (James 3:2). The implication is, of course, that if a man is imperfect, he will offend in word. Brigham Young used to say that no man, if allowed to speak, could possibly avoid revealing his true character. (*BYU Studies*, Autumn 1970, p. 61.)

The first thing, then, for me to teach my children, if I want them to be discerning, is simply to listen to the many ways language is used around them. Easy as that sounds, listening is, for most people, difficult. Particularly when I feel ill at ease, I find myself thinking about how I'm coming over and what I'm going to say next, rather than listening to what's being said. In this, I belong to that group of people who "seeing, see not" and "hearing, hear not," who are so preoccupied with justifying themselves that they have blinded their eyes and stopped up their ears. This is, of course, no small group of people. The Lord, in the Doctrine and Covenants, repeatedly says to his people, "Hearken, and listen" or "hearken and hear" or "hearken ye and give ear." And when they still don't listen, he changes his tone of voice. This is what Nephi said to his brothers: "Ye are swift to do iniquity but slow to remember the Lord your God. Ye have seen an angel, and he spake unto you; yea, ye have heard his voice from time to time; and he hath spoken unto you in a still small voice, but ye were past feeling, that ye could not feel his words; *wherefore, he has spoken unto you like unto the voice of thunder,* which did cause the earth to shake as if it were to divide asunder." (1 Nephi 17:45.) What must be the frustration of the Lord when his children will not listen, no matter how he tries to get through to them. This is what he says in the Doctrine and Covenants: "O, ye nations of the earth, how often would I have gathered you together as a hen gathereth her chickens under her wings, but ye would not! How oft have I called upon you by the mouth of my servants, and by the ministering of angels, and by mine own voice, and by the voice of thunderings, and by the voice of lightnings, and by the voice of tempests, and by the voice of earthquakes, and great hailstorms, and by the voice of famines and pestilences of every kind, and by the great sound of a trump, and by the voice of judgment, and by the voice of mercy all the day long, and by the voice of glory and honor and the riches of eternal life, and would have saved you with an everlasting salvation, but ye would not!" (D&C 43:24-25; see also D&C 88:88-90.)

Difficult as it may be, I need to teach my children to listen to the Lord, and to other people with discernment. The place to begin, it seems to me, is in the home. When my children don't hear me, what I learn from the scriptures is that I, too, must be willing to change my way of speaking. Sometimes when my children don't listen to me, I am prompted, "Listen to them first." At other times, when they seem to me willfully disobedient, they have just tuned me out and become "mother deaf." Then I ask them to repeat back to me the instructions I have given them, to make sure they have heard. Still other times, I, like the Lord, must speak sharply. But it has to be done in the Lord's way. I cannot be thinking in the back of my mind, as I've sometimes caught myself doing, "I really shouldn't be getting angry, but I'm so busy that I don't have time to give this child the attention he needs." When this happens, my feelings of guilt show and the rebuke is ineffective. But when the rebuke is for the sake of the child—not an expedient for me when I've reached the end of my rope—then I have a chance of reaching my child.

I have also come to realize that when a child, or an adult for that matter, stops hearing others, he frequently quits hearing himself too, and needs to be shown what he sounds like. On one occasion, my husband was questioning my six-year-old about a certain infraction. My son quickly denied any responsibility, but then seeing a knowing look on my husband's face and figuring a lie would only make matters worse, said instead, "I mean, I did do it." I could see what he was doing, and simply told him what his verbal acrobatics sounded like. He was so uncomfortable listening to me that he ran out of the room — but he had gotten the message.

I believe that half the battle will be won if I can teach my children to listen. What remains after that is helping them discern what the people they hear every day are doing with language. I know a father who points out to his children how TV advertisers use language to manipulate them, which of course makes his children determined not to be manipulated. I like that way of teaching. It's not enough to tell children, or adults for that matter, not to be disrespectful or quarrelsome or sneaky, or on the other hand to tell them to be honest or polite or kind. For these words to mean anything to them, they need examples — from literature, especially the scriptures, as well as day-to-day, commonplace ones. And then they need to see for themselves the good or evil in the examples, to feel it, to experience it. Teachers and parents can help, but children must see the good or evil themselves. Our children are innocent because they haven't had enough experience to judge between good and evil, just as Adam and Eve were innocent because of their lack of experience. Only by experiencing good and evil — not necessarily by doing wrong, but by coming to see situations in moral terms — will children come to love good and hate evil.

Nephi, I believe, if he lived today, would also have said something about the language of TV advertisers. He was interested in people's language, and he writes to us as if we shared that interest. He records what people say and then tells us the actions they performed by speaking as they did. For example, "After this manner was the language of my father in the *praising* of his God . . ." (1 Nephi 1:15); ". . . after this manner of language did I *persuade* my brethren" (1 Nephi 3:21); "And after this manner of language had my mother *complained*" (1 Nephi 5:3); "And after this manner of language did my father, Lehi, *comfort* my mother, Sariah . . ." (1 Nephi 5:6); "And after this manner of language did my father *prophesy* . . ." (1 Nephi 10:15). Would that my children were as aware of the many voices they hear and as able to see them for what they are.

But where to begin? Evil has many faces, and I'd like

my children to recognize them all — no small task. The place to start, I've decided, is with those evil ways of speaking that people I know, myself included, are particularly susceptible to. Two such evils are *murmuring* and *flattery,* both exaggerated ways of speaking, the one overdoing the negative, the other the positive. Fortunately, goodness is not so many faced. I've found that *plainness* is probably the term most frequently used in the scriptures to describe the kind of language my children should be attracted to.

I like the word "murmur." It sounds like what it means. But my liking doesn't go beyond the sound of the word. True, there are examples in the scriptures of justified, or at least uncondemned, complaining. When, in the Book of Mormon, for instance, unbelievers persecuted the Church, the Church *complained* to Alma. (Mosiah 27:1.) And when prophets of the Lord were secretly put to death by unrighteous judges "a *complaint* came up unto the land of Zarahemla." (3 Nephi 6:24-25.) Job, King David, and the childless Hannah all had their complaints, and one can't help feeling for them in their sorrows. But there are other complainers, a large group of them, that I hope my children will be wary of — those whose murmuring, grumbling spirit seems to color their whole outlook, attitude, and personality. Their spirit, from my experience, is highly contagious, the kind I would like somehow to "immunize" my children against. Fortunately for me, the scriptures talk a lot about these complainers.

The two classic groups of murmurers are the children of Israel under Moses and Nephi's rebellious brothers in the Book of Mormon. The similarities between these groups are remarkable. They were both wandering around in a wilderness, waiting to enter a promised land. (Actually, that's what we're all doing, as Lehi's dream with the dark and dreary wilderness suggests.) And both groups had prophets leading them to their promised lands — Moses and Aaron in the first case, Lehi and Nephi in the second. And both imputed bad motives to their prophet leaders.

This brings me to something I've noticed about murmurers in the scriptures: they like to impute bad motives

to their leaders. For example: "And Moses sent to call
Dathan and Abiram, the sons of Eliab: which said, We
will not come up: Is it a small thing that thou hast brought
us up out of a land that floweth with milk and honey, to
kill us in the wilderness, except thou make thyself
altogether a prince over us?" (Numbers 16:12–13.) Of
Laman and Lemuel, Nephi says, "Yea, they did murmur
against me, saying: Our younger brother thinks to rule
over us; and we have had much trial because of him;
wherefore, now let us slay him, that we may not be afflicted more because of his words. For behold, we will not
have him to be our ruler; for it belongs unto us, who are
the elder brethren, to rule over this people." (2 Nephi
5:3.) And also, ". . . for behold they did murmur in many
things against their father, because he was a visionary
man, and had led them out of the land of Jerusalem, to
leave the land of their inheritance, and their gold, and
their silver, and their precious things, to perish in the
wilderness." (1 Nephi 2:11.) Both groups of murmurers
accuse their leaders of trying to lord it over them and also
of trying to bring them to ruin and death. This is a bit inconsistent. After all, Moses and Nephi could hardly have
gloried over being kings of corpses. Being unrighteous
and seeking dominion themselves, these murmurers seem
quite unable to understand what motivates their prophet
leaders.

Notice also how the murmurers paint the past
unrealistically rosy. Egypt was not a land flowing with
milk and honey, at least not for the Israelites. And the
Jews at Jerusalem were not "a righteous people" (1 Nephi
17:22) as Laman and Lemuel claimed even after those
same Jews had tried to kill Lehi. Something else that is
unrealistic: the murmurers speak of their "fears" for the
future as if they were certainties. Laman and Lemuel say,
". . . and after all these sufferings *we must perish in the
wilderness with hunger*." (1 Nephi 16:35.) When Sariah
takes on the complaining spirit, she says, "Behold thou
hast led us forth from the land of our inheritance, and *my
sons are no more, and we perish in the wilderness*." (1 Nephi
5:2.) Note how she uses the present rather than the future
tense. The children of Israel, on learning that the promised land was inhabited by giants, say, "Would God that

we had died in the land of Egypt! or would God we had died in this wilderness! And *wherefore hath the Lord brought us unto this land, to fall by the sword, that our wives and our children should be a prey?*" (Numbers 14:2-3.) They don't qualify their fears in the least, even after all the miracles they have seen. Theirs is an example of extreme faithlessness. Not to be outdone, though, Laman and Lemuel, just after being promised by an angel of the Lord that Laban would be delivered into their hands, say, "How is it possible that the Lord will deliver Laban into our hands? Behold, he is a mighty man, and he can command fifty, yea, even he can slay fifty; then why not us?" (1 Nephi 3:31.)

Perhaps the most frightening thing about murmurers is that they continue murmuring even in the face of overwhelming evidence that their complaints are unjustified. They almost seem, in a perverse way, to enjoy their role. Laman and Lemuel, on at least two occasions, could have returned to Jerusalem if they had wanted to. But they preferred to be the tag-along grumblers. The children of Israel, when the Lord wanted them to enter the promised land, threatened to return to Egypt — that is, until the Lord changed his mind because of their faithlessness and commanded them not to enter. Then they changed their minds too, and wanted to enter. Moses incredulously asks them, "Wherefore *now* do ye transgress the commandment of the Lord?" (Numbers 14:41.) It's as if they felt obligated, no matter what the Lord might do, to find something to do or say against it.

These murmurers are one extreme. Their opposites are the good and great people of the scriptures who murmur only when there is nothing else left to do. They are reluctant to complain, and avoid it whenever possible. Captain Moroni was such a person. In censuring Pahoran for his apparent neglect in not sending provisions and reinforcements to the Nephite armies, Moroni says, "And now behold, I say unto you that myself, and also my men, and also Helaman and his men, have suffered exceeding great sufferings; yea, even hunger, thirst, and fatigue, and all manner of afflictions of every kind. *But behold, were this all we had suffered we would not murmur nor complain.* But behold, great has been the slaughter among our people; yea, thousands have fallen by the sword, while it might have otherwise been if ye had rendered unto our armies sufficient strength and succor for them. Yea, great has been your neglect towards us." (Alma 60:3-5.) Helaman was of a similar spirit. Needing reinforcements too, he tries to think of all the possible reasons why he hasn't received them — maybe Moroni has been unsuccessful and needs all the troops, or maybe there is some faction in the government — and adds that if Moroni needs the troops, then he (Helaman) doesn't want to murmur. How different their spirits are from those of Laman and Lemuel and the Israelites.

Why are good people reluctant to murmur? Perhaps part of the answer can be inferred from King Mosiah's instructions to his people: "And many more things did king Mosiah write unto them, unfolding unto them all the trials and troubles of a righteous king, yea, all the travails of soul for their people, and also all the murmurings of the people to their king; and he explained it all unto them. And he told them that these things ought not to be; but that the burden should come upon all the people, that every man might bear his part." (Mosiah 29:33-34.) What this tells me is that irresponsibility goes hand in hand with murmuring. It is easier to complain about the government, about the Church, about one's spouse or children, than to help bear the responsibility for them. Responsible people look to themselves before complaining.

This much learned, I need to teach my children about murmuring — from the scriptures as they are able to understand them, and from day to day situations as they experience them, even if that means telling them on occasion when "mama has been complaining and shouldn't have." I also need to show them the positive side — when someone didn't complain but could have; what good people do instead of complain; and how they complain when they must.

I'd always thought that "flattery" meant "insincerely praising someone in order to get favors from him." As a result, I've never understood its use in the scriptures. Actually, "flattery" has several different but related meanings, and the meaning that I think fits best most often in

the scriptures is "portraying something too favorably."
Flatterers in the scriptures portray sin and sinners,
themselves especially, too favorably. They misrepresent
with fair speeches and specious reasoning, subtly appealing to the base, carnal desires of their listeners in order to
fulfill their own base, carnal desires. These are just the
kind of people, particularly because of their subtlety, that
I want my children to be wary of.

In the Bible, Solomon tells of the flattery of an
adulterous woman who says to a youth, "I have peace offerings with me; this day have I payed my vows.
Therefore came I forth to meet thee, diligently to seek thy
face, and I have found thee. I have decked my bed with
coverings of tapestry, with carved works, with fine linen
of Egypt. I have perfumed my bed with myrrh, aloes, and
cinnamon. Come, let us take our fill of love until the
morning: let us solace ourselves with loves. For the good-
man is not at home, he is gone a long journey: He hath
taken a bag of money with him, and will come home at
the day appointed." (Proverbs 7:14–20.) Notice how, by
speaking of her vows and offerings, the woman flatters
herself, pretending to be more holy than she is. She also
flatters the youth, saying she has sought him "diligently,"
as if he were some hard-to-find dignitary. Then she
speaks of the beauty of her bed, diverting attention from
the ugliness of her betrayal, as if to say, "Morality? I have
said nothing about morality." She continues, ". . . let us
solace ourselves with loves," flattering herself and him that
they are poor put-upon creatures who deserve the comfort
of love, though illicit. Finally, she sends two different
messages in the last line. First, she explains why she needs
solace: her husband has gone on a long journey, leaving
her all alone, no doubt in a big house. How sad! At the
same time, of course, she's telling the youth they needn't
worry about getting caught. Solomon concludes, "With
her much fair speech she caused him to yield, with the
flattering of her lips she forced him. He goeth after her
straightway, as an ox goeth to the slaughter, or as a fool to
the correction of the stocks; Till a dart strike through his
liver; as a bird hasteth to the snare, and knoweth not that
it is for his life." (Proverbs 7:21–23.)

The typical Book of Mormon flatterer, as Samuel the

Lamanite describes him, is one who is received as a prophet because he speaks flattering words to the people and tells them that all is well. (Helaman 13:28.) Such was Sherem, the anti-Christ, of whom Jacob wrote, "He was learned, that he had a perfect knowledge of the language of the people; wherefore, he could use much flattery, and much power of speech, according to the power of the devil." (Jacob 7:4.) Jacob gives us an example of Sherem's speech — to me, a scriptural gem. Here is the speech. The italicized words need to be read with emphasis in order to bring out Sherem's craftiness. The comments in parentheses spell out the subtleties and innuendos, as I see them.

Brother Jacob,
    (Notice folks, the great brotherly affection I feel for people, even for a wretched blasphemer like Jacob.)
I have sought *much* opportunity that I might speak unto you;
    (I want you all to realize that I just wouldn't have spent so much of my valuable time and effort trying to track Jacob down if what I had to tell him wasn't really important.)
for I have heard and also *know* that thou goest about much, preaching that which *ye call* the gospel, or the doctrine of *Christ.*
    (You see, I act on knowledge. But Jacob, here, and his kind, let their imaginations get the better of them — "Christ" indeed!)
And ye have led away much of this people that they *pervert* the *right* way of God, and keep not the law of *Moses* which is the right way;
    (You see everybody, it can't be both Moses and Christ. I'm for Moses. If you follow old freethinking Jacob, you'll end up a heretic.)
and convert the law of Moses into the worship of a being which *ye say* shall come many hundred years hence.
    (The law of Moses is tried and true, something solid we've had for years. Are you going to abandon it for a whim, a ridiculous figment of Jacob's imagination? Very tricky, that Jacob — conjures up a mysterious superman who he then tells us won't be around till we're long gone. Can you beat that?)
And now behold, *I, Sherem, declare* unto you that this is *blasphemy;*
    (Note it well, everybody, that I, the great Sherem, authority of things religious, upholder of the right way, foe of all who seek to lead people astray, I unequivocably state that this is *blasphemy.*)

for *no* man knoweth of such things; for he *cannot* tell of things to come.

> (It's blasphemy to speak of God without knowledge. And when Jacob speaks of God, that's what he does. He can't know what is to come. So you see, Jacob is a blasphemer. And believe me, there isn't anything worse than that.)

(Jacob 7:6–7.)

Poor Sherem—exerting all his powers of subterfuge and slander to make himself look important. It is ironic, but true to form, that Sherem should accuse Jacob of what he himself is guilty of—blasphemy and perverting the right way of God. His guilt and lack of knowledge about the things of God become obvious in his conversation with Jacob. He contradicts himself twice: first by saying that he knows there will never be a Christ (verse 9), just after having said that no man can know of things to come; second by denying the Christ but saying he believes the scriptures which testify of Christ (verses 10–11). In an expression of humility so at odds with Sherem's speech, Jacob tells us how he was able to confound Sherem. He writes, "Behold, the Lord God poured in his Spirit into my soul, insomuch that I did confound him in all his words." (Verse 8.) The power of God in a humble prophet confounds the "power of the devil" (verse 4) in an arrogant anti-Christ.

There are, of course, many other flatterers in the scriptures—Korihor, another Book of Mormon anti-Christ, for one, and the arch-flatterer himself, Satan, for another. No doubt today's world is even richer than the scriptures with examples of flattery. One evening, for example, in trying to understand flattery better, I asked my husband to flatter me a little (in the scriptural sense). He appeared lost in thought for so long that I forgot what I'd asked him and started doing something else. Then he said, "You know, Sandy, I don't think you should worry so much about getting angry with the kids. After all, it's only a natural reaction." My immediate feeling was one of relief, because I'd been concerned about that. I even thought, "Well, maybe I'm doing all right after all," before I realized that this was the flattery I had asked for. I was amazed I had bought it so quickly, just after having talked about it. I realized at that moment how much of what we hear from popular "preachers" today is flattery, appealing as it does to our desires to be justified in what we do. "I'm O.K. You're O.K." we tell each other soothingly, and continue our eating, drinking, and merrymaking. Now, this is not to say that I have all the answers—no one (I think) knows this better than I do. But I do think the answer lies closer to "Lord, be merciful to me, a sinner," than to "Sin is only natural." At any rate, I am convinced that if I and my family can just learn to see flattery for what it is, which I expect will take many examples and a lot of thought and prayer, then it will be relatively easy to avoid falling prey to it.

At the conclusion of his conversation with Jacob, Sherem asks for a sign and is given one; he is struck down by the power of God for his blasphemy. Then, on the verge of death, Sherem asks to speak to the people. At this point, Jacob draws a contrast which I find very instructive. He says, ". . . and he [Sherem] spake *plainly* unto them and denied the things which he had taught them, and confessed the Christ, and the power of the Holy Ghost, and the ministering of angels." (Jacob 7:17.)

Contrary to the language of all sin—whether it be "optimistic" flattery or "pessimistic" murmuring or contention or boasting or lying or whatever—is the language of plainness. Jacob continues, "And he spake *plainly* unto them, that he had been deceived by the power of the devil. And he spake of hell, and of eternity, and of eternal punishment. And he said: I fear lest I have committed the unpardonable sin, for I have lied unto God; for I denied the Christ, and said that I believed the scriptures; and they truly testify of him. And because I have thus lied unto God I greatly fear lest my case shall be awful; but I confess unto God." (Jacob 7:18-19.) How different this speech of Sherem's is from his previous one. It is simple, sincere, straightforward, with nothing hidden, nothing oblique.

When the Lord speaks, he speaks plainly. Nephi says, "The Lord . . . doeth nothing save it be plain unto the children of men." (2 Nephi 26:33.) The angel in Nephi's vision of the last days speaks of "the plainness which is in the Lamb of God" (1 Nephi 13:29) and describes the scriptures as "plain and pure, and most precious and easy to the understanding of all men" (1 Nephi 14:23).

What are the characteristics of plain speech? Well,

first of all, it tells the truth. Jacob says, "The Spirit . . .
speaketh of things as they really are, and of things as they
really will be; wherefore, these things are manifested to us
plainly, for the salvation of our souls." (Jacob 4:13.) Also,
it speaks to our understanding. In his introduction to the
Book of Commandments, the Lord says, "These commandments are of me, and were given unto my servants
in their weakness, after the manner of their language, *that
they might come to understanding.*" (D&C 1:24.) This means
to me that the Lord takes account of our weaknesses and
our limited understanding when he speaks to us (like a
parent carefully choosing his language when explaining to
a four-year-old why we don't fall off the earth if it's
round), and that he would probably speak to us differently if we had greater understanding. In the Doctrine
and Covenants, for instance, the Lord tells a group of
elders that "the first shall be last, and the last shall be first"
(D&C 29:30) and then qualifies this, saying, ". . . speaking unto you that you may naturally understand; but unto myself my works have no end, neither beginning; but it
is given unto you that ye may understand, because ye
have asked it of me and are agreed" (D&C 29:33).
Another example is Jesus speaking in parables during his
earthly ministry because the people were hardened and
would not understand more direct forms of speech. Paul
says, "Let your speech be alway with grace, seasoned with
salt, *that ye may know how ye ought to answer every man.*" (Col.
4:6.) This combination of speaking the truth and speaking it in a way that will be understood is no easy task. It
requires taking people from their present understanding
to a better one, neither talking down to them and giving
them what they want to hear but what isn't true, nor talking above them and giving them things they can self-
righteously go around saying without understanding.

Plain speech aims at our improvement, our edification
and enlightenment. In the Doctrine and Covenants, the
Lord gives a pattern for discerning between men who are
of God and those who aren't: "He that speaketh, whose
spirit is contrite, whose language is meek and edifieth, the
same is of God if he obey mine ordinances." (D&C
52:16.) On the one hand, then, are those speaking plainly
for our edification; on the other are those whose spirits are

not contrite and whose language is not meek — those using their speech to vaunt themselves, to flatter and to please themselves. "And I taught them because they were pleasing unto the carnal mind," says Korihor of his blasphemies. (Alma 30:53.) Paul says, "We speak; not as pleasing men, but God, which trieth our hearts." (1 Thessalonians 2:4.) The truth is in Christ and so, to speak it, one cannot turn inward, magnifying one's own importance and in a thousand different ways saying, "Look at me." Then one's speech is not plain. It aims at something other than what it purports to, and comes out twisted and distorted.

I hope my children will come to recognize and love words of plainness, particularly, and this is the test, when those words speak against their own misconduct. Laman and Lemuel were good at misinterpreting Nephi's plainness. Lehi says to them, "And ye have murmured because he hath been plain unto you. Ye say that he hath used sharpness; ye say that he hath been angry with you; but behold, his sharpness was the sharpness of the power of the word of God, which was in him, and that which ye call anger was the truth, according to that which is in God, which he could not restrain, manifesting boldly concerning your iniquities." (2 Nephi 1:26.)

How do I teach my children to seek out and to listen to those who speak plainly? Since Babel, the languages of the earth have been confounded, and not only in the literal sense. I believe that the confusion that occurred at Babel is a type of a more insidious confusion that exists when people use language unrighteously. There was a time when the languages of the earth were not confounded in either sense. This is what Moses says about that time: "And God revealed himself unto Seth, and he rebelled not, but offered an acceptable sacrifice, like unto his brother Abel. And to him also was born a son, and he called his name Enos. And then began these men to call upon the name of the Lord, and the Lord blessed them; And a book of remembrance was kept, in the which was recorded, in *the language of Adam,* for it was given unto as many as called upon God to write by *the spirit of inspiration;* And by them their children were taught to read and write having a language which was pure and undefiled. Now *this same Priesthood,* which was in the beginning, shall be in the end of the world also." (Moses 6:3-7.) This says to me that both the Adamic language and the priesthood are names for the language and spirit of inspiration. This is the language Nephi referred to when he said that after a person is baptized by fire and the Holy Ghost, he can speak "with a new tongue, yea, even with the tongue of angels." (2 Nephi 31:13-14.) This is what the prophet Zephaniah foresaw when he said, "For then will I turn to the people a pure language, that they may all call upon the name of the Lord to serve him with one consent." (Zephaniah 3:9.)

The children of Adam were taught to read and write from a book of remembrance kept by inspired men—their fathers. They must have become very familiar with the language and spirit of inspiration. May my children become familiar with it, too—by reading the scriptures, by hearing the prophets, and hopefully by listening to their parents—so familiar, that they will perceive discord in the ugly voices they hear, just as easily as they perceive it when their father plays one of their favorite Primary songs with one note deliberately wrong.

Afterword

Arthur Henry King

The scriptures are the greatest writing. But there is an important difference between scripture and other great writing, and that is something we need to hold on to because it gives us the interpretation of all writing. That is, the scriptures always tell the truth, and no other writing always does. The rest of great writing tells a great deal of truth, but does not tell the truth all the time. What the scriptures have in common with all great writing, that of Homer, Virgil, Dante, Shakespeare, and Goethe, is that they offer us a profound comment on human life and its destiny.

The scriptures tell us the truth about the people they describe. They do not idealize, but show us people as they are, not better, not worse. "Thou art the man," said the prophet Nathan to David when he had caught him in the net of a parable. We too are the men and women. What the scriptures say about others is true of us. Human virtues and vices are still the same as they were when the scriptures were written. Let us never read the scriptures under the impression that we know better; we do not, nor shall we. We read the scriptures to find out what they, as writings above us, have to tell us. There is no question of naiveté, of primitivism, of coarseness, of insufficiency, of inappropriateness, about the scriptures. A cultured person, like the man who wrote the history of the court of David, knew exactly why he left something out, put something in, or placed things where he did. This inspired genius was as "civilized" as Henry James and much more deeply certain about right and wrong.

If it's in the scriptures, we had better accept it, because if we don't, we are going to lose something. There are some people in the scriptures, like Joshua or Ruth, whose faults we know nothing of, and we do not need to know. Others, like Sarah or David, have faults that we are told of for our own good. We are meant to see their virtues and vices and to learn from both. "Don't read that chapter, it's not very nice." Who would dare speak of the word of God in that way? The word of God is the history of Tamar (2 Samuel 13) as well as the first chapter of Genesis. There is only one perfect person in the scriptures, the Lord himself.

Now the truths we find in the scriptures are not couched in the prose appropriate to a scientist announcing a discovery to the world for the first time and trying to persuade other people to believe it. The language of the scriptures is the language of the whole man, emotive language, which, like the language of other great writing, not merely tells us the truth, but enables us to feel the truth and exhorts us to follow the truth.

Scriptural language, unlike scientific language, makes use of the various figures of speech commonly found in great writing. In the past, the schoolboy knew the names of at least fifty such figures and could cite you examples of each. The important thing is to be able to feel their impact. But I never realized until I went to stay with an uncle who was a botanist how much more I could enjoy flowers when I knew their names. A rose by any other word would smell as sweet; but Juliet had her Romeo to make the rose do that. I don't believe that a rose without a name would smell as sweet. When we know the names of flowers, we know the flowers better, we can identify them better, we know more about them.

I do not want to involve you in fifty terms. But here are twenty or so fairly important ones:

1. Repeated initial words — anaphora:

Cry unto him when ye are in your fields, yea, over all your flocks. *Cry unto him* in your houses, yea, over all your household, both morning, mid-day, and evening. Yea, *cry unto him* against the power of your enemies. Yea, *cry unto him* against the devil, who is an enemy to all righteousness. *Cry unto him* over the crops of your fields, that ye may prosper in them. (Alma 34:20-24.)

2. Repeated ending words — epistrophe:

Therefore I command you to repent — repent, lest I smite you by the rod of my mouth, and by my wrath, and by my anger, and your sufferings be sore — how sore *you know not,* how exquisite *you know not,* yea, how hard to bear *you know not.* (D&C 19:15.)

3. Repeated adjacent words — epizeuxis:

Tarry ye, tarry ye in this place, and call a solemn assembly, even of those who are the first laborers in this last kingdom. (D&C 88:70.)

4. Words repeated in reverse order — antimetabole:

Wo unto them that call *evil good,* and *good evil,* that put *darkness* for *light,* and *light* for *darkness,* that put *bitter* for *sweet,* and *sweet* for *bitter!* (2 Nephi 15:20.)

5. Irregularly repeated words — epanalepsis:

And if men come unto me I will show unto them their weakness. I give unto men weakness that they may be *humble;* and my grace is sufficient for all men that *humble* themselves before me; for if they *humble* themselves before me, and have faith in me, then will I make weak things become strong unto them. (Ether 12:27.)

6. Repeated word roots — polyptoton:

But let him ask in faith, nothing *wavering.* For he that *wavereth* is like a *wave* of the sea driven with the wind and tossed. (James 1:6.)

7. Repeated structures — parison:

And *we talk of Christ, we rejoice in Christ, we preach of Christ, we prophesy of Christ,* and we write according to our prophecies, that our children may know to what source they may look for a remission of their sins. (2 Nephi 25:26.)

8. Repeated ideas — parallelism:

She stretcheth out her hand to the poor; yea, *she reacheth forth her hands to the needy.* (Proverbs 31:20.)

9. Ideas repeated in reverse order — chiasmus:

He that *findeth his life* shall *lose it:* and he that *loseth his life* for my sake shall *find it.* (Matthew 10:39.)

10. Chained repetition of words or ideas — climax:

And the first fruits of repentance is *baptism;* and *baptism* cometh by faith unto *the fulfilling the commandments;* and *the fulfilling the commandments* bringeth *remission of sins;* and *the remission of sins* bringeth *meekness and lowliness of heart;* and because of *meekness and lowliness of heart* cometh *the visitation of the Holy Ghost,* which *Comforter* filleth with hope and perfect *love,* which *love* endureth by diligence unto prayer, until the end shall come, when all the saints shall dwell with God. (Moroni 8:25-26.)

11. Contrasting ideas — antithesis:

. . . for *the letter killeth,* but *the spirit giveth life.* (2 Corinthians 3:6.)

12. Repeated initial sounds — alliteration:

And the *first* *fruits* of repentance is baptism; and baptism cometh by *faith* unto the *fulfilling* the commandments; and the *fulfilling* the commandments bringeth remission of sins. (Moroni 8:25.)

13. Repeated ending sounds — homeoteleuton:

As*k*, and it shall be given unto you; see*k*, and ye shall find; knoc*k*, and it shall be opened unto you. (3 Nephi 14:7.)

14. Repeated initial and ending sounds — paromeon:

And above all things, clothe yourselves with the bond of charity, as with a mantle, which is the bond of *p*erfectne*ss* and *p*ea*ce*. (D&C 88:125.)

15. Irregularly repeated consonant sounds — consonance:

O LOR*D* my Go*d*, in thee *d*o I put my trust. (Psalm 7:1.)

16. Irregularly repeated vowel sounds — assonance:

Wh*y* h*i*dest thou th*y*self in t*i*mes of trouble? (Psalm 10:1.)

17. Rhyme:

All we like sheep have gone astr*ay*; we have turned every one to his own w*ay*; and the Lord hath laid on him the iniquity of us all. (Isaiah 53:6.)

18. Repetition of the number of syllables — isocolon:

They shall build, and another shall not inherit it [13 syllables]; *they shall plant vineyards, and they shall eat the fruit thereof* [13 again]. **Even so. Amen. (D&C 101:101.)**

19. Unusual word order — hyperbaton:

Then Agrippa said unto Paul, *Almost* **thou persuadest me to be a Christian. (Acts 26:28.)**

20. Figurative comparison — metaphor:

Behold, I am God; give heed unto my word, which is quick and powerful, *sharper than a two-edged sword, to the dividing asunder of both joints and marrow;* **therefore give heed unto my words. (D&C 6:2.)**

21. Comparison using "like" or "as" — simile:

And *as* **Moses lifted up the serpent in the wilderness,** *even so* **must the Son of Man be lifted up. (John 3:14.)**

22. A part put for a whole or a whole for a part — synecdoche:

. . . and every *tongue* **shall confess, while they hear the sound of the trump . . . ["tongue" is used for "person"]. (D&C 88:104.)**

23. Something associated used for the thing itself — metonymy:

God forbid that I should glory, save in *the cross* **of our Lord . . . ["the cross" is used for the "the atonement"]. (Galatians 6:14.)**

24. A seeming contradiction — oxymoron:

They are walking in *darkness at noon-day.* **(D&C 95:6.)**

Clearly, then, the language of the scriptures, like that of other great writing, is rich with details. And so, like great writing in general, much can be gained by reading the scriptures aloud. There are two habits that have developed in our time — they're not very old, either of them. One is rapid reading, and one is silent reading. I have nothing against speed-reading, provided that it's kept to the valueless material for which it is valuable. But when we study great writing, we must study, not as quickly as possible, but as slowly as possible; because the more quickly we read, the fewer our thoughts will be. But the more slowly we read, the more thoughts will come thronging in. It's not the speed at which we read, but the speed at which thoughts come that counts.

Those who fail regularly to read aloud great writing and the greatest of all, the scriptures, are losing something inestimable. It was the practice in the ancient world to read aloud to oneself as well as to other people, and it was a general practice in Britain and other countries to do so until the nineteenth century. It is only inferior stuff that does not gain by being read aloud.

Our voices have wisdom — they know things that we don't know they know. They have been with us all our lives and they have undertaken a lot of things. When we use our voices, we may be aware of some of the things we are doing, but most of what we are doing we are not in the least aware of, just as when we are speaking we often say things that we think have some meaning that other people may share a part of, but there may be another part they pick up that we weren't thinking of but that is nevertheless there. We must therefore trust our voices to be able to tell us things that we wouldn't know if we didn't use our voices. Practiced readers may not need to see a text beforehand to give it a correct reading. In some mysterious way, the voice immediately picks up and goes ahead with the eyes. If we listen to our voices, we shall learn things that we wouldn't get in any other way. The voice carries us, the voice sums up and coaches us in terms of our lives. It is the carrier to us of inflections, feelings, all sorts of things coming from our inside from moment to moment, things we have not planned for.

If we are not in the habit of listening to our voices, we should tape ourselves and play ourselves back. It is quite something to find out how we ourselves speak. I do not try to teach people to read aloud. Often they can read rather well. But I do try to show them that when they are reading aloud, they are over and over again making choices about the simplest things. A verse of scripture, for example, can have a number of different meanings or shades of meaning according to the stress we choose to give it. One outstanding example is the first verse of the Gospel of John: "In the beginning was the Word, and the Word was with God, and the Word was God. The same

was in the beginning with God." That is one way of doing
it, a way in which we are thinking mainly about getting
the plain sense, the plain antithetical sense out of that
verse. There is another way of doing it, which we might
almost call worship. It would go like this: "In the beginning was the Word, and the Word was with God, and the
Word was God. The same was in the beginning with
God." Now that is what I call a rhetorical stress intended
to convey the supreme importance of the Deity. It is a
very different way of reading from the first. The possibility of reading it either way is there in the Greek too. The
point about it is not that one or the other is the correct
reading, but that they are doing slightly different jobs; we
have one experience when we read it one way, and
another when we read it another way. And both of those
experiences are valid. But if we just read it to ourselves
without reading it aloud or hearing it read aloud, those
differences will not be clear. Reading aloud, then, is one
of the ways — one of the best ways — for stimulating
thought, one of the best ways for seeing that scripture is a
shimmering jewel that will show different lights according
to the way in which the light plays upon it, and not just a
plain piece of dull stuff.

That is what we can gain by monitoring ourselves and
seeing where we are putting stress. Perhaps most important is that we read to one another regularly, particularly
as families, listening to each other and telling each other
what we are hearing. And we need to begin when our
children are as young as possible. We need to help each
other learn to read sufficiently well, not merely to be
understood, but to convey some sense of what is there to
be conveyed, which is, after all, not simply plain sense,
but high emotion, too. Great writing is intended to appeal
to the whole of us and not simply to our reason or to our
power to solve a puzzle.

Conveying the emotions is important. How are we going to do it? When I was at Cambridge, there were two
opposing schools. One school said, "Read to make
yourself clear but don't read in such a way as to impose
your emotions on other people. Let them have *their* reactions to the thing." The other school said, "Read with
your whole soul; put into it whatever feelings you can find

to put into it." But alas, those who do that may readily degenerate into second- or third-rate actors. It's one thing to read with a feeling that you genuinely have, but it is another thing to read *in order to* make other people feel; it seems to me that that is manipulation and a sin, except in an actor. To make other people feel, without feeling yourself — there is something profoundly wrong with that. When I was an undergraduate at Cambridge, I held to the other school, which was "Read as well as you can, read warmly if you will, but allow other people to have their emotions for the thing and don't impose what you affect to be your own." There's a great deal to be said for that. Moreover, we must remember, if we go back to what I said about the voice just now, that the voice carries us, that the voice knows more than we know. Let us leave it to our voice to be sincere; let's not manipulate that either. There's all the difference in the world between speaking straightforwardly and manipulating or attitudinizing. So, rather than trying to *put* feeling into our reading, let us just read and then after look to see what feelings came out.

If I had to summarize the difference between the language of the scriptures and that of science, it would be this: science conveys truth as information; the scriptures convey truth as experience. The scriptures are not abstract writing. They may be parables, like the parable of the prodigal son (or, as I prefer to call it, the parable of a father and his two sons). We do not need to argue about the significance of the forgiveness or repentance — or even envy — in this parable. Its aim is to make us feel like forgiving, feel like repenting, dislike envy. This is the greatest short story in the world, and it has been made for us in order that we may experience forgiveness and repentance. It's the experience that counts. How are we to forgive unless we feel forgiveness? How are we to repent, unless we feel repentance? If we miss those experiences, we've missed the point of the parable.

The same is true of a story like the life of David. The lessons are embedded in the story without our needing to pull them out and argue about them. After all, Nathan was better able to convey his message to King David through a parable than by argument or any other means.

When the Lord uttered the Beatitudes, he did not say, "Blessed is peace," but "Blessed are the peacemakers." He did not speak of guilelessness, but said, "Blessed are the pure in heart." He did not say, "Blessed is persecution," but "Blessed are ye when men shall revile you." The ultimate reality is not peace, but peacemakers, and peace exists only in peacemakers. The ultimate reality is not mercy, but people with mercy in their hearts.

Even when Paul is talking about apparently abstract "concepts," he does not define them or argue about them, but makes a poem about them, as he does in the thirteenth chapter of the first book of Corinthians about "charity."

It is not "concepts" with which we are concerned in scriptural writings. We must not lose the great traditions of our forefathers, who knew how to handle and respond to the language of scripture but would have raised their eyebrows at "concepts." Unless we become as little children, we shall not be able to read the scriptures properly; we shall see or try to see all sorts of intellectual things, reading into the scriptures the philosophies of men when we should be responding to what the scriptures themselves have to give us.

When Jupiter and Mercury left the hospitable cottage of Baucis and Philemon, they gave the old couple the gift of an inexhaustible pitcher; however much was poured out of it, the pitcher remained full. The scriptures are like that pitcher; however much they have given us, they have more to give. We drink them for life; we shall drink them forever.

The scriptures speak directly to us. They can be understood by all who will listen. They are not written for philosophers, historians, or literary men; they are written for us all. They are eternal.

Index